THE HOLY SPIRIT

Edited by
Dow Kirkpatrick

*Prepared under the direction
of The World Methodist Council*

Designed by Paul Behrens
Library of Congress Catalog Number: 74-83375
S513 B

CONTENTS

PREFACE

A theology of *The Holy Spirit* is urgent business in today's church. The Fifth Oxford Institute on Methodist Theological Studies was called in the summer of 1973 to address that need.

Pentecostalism demonstrates a sensational vitality and commands a reassessment by main line churches. If grandchildren of the Wesleyan Evangelical Revival are confused by the charismatic return, perhaps a fresh reminder of our own heritage would give clarity. Churches born of the missionary movement may still be close enough to the Bible and sufficiently distant from traditional structures to speak a clear word regarding the Spirit and ministry. Furthermore, we perceive the emphasis given to the renewal of the church during the past decade as related to the liberating activity of the Spirit. Renewal has brought forward the ministry of the laity. These and other currents running through the church today underline the importance of a new depth study on the doctrine of the Holy Spirit.

The Oxford Institute of the World Methodist Council is grateful to Tidings for making the papers from the Fifth Institute available to the whole church. These papers take their place alongside previous Institute offerings: *Biblical Theology and Methodist Doctrine* (1955); *The Doctrine of the Church* (1962); *The Finality of Christ* (1965); and *The Living God* (1969). The last three volumes were published by Abington Press, Nashville, Tennessee, USA.

My personal gratitude is deep for the co-secretaries from Great Britain: Prof. Raymond George, Wesley College, Bristol; and Prof. Brian Beck, Wesley House, Cambridge.

Through ten days of discussion, one central issue divided lecturers and members: *whether the Spirit works only in and through the church, or whether the Presence may be discerned in movements outside the People of God?*

A debate between Dr. Richard Tholin (USA) and Dr. Geoffrey Wainwright, recently from the Faculté de Théologie Protestante, Cameroun, West Africa, sharpened the issue on the proposition: "The Spirit can be discerned where the Name is not named." Dr. Tholin, whose paper is included here, had no difficulty showing how the Spirit urges believers to social justice. Dr. Wainwright insisted the Bible speaks of the Spirit almost exclusively as working within the People of God. It would be more biblically consistent, he contended, to ascribe God's work outside the church to the *Logos*. In each instance, the speakers were putting forward positions strongly dividing the Institute.

It was agreed that the king of Babylon, for example, was used by God to chastise the People of God. The question was: Is the Holy Spirit, strictly speaking, active in the king or in the prophet who discerned the action of God through the king, or in both? A diversity of opinion persisted, as it undoubtedly does throughout the church. In worship and discussion, however, Institute members were aware of strong elements of unity —the most assuring benefit of the work of the Spirit in our midst.

The one hundred participants who gathered at Lincoln College, Oxford, from all parts of world Methodism bore marks of the glory and limitations of our *koinonia*. Churches with few financial resources and great distances from England were not as fully present as they should have been. Some correction was furnished by the impact of non-Anglo-American delegates.

The Warden of the Institute was Prof. José Miguez-Bonino, of Buenos Aires. Prof. E. Bolaji Idowu, Ibadan, Nigeria, related the Spirit of God to the vital forces in traditional African religion. Dr. Stanley Samartha of the World Council of Churches Department on Dialogue with People of Living Faiths and Ideologies, and Dr. Daniel Arichea, from the Philippines and Thailand, kept the Asian perspective alive in all discussions.

The most significant addition over past Institutes was the larger number of women. Male patterns, however, continue to shape the process. Challenge came not only from the women and some men, but also from the theological critique by Dr. Tholin and Father Meyendorff. Each in separate ways claimed the feminine gender for the word "Spirit." The difficulty of achieving in such a gathering a balance of youth, women, and non-whites results from the same imbalance at leadership levels in the church.

We turned to theologians from other confessions for their distinctive contributions on the two more "theological" questions: the definition of the relation of the Holy Spirit to the Incarnation and to the Godhead. Prof. Maurice Wiles, Regius Professor of Divinity at Oxford, took the first. Fr. John Meyendorff, St. Vladimir's Orthodox Theological Seminary, New York, and chairperson of Faith and Order of the World Council of Churches, the latter.

Appreciation is acknowledged to those already named and to the other readers whose lectures are included in this volume: Prof. André Pieters, President of the United Protestant Church and its seminary in Brussels; Dr. Thomas Langford, Dean of Duke Divinity School, USA; Dr. Peter Stephens, Wesley College, Bristol, England; Prof. Walter Hollenweger, another non-Methodist, who shared his life experience and expert understanding of worldwide pentecostalism.

One can only wish it might have been possible to have shared our experience of the Spirit's movement

in the evening led by Dr. Hycel Taylor, Professor of
the Black Experience, Garrett-Evangelical Theological
Seminary, USA, on "Spirit and Soul—the Black Experience;" in the Bible studies by Dr. Morna Hooker,
Methodist laywoman, Lecturer in New Testament, Oxford University; and in numerous worship occasions.
The Warden's sermon is part of this volume as an
illustration of how the theology of the Spirit is
preached.

The church in our time is searching for renewal of
its life. The vitality which marks its history clearly
resulted from the activity of the Holy Spirit. The same
Spirit stirs today. Whether a book becomes the instru-
mentality of the Spirit may be debated. Yet this volume
is sent forth with the prayer:

> Come, Holy Ghost, our souls inspire,
>   And lighten with celestial fire.
> Thou the anointing Spirit art,
>   Who dost thy seven-fold gifts impart.
> Thy blessed unction from above
>   Is comfort, life, and fire of love.
> Enable with perpetual light
>   The dullness of our blinded sight.
> Anoint and cheer our soiléd face
>   With the abundance of thy grace.
> Keep far our foes, give peace at home;
>   Where thou art guide, no ill can come.
> Teach us to know the Father, Son,
>   And thee, of both to be but One;
> That through the ages all along,
>   This may be our endless song:
> Praise to thy eternal merit,
>   Father, Son, and Holy Spirit. Amen.
>   *(Veni, Creator Spiritus)*

Dow Kirkpatrick

Evanston, Illinois, U.S.A.
1974

The Spirit of God in the Natural World

E. Bolaji Idowu

Somewhere in America and Britain, or between those two countries, a "head" was conceived and created. In my language, a head implies a destiny. This prefabricated "head," bearing the specifications "the Spirit of God in the natural world," was sent to me in Nigeria with the request that I should create a "body" worthy of it—a "body" which would enable it to fulfill its destiny. I was thus left to my devices in investigating the actual destiny which this "head" was meant to fulfill in order to create for it an appropriate "body." This led inevitably to the question of definition.

The "head" can be sectioned, roughly, for the purpose of the definition, into two parts. The first part is the phrase "the Spirit of God." Shall we take it for granted that we all understand what this means? After all, we have our Bibles; we have our theological books. I hope, however, that we are not being so supercilious as to think that we can define "the Spirit of God" accurately on the ground that we are able to read about the subject in books. I hope that we have enough theology to be aware of the fact that we cannot define "the Spirit of God" except insofar as the Spirit vouchsafes to us his own definition by self-manifestation through personal experience. I hope that we keep in mind both the promise and the implied warning of Scripture: "I will not leave you desolate; I will come to you. . . .Judas said to him, 'Lord, how is it that you will manifest yourself to us, and not to the world?' Jesus answered him, 'If a man loves me, he will keep my word, and my father will love him, and we will

9

come to him and make our home with him.' " (John 14:18-23)

The second section of the "head"—"in the Natural World"—I have found rather baffling, for the immediate question which it poses is this: Which world is not natural? Does such a world exist? Theologically, we may answer appropriately that such a world exists. But then, we are thinking of the whole world which is in the grip of sin—the fallen world of which St. John's Gospel and the Epistles, the Epistle to the Romans and, in fact, the whole Bible speaks.

I have the feeling, however, that the reference of this section of the "head" is not to the whole world. By a process of divination, I have come to see that it is referring to that theoretical, abstract creation which has been given the specious nomenclature of "the Third World"—that is, the remainder of the world, when Europe and America have been subtracted from it. But, is it not a theological tragedy that the church has not only given her blessing to this heresy but has helped to promote it by adopting and using it as a convenient handle? How can the church which has her basis on "In the beginning, God created the heavens and the earth" . . . , "The earth is the Lord's and the fulness thereof, the world and those who dwell therein" . . . , "The Lord is the everlasting God, the Creator of the ends of the earth . . ."—how can the church afford to seek to cut the ground under her own feet by such culpably careless conformity to the form of the world? The church came into being to heal the world of personal and racial schizophrenia. By contributing to the erroneous notion of a compartmentalized, trichotomized world, she is only violating her spiritual and moral responsibility, with the result that she is aiding and abetting the perpetuation of the curse of Babel.

I proceed on the assumption "the natural world" refers, in particular, under my terms of reference, to the world out of which Europe and America have been subtracted! To deal with "the natural world" in this sense is a "tall order," indeed. The section of the world covered is overwhelmingly wide; and only an unscrupulous pretender will claim to be able to speak out about the whole of such a wide area. Even if one had the time to consult all the literature that is in existence on the subject, one would still find oneself in difficulty. It is being realized more and more today that the world has been treated to too many traveler's tales, anthropological fabrications, sociological guesswork, and enthusiasts' distortions—matters relating to this area of the world.

The area under our reference is a wide, wide world of various cultures and varieties of religious experiences which are expressing themselves by various categories each of which can only be fully understood by those who are actually and personally involved in the experiences. This explains why the Western World has been blundering lamentably when it tries to invent terms issuing out of its own preconceived notions for something totally outside its own immediate experience.

Let me narrow down my discussion to Africa. Even here, I must give the warning that I can only be selective and restrict myself to areas about which I have firsthand knowledge, or areas about which I believe that those who have done research there have been sufficiently discerning.

African experience of, concept of, and teaching about, the Spirit are bound up in their experience of, concept of, and teaching about, the living Source-Being. That is, it is not often that they speak of "the Spirit of God" in the kind of distinctive, almost separative way in which Christian doctrine tends to speak of him. There are African names for God which, in fact, should be properly translated Spirit, like the Nuer's di-

vine name, *Kwoth;* or the Igbo divine name, *Chukwu*—
the Infinite or Undimensional Spirit who is Source-
Being; or the Yoruba *Orise* which means the Source-
Being. According to Evans-Pritchard, the Nuer believe
that Kwoth is "the very Spirit of the universe;" he is
"the Spirit of the sky" or "the Spirit who is in the sky."

The most vital aspect of African experience of the
Spirit is implied in their knowledge of God as Source-
Being, which implies his immanence as well as his
control and maintenance of the universe. This is an
area where Western investigators—those who go out
to research as well as the stay-at-home ones—have
erred exceedingly.

Writing about the concept of God among the Mende
of Sierra Leone, K. Little observed: "In the beginning,
there was. . .God. All life and activity. . .derive from
him. . . In addition, he invested the whole universe
with a certain non-material kind of power or influence
which manifests itself in various ways and on specific
occasions in human beings and animals, and even in
natural phenomena. . . ." And Placide Tempels, writing
on the Bantu in his book, *Bantu Philosophy,* read into
their belief something to which he gives the name of
"vital force," which appears to be the metaphysical
generator and ruler of the universe. Says he, "Force
is the nature of being, force is being, being is force."

Africans do not speak in terms of a computerized
universe, a world charged with a self-generating, self-
directing force which in its turn maintains the universe.
As I have said, Africans see God as Source-Being; he
gives being to all. All live and have being because he
continues in being and governs all things by his own
living power. Both K. Little and P. Tempels, like those
who have been making a toy of the word *mana,* have
seen without recognizing, observed without understanding, what Africans know and experience about
the control and maintenance of the universe. There is

an undeniable sense of this *dunamis,* but its secret eludes them. As I have observed, it would seem that the real problem of Tempels was one of communications. He keeps surfacing again and again and correcting himself: he observes correctly, "The sage 'par excellence' is God who knows every being, who comprehends the nature and quality of each . . . . God is force; possessing energy in himself, the mover of all other forces. . . ."

John Middleton observes correctly that Lugbara see God as being "the ultimate source of all power and of the moral order . . . ." And Godfrey Linhardt discovered that to the Dinka, *"Nhialic* is figured sometimes as a being, a personal supreme Being even, and sometimes as a *kind* of being and activity which sums up the activities of a multiplicity of beings. . . . The Dinka are in a universe which is largely beyond their control where events may contradict the most reasonable human expectation. The divinity who is sometimes a kindly Father is also the divinity which is manifested in the non-rational forces of nature and hence has non-rational as well as rational attributes."

According to African belief, all powers and authorities "in heaven" or on earth derive from Source-Being. They *are* because he permits or commissions them and *are no more* when he withdraws from them. I will illustrate this from three categories of beings:

1. *The divinities.* These are ministers with portfolios in the theocratic kingdom of the universe. Recently, an Irishman, a professor of political science, argued this point with me. He thought it was wrong to speak of theocracy in Africa. This is because he has been led astray by appearances. Where the divinities or spirits are recognized, they are known always to be derivatives from deity. An African pressed for an answer may say that God "created" them. In reality, the oral traditions show that they were brought into being by him; one

could almost say that they were engendered. Anyway, they have no absolute existence, their powers are delegated. That is why, very often in Africa, the name of the divinity in each locality either derives from the name of deity, or that deity and the divinities bear the same generic name and are distinguished by qualifying words or suffixes.

2. *The human*. Essential being is put into humanity by deity. Without this, one would not be a person. While an arch-divinity may be commissioned to fashion physical parts, it remains the absolute prerogative of Source-Being to put something of himself into an individual to give that person personality and life. And one remains a true personality only by maintaining a good relationship with Source-Being. Here again, it is illuminating that the name for the essential person derives in one way or another from the divine name. One may summarize African belief in this context with the word of the Psalmist: "When thou hidest thy face, they are dismayed; when thou takest away their breath, they die and return to their dust." (Psalms 104:29)

3. *Society*. Society is God's ordinance. John Middleton observes that to the Lugbara, "God is not outside society, but rather above it completely. . . .He is said to be 'behind' all people and all things, as their creator, and may be in indirect contact with all forms of social action. His presence unites them into a simple scheme, of which the divisions are complementary and cannot be understood in isolation."

The Yoruba structure will afford an apt illustration. In the Yoruba system of government, *the* Scepter belongs to Olodumare (Source-Being). When the earth was to be created and equipped, it was the sceptre given to the archdivinity which enabled him to carry out his assignment and accomplish the task. When the sixteen persons who formed the nucleus of the inhabitants of the earth came to possess the earth, their leader was vested with authority which came from Source-Being through the arch-divinity. Thus, today, all kings and rulers of Yorubaland are regarded as derivatively divine rulers. This should be elaborated further, for emphasis. At the installation of the Ooni of Ile-Ife (the spiritual head of Yorubaland), he has to worship at several temples: at one he receives his title; at another he receives the crown, but neither the title nor the crown makes him the ruler of the people. It is when he has worshipped at the temple of the arch-divinity and received the scepter that he becomes the ruler of the people with derivatively divine quality of rulership. The ritual at this temple is sacramental: The ruler-to-be must eat part of the divine being, symbolized in scrapings from the effigy of the arch-divinity and mixed with certain other ingredients. The ruler literally "eats" kingship or royalty from something out of the body of his predecessor (meaning that royalty is an unbroken continuity), and from something of the divine, to give him the divine quality of kingship. Thus, the honor, regard, and veneration given to him are consequent upon the divine quality. Two things become important now: It is expected of him to become endued with charismatic virtues. Once he loses the divine scepter, people know it and he himself will decide "to go and sleep," or this will be demanded of him. He has finished and he has nothing more to do on earth. What happens in the case of Ooni is true of every Yoruba ruler who is in the right tradition.

It must be observed that the rituals and sanctions of rulership are being overlaid by the current political situations in Africa. With the coming of colonial rulership and the consequent subordination of African rulership to the colonial royalty, the making of kings and rulers in Africa has become a dual undertaking—the traditional ritual which is the really meaningful one to

the people, and the sanction and giving of the royal
staff by the colonial ruler, which is a mere imposition
with outward recognition by the "outsiders." The colonial system has been inherited by the current political
structures in Africa. Who knows whether it is not this
violation of religious traditions and the imposition of
political, often unedifying, systems, upon Africa which
are making for the societal chaos which we are facing
today!

The main point, however, is that by and large, the
basis of kingship is still the sacramental ritual of
scepter-receiving. The scepter is a moderating factor.
The ruler cannot rule according to his own whims and,
technically, he cannot become a tyrant (although, in
practice, like several of his counterparts in history who
have the consciousness of divine quality, he could
develop a royal megalomania); it also keeps the people
law-abiding because they know that in respecting and
obeying the king, they are respecting and obeying the
divine will. Here again the current political system in
Africa, where the President or Prime Minister now has
political precedence over the natural ruler, is posing a
problem.

The king, according to the traditional constitution,
is a cohesive factor in society. But this is in consequence of the fact that Source-Being is fundamentally
and ultimately the cohesive factor of society.

In this connection, we must bring in the factor of
covenant which is vital to the being of society in
Africa. Every person born into traditional African society is born into a covenant relationship, with a
tutelary divine power (and consequently with Source-
Being) and with his fellowbeings in the same covenant
group. Whether covenant is a community covenant,
between two persons, or among a group of persons for
any special purpose, the divine will is always supreme.
Every entry into a covenant situation, or every

covenant-making, is governed and under the superintendence of the divine Spirit.

Incidentally, if we are failing in our evangelistic efforts anywhere in Africa, the reason is to be found in the fact that Christianity is still to be presented as covenant faith, covenant between the living Lord and the believer. African elders are telling us rather loudly that Christianity is a fashionable religion with little spiritual and moral anchor. Hence the rise of the independent churches which had their origins in protest against "unspiritual Christianity;" and hence the resurgence of certain African cults as a danger signal.

The experience of the transcendence-immanence of Source-Being is ever a reality to Africans. They recognize the greatness, the majesty, the all-purity of Source-Being. They are also aware of his presence in the world as Source-Being who gives being and continuance in being to the world and its fullness. Thus, the Nupe of Nigeria say, "Soko (Source-Being) is far away;" and at the same time say, "Soko is in front, Soko is in the back." The Igbo call Source-Being "the Great Spirit of the skyey heaven" and at the same time, "the Infinite Spirit of the created order." The Edo sum it all up when they give him the name of "Osanobwa"—"Source-Being who carries, sustains, or maintains the created order." The Yoruba express the concept of the transcendence-immanence in the myth of the abortive *coup d'état* organized by the hosts of heaven to wrest the government of the created order from Source-Being. They demanded of him to let them run the universe for an experimental period of sixteen years. He gave them the freedom to make the experiment for sixteen days to begin with. For that period he left things entirely in their control. It was not yet eight days, however, when the machinery of the universe ground to a standstill and a threat of total extermination came upon all creatures. The hosts of heaven had to hurry back and confess their folly; then Source-Being set things in motion again and all was well. It is the belief of the Yoruba that things go well when the human submits to Source-Being; things become very difficult when humans seek to act independently of him.

One more important point: The *Paraclete* is an ever-present reality to Africans. Unfortunately, the situation is affected by the curse of Babel. This needs careful explanation. Everywhere in Africa (as far as I can judge) we have not only the belief that it is the spirit which Source-Being puts into an individual that makes a person of that individual, but also that one has a spiritual counterpart which is a companion and guide throughout life. This companion, guardian-angel, or counterpart, is called either by the same name, derived from the name of Source-Being, as that of the "inner person," or by another name which is descriptive of his function. The significance of this fact to Africans is that the "essential person" as well as the spiritual counterpart has a cult which symbolizes the fact of the strong belief that apart from the spiritual, the material has no cohesion or meaning, and will therefore be ineffectual. One must therefore keep in good relationship with the companion by means of sacramental rituals.

I have given the companion the name *paraclete* because it is my conviction that the idea of the *paraclete,* in connection with the nature of Source-Being, has ever been present with us in one form or another. With the curse of Babel the sense of that which is the cohesive factor of integrated personality, both of the individual person and of the corporate being of society, was lost. And while, therefore, we retain the sense of the inevitability of the spiritual companion for real, meaningful life, we can now only see, in consequence of spiritual astigmatism, the companion in terms of ourself alone. Thus, each person in Africa has a guardian angel who not only guides and protects selfishly and possessively, but even also enters into conflict with, or is afflicted by, another person's *paraclete*—even the parents,' or wife's, or husband's *paraclete*. The *paraclete* may turn against one if the person does not keep the *paraclete* in a state of contentment.

This is the point at which Christianity should come to the rescue. Jesus Christ came to deliver from the curse of Babel. The church, born on the day of Pentecost, is meant to reverse the curse of chaotic misunderstanding into the *koinonia* created by oneness of spirit which is oneness in the Spirit. The church, by her nature, is in a position to unify the world of Africans by showing them that the multitude of conflicting or friendly *paracletes* are only shadows, in their minds, of the *Paraclete*—Creator Spirit by whose aid the world's foundations first were laid; the One who creates all things new, controls our will, subdues the rebel in our souls. This is the Spirit of Source-Being whom Africans believe to be the One who brings all into being, sustains and controls the created order and gives life that is real and meaningful to human beings. As they believe there is only the one Source-Being, so must they believe in the only one *Paraclete* for their own permanent well-being.

The Holy Spirit and People of Various Faiths, Cultures, and Ideologies

S. J. Samartha

When we speak of the Spirit we think of life and its unpredictable growing points, of truth and moments of enlightenment. We also think of inspiration, creativity, and boundless freedom. The ultimate source of all these is God himself. Any attempt to understand God's activity in the world must acknowledge that we are groping after a mystery. Therefore, the limitation of words and the inadequacy of conceptual forms are perhaps nowhere more consciously to be acknowledged than in a discussion on the Holy Spirit.

The subject itself has become important for at least two reasons. First, it is being increasingly recognized that all human life, not just an artificially isolated segment called the "religious" dimension, comes within the purview of God's activity. Second, there is the existential fact that *all* human beings, not just Christians but people of all living faiths, cultures, and ideologies, share a common future, either for survival or for annihilation. This makes them inter-dependent in their search for the meaning of life and existence. The theological significance of this fact cannot be ignored any longer. That all people are open to the activity of God's Spirit seriously challenges a legalistic dogmatism which limits the work of the Spirit to a narrow segment of time, to an isolated bit of geographic location, and to the history of a particular people. The Spirit of God cannot be regarded as the monopolistic possession of the Judaeo-Christian tradition imprisoned within the steel and concrete structure of Western dogma and a permanent Atlantic Charter. As Metropolitan Khodr remarks, "It is totally inconceivable that theologians should speak authoritatively of the relation between Christianity and the religions without having first, critically yet creatively, integrated the data from outside Christianity into their thinking."[1] Therefore, what we seek here is not so much to extend the work of the Holy Spirit outside the hedges of the church as a more inclusive doctrine of God himself. A more sensitive recognition of the wider work of the Holy Spirit may also help us to broaden our understanding of God's saving activity, thus correcting what our Orthodox friends describe as a "Christo-monistic tendency" that seems to dominate Protestant theology, and preventing our conceptions of God from becoming too small and too static.

I.

Certain observations are necessary at the outset. There is the question of terminology—the Spirit, the Spirit of God, the Holy Spirit, and the Spirit of Christ. It would be unwise to attempt a clarification of the terms here on the basis of biblical exegesis. That is a task for more competent biblical scholars. All these terms refer to the activity of God in the world. To draw any sharp lines of demarcation between them is like trying to slice a flowing river with a razor blade; it cannot be done. Moreover, we acknowledge that we speak within the community of Christians who believe in God through Christ in the fellowship of the Holy Spirit. We are already in dialogue with people of various faiths and ideologies, and who therefore seek to recognize, interpret and understand this larger relationship in the light of our faith. In the Christian understanding of God and his activity, his transcendence is balanced by the doctrine of the Holy Spirit. But there are divergent views regarding the latter. There are those who reserve the use of the term "Holy Spirit" to God's relationship with personal beings and who emphasize that, strictly speaking, the term Holy Spirit should be reserved exclusively to describe God's activity in making Christ known, (John 7:39) in assuring his continuing presence in the church, and finally presenting them to himself as sons and daughters in Christ. (Galatians 4:6, Romans 8:9-16) There are others who seem to be reluctant even to raise this question positively in relation to people of other faiths. Discussing the connection between Spirit and mission, Berkhof points out that in Roman Catholic theology the Spirit is institutionalized because he is regarded mainly as the soul and sustainer of the church. In Protestant theology the Spirit is individualized because he is regarded mainly as the awakener of individual spiritual life in justification and sanctification. He rightly concludes that both these lead to a "common pattern of an introverted and static pneumatology."[2] He makes no reference to the possible work of the Spirit in the world of other religions, but in discussing the work of the Spirit in the "secularized" world he says, "The Spirit is not locked up in the church."[3] Does this mean that there is more willingness to recognize the work of the Spirit in the "secularized" world than in the world of millions of people who follow "religions" other than the Christian? In many of the more recent books on the Holy Spirit there is no reference at all to the possible work of the Spirit among people of other faiths. The discussion is almost entirely limited to the church and to the "secular" world. There are others, however—of the Orthodox tradition, for example—who refuse to limit the work of the Holy Spirit to the area of rational beings only but would include all creation within the scope of his presence and activity.[4] This would, by implication, have a more generous attitude toward recognizing the work of the Holy Spirit among people of other religions.

A whole series of questions might then be raised which would have to be discussed in fresh ways for many years to come. For example, how do Christians clarify to themselves theologically the relationship between the work of the Holy Spirit in the church and the activity of God's Spirit among people of different religious traditions and ideological persuasions? Is it the same Spirit that brooded upon the waters over *all* creation, that spoke through the prophets of the Old Testament, that was with Jesus at the critical points of his life and ministry, that manifested itself in "the outpouring" in Acts which also activated Yajnavalkya, the Buddha, the Prophet Mohammed, and, why not— Mahatma Gandhi, Karl Marx, and Mao Tse-tung? Or is there a qualitative difference? Should we seek a difference? Why? If so, on the basis of what criteria? These are not easy questions but their implications are serious not only because they touch such topics as revelation, mission, peace, justice, and co-operation with people of other faiths, but also because the question of truth is involved. It certainly makes a difference whether we regard the work of the Holy Spirit as exclusive or inclusive. The style of Christian life and the Christians' attitude toward others would be different depending upon whether we regard God's truth to be confined to the historical limits of the church or whether we accept his truth to be as free as his Spirit, active at all times and working among all people.

A further consideration pertains to the nature of the sources from which we derive our theological observations. Here we immediately face the fact that neither the testimony of the Scripture nor the tradition of the church gives clear and consistent guidelines to discuss the larger work of the Holy Spirit. The Old Testament does make brief references to the Spirit of God and his concern with other nations and individuals (see, for example, Amos 9:7). George S. Hendry remarks that the New Testament contains no trace of any understanding of the Spirit as the principle that animates human life as God's creature. Hendry draws attention to the fact that the activity of the Spirit is mentioned at the decisive points in the life and ministry of Jesus Christ—his conception, baptism, temptation, first preaching, the casting out of the demons, perhaps his death on the Cross. He goes on to say: "Thus the action of the Spirit is literally Christocentric inasmuch as it is always centered on Christ, whether it comes before or after the Incarnation. There is a difference in distribution and degree, but none of focus. The New Testament knows no work of the Spirit except in relation to the historical manifestation of Christ."[5] The question which immediately arises is obvious: How then can any criteria be derived from the New Testament to discuss the work of the Holy Spirit in relation to people of other religions when the New Testament writers were concerned exclusively with the work of the Spirit within the community of the faithful? Even in the Fourth Gospel the Spirit is the "remembrancer," not innovator. The Spirit's function is not to originate truth, but to recall, to represent, the scope of which is limited to the believing and expectant community of Christians. The references in the New Testament should be regarded as warmly personal, intensely joyful, and strongly affirmative statements of the early Christian community in the pre-Constantine era about the work of the Holy Spirit in their personal and community life. They surely cannot be regarded as negative statements or judgments on people of other religions about whom they knew nothing or very little. How then can theologians use them *now* as criteria to pass judgments on Hindus, Buddhists, Muslims, and others?

Historically, as soon as the Christian faith moved into the wider world of Greek culture and philosophy with its different religions and lofty view of the human spirit, the question of the larger work of the Holy Spirit was bound to arise. In the aspiration of the human spirit, in the very core of the created being, St. Augustine, for example, did recognize an ontological affinity between the Creator and creature. "Man was so created that by means of that in him which transcends he should attain to that which transcends all things, that is the true and best and only God."[6] The theological emphasis of Clement of Alexandria and Origen are well known in this connection. Gregory Nazianzen says that philosophers such as Plato and Aristotle "have caught a glimpse of the Holy Spirit."[7] Irenaeus sums up the general trend in Patristic tradition in the words, "There is but one and the same God who, from the beginning to the end by various dispensations, comes to the rescue of mankind."[8] The Orthodox tradition, following these insights, strongly emphasizes a more generous attitude toward others. Metropolitan George Khodr's address to the Central Committee of the World Council of Churches at Addis Ababa in 1971, dealing with the topic "Christianity in a Pluralistic World—the Economy of the Holy Spirit," drew a good deal from these Fathers and developed its implications to contemporary attitudes toward people of other religious traditions, and more particularly to a new style of "mission." It was not surprising, however, that the strongest criticisms against his position came from Protestant theologians, particularly those heavily influenced by Karl Barth and the dominant ideas of the Heilsgeschichte school.

It is significant that Karl Barth's section on "The Revelation of God as the Abolition of Religion" comes in the context of his discussion on "The Outpouring of the Holy Spirit."[9] It is well known that Barth's judgment on "religion" as "ideology," "self-righteousness," and "unbelief" applies both to Christianity and

other religions and that it has influenced generations
of theologians and missiologists in their understanding
of the work of the Holy Spirit and their attitude to
people of other faiths. If the premises of Karl Barth
are taken for granted, then the rigor of his logic would
probably lead to his conclusions. In the complex and
highly sophisticated discussion, it is fairly clear what
Barth means by "true religion." "That there is a true
religion is an event in the act of the grace of God in
Jesus Christ. To be more precise, it is the outpouring
of the Holy Spirit."[10] He goes on to say, ". . . in the
very encounter with God, the site of which we call
Peniel or, it may be Evangelical Reformed Christianity,
that the face of God is seen, and therefore Peniel or
Evangelical Reformed Christianity is the true religion." [11] And he goes further in drawing the implication,
"And it (Christianity) alone has the commission and
authority to be a missionary religion, i.e., to confront
the world of religions as the one true religion, with absolute self-confidence to invite and challenge it to abandon its ways and to start on the Christian way." [12]

A few remarks may be made on this because of its
implications to our attitudes to, and relations with,
people of other religions. First, there is the use of the
word "religion." In this and numerous other similar
discussions coming from the West, the category of
"religion" and the norms of theological debate derived
entirely from within one dominant, historical culture
and thought pattern are used to measure and dismiss
apparently similar categories in other cultures. Thus it
is almost wholly taken for granted that Barth's description of "religion" as "unbelief" includes Hindu-
ism, Buddhism, Islam, the Primal World Views, etc.,
and that "true religion," that is, that which is the
bearer of God's revelation through the Holy Spirit,
cannot be found among them. Is this conclusion justifiable? In many of these cultures the totality of life is

not split up into the "religious" and the "secular," and
the word "religion" is not used in the same conceptual
way as in the Western context. *Dharma,* for Hindus
and Buddhists for example, is far more inclusive than
what is denoted by "religion" in the West. It is both
a way of life and a view of life that is much more inclusive. In addition to this, granting that for Christians
"Peniel" or "Evangelical Reformed Christianity" or
Methodism are the sites of God's encounter with humanity, does it follow that one should declare that
Banaras, or Bodh Goya, or Mecca are outside the
orbit of God's Spirit."[18]

Second, it limits "religion" very much to "belief"
and "systems of thought" where people of other faiths
are concerned. A long discussion on certain religions,
e.g., *Yodo-Shin* and *Yodo-Shin-Shu,* and on the Indian
Bhakti religion deals with ideas and techniques, not
with *people* and their inner struggles to understand the
relation between grace and freedom in other cultures.
One of the most important lessons some Christians
have learned reluctantly through the experience of actual dialogues is this *viz.,* that there can be no dialogue
between "religions," between Christianity and Hindu-
ism, between one "belief" and another. Dialogue can
take place only between *people,* living persons, sharing
the conflicts, ambiguities, tragedies, and hopes of human life. The co-existence of particular religions might
provide the historical context in which such living
encounters might take place. When a Christian and a
Hindu or a Muslim or a Marxist meet, sharing the
mystery of existence, longing for salvation and liberation, groping for meaning and struggling for strength,
can one limit the work of the Holy Spirit only to the
Christian partner?

Third, there is the difficult question of the relation
between the human spirit and the Holy Spirit, between
human freedom and the grace of God in the work of

salvation. It is obvious that the crucial point here—as
with the Reformers—is the primacy of God's grace.
But while acknowledging this, is it justifiable to state
it in such a way as to deprive persons totally of their
freedom in encounter with the Gospel? (A similar
point was at issue in the *Bhakti* religion—the well-
known *markata nyāya* and *mārjāla nyāya*—in the persistent debates between the priorities of *Sankara* and
Ramanuja.) Can persons be deprived of active spirit,
which is the principle of their freedom, creativity, and
transcendence without ceasing to be human? Or, as
Hendry puts it, granting that as Christians we appre-
hend God through Christ in the Holy Spirit, does it
follow that apart from this spiritual relation, God and
humanity stand completely unrelated to each other?
To answer this in the affirmative would not only be
"to maintain the sovereignty of grace at too great a
cost," but also to ignore the presence and fruits of
grace in the lives of countless people of other faiths.

This leads to a fourth observation *viz.,* the question
of authority to which some reference was made earlier.
A discussion on the larger work of the Holy Spirit
cannot limit itself to the Scriptures alone. It must also
take into account the different trends within the tradition of the church during the centuries. But if we
are serious when we say we believe in the *living* God
who is the Lord of history, then the present, the contemporary historic context in which people of various
faiths are inter-dependent and have to live together as
neighbors, is equally important. Thus scriptural evidence, the trends in the tradition of the church, and
the sensitivity of Christians to the guidance of the
Holy Spirit, *now* in obedience to the *living* God and
in relation to other people, must all be taken into
account. Therefore, it is important to break out of the
narrow corridors of *Heilsgeschichte* theology which,
as a hermeneutical method, has unduly dominated bib-

lical studies for decades—and as a consequence of
which, Christian attitude toward people of other religious traditions has been almost exclusively negative.
Its narrow view of revelation, and exclusive attitude
toward the work of the Holy Spirit, have marked
Christians with an arrogance which is at variance with
Christ-like humility. It has confused Christian communities wherever they have sought to be responsibly
involved with their neighbors in tackling common concerns in society. In recent years it has been challenged
on various grounds. For one thing, it is now more
clearly recognized that the Bible contains many theolo-
gies and different historical perspectives. Therefore, no
single method of interpretation should be taken as the
norm to judge all others. For another, there are many
who question whether Israel's faith and conception of
history was as "distinctive" or "unique" in the ancient
world as it is claimed. Bertil Albrektson remarks that
a detailed comparison of Near Eastern and biblical
texts have convinced him that on point after point
"the Old Testament has no real claim to a special kind
of history that is in any way distinct from its environ-
ment."[14] More important, the basic assumption that
there are two kinds of history—*Geschichte* and *Historie*
—is seriously questioned by many scholars as being unnecessary and artificial. Weiss says the distinction between two levels of history "is not only necessary but
an exercise in self-defeat."[15] Lastly, one should ask the
question: Are *Heilsgeschichte* and the attitudes engendered by it really relevant to Christians *now* in
inescapably multi-religious and multi-cultural societies
struggling with the question of how to live together in
peace and harmony? Or does it merely refer back to
certain ideological assumptions of the colonial era?[16]
"Contemporary theology must therefore transcend the
notion of 'salvation history' in order to recover the
meaning of *oikonomia*. The economy of Christ cannot

be reduced to its unfolding in history; the heart of it
is the fact that it makes us participants in the very life
of God. It must involve reference to eternity and to
the work of the Holy Spirit. For inherent in the term
of 'economy' is the idea of mystery."[17]

II.

It would be premature and less than helpful to
attempt any systematic treatment of the topic before
us. The data are insufficient, criteria have to be developed responsibly and the insights gained through
actual dialogues have to be carefully evaluated. The
most that can be done at this stage is to give reasons
to reject the negative attitudes, to raise exploratory
questions in more positive ways, and to emphasize the
context of living in dialogue in which this question
can more fruitfully be discussed in a more challenging
manner. In view of the lack of authoritative guidelines,
perhaps it would be wiser at this stage in our relationships with people of other faiths to look for existential
criteria rather than conceptual criteria. In other words,
the question seems to be not what theological reasons
we can advance to ourselves and to our fellow theologians to justify why we are talking kindly to our neighbors of other faiths—sometimes condescendingly—
but how do we understand the work of the Spirit in
our relationships to each other and to God in a world
that is becoming increasingly inter-dependent? Certain
points seem to be fairly clear.

1. There is little said in the Scriptures on the question of the relationship between the Holy Spirit and
people of other faiths. What is said about the Spirit's
activity is within the context of the life and work of the
believing community and should not be regarded as
negative judgment on Hindus, Buddhists, Muslims, and
others today. Therefore, one may at least raise the
question whether it is the most fruitful attitude to claim
the authority of the Scriptures for an exclusive or an

inclusive attitude toward the work of the Spirit in relation to people of other faiths.

2. Sufficient weight must be given to the fact that within the tradition of the church there are divergent tendencies in the Catholic, Orthodox, and Protestant heritages and that, therefore, it is possible for Christians to hold different views on the work of the Holy Spirit in relation to people of other religions. No one particular tendency can be regarded as the norm to judge others. Perhaps there is need for clarification of related questions within the Christian tradition itself, e.g., it would be worthwhile to see what the real issues are if the position of the early Greek Fathers is confronted with that of the Reformers, not in abstract debate, but in the living context of multi-religious and ideological relationships. The real issue may turn out to be not how the two might be theologically divergent but how, together as Christians, those who feel persuaded to follow these respective tendencies relate themselves *now* to others under God. The present and future dimensions of our response to the guidance of the Spirit are more important than obsessive clinging to the controversies of the past.

3. The context of living in dialogue is of particular significance and has to be taken more seriously. Perhaps it is too early to draw theological conclusions on the basis of insights gained and lessons learned in recent meetings. It must be emphasized that our concern here is not just with organized inter-religious meetings limited to intellectual exchanges. Murray Rogers rightly points out that to those who belong to the monotheistic family "true religion" is always a dialogue. First, it is a dialogue of God with us, followed by our response to him, as was most vividly lived by our Lord Jesus Christ. Second, it is dialogue between persons in sharing our experience and knowledge of the mystery of God in Christ. "This human exchange is always a

giving and receiving used by the Holy Spirit to awaken and to bring nearer to fulfillment what was already implanted by God in every man in the first step of creation, the first innumerable calls to participate in the Divine Life."[18] In a real sense, therefore, the Holy Spirit is not a subject for reflection and talking, but for prayer and meditation. Third, it is an inner dialogue within us, with God, in "the cave of the heart," at the very source of our consciousness.

But one should also take into account those who do not belong to the "monotheistic family" of religions. There is a vast unexplored area here which, in the past, has been more or less dismissed as being outside the realm of revelation. For example, a fresh examination of the Hindu view of *ātman* and of *shakti* in connection with the nature and work of the Spirit is yet to be done. The experience of and attitude toward spirits or Spirit in primal world-views, e.g., in Africa, is yet another area to be explored.[19] There is also the question whether God's activity through the work of the Spirit should be confined to the realm of "religions" only, and whether the connection between Spirit and history is the exclusive mark of the Judaeo-Christian tradition. If the prophet, inspired by the Spirit, should *then* describe Cyrus as "The Lord's shepherd" (Isaiah 44:28), and as "his anointed whose right hand I have grasped" (45:1), why not Mahatma Gandhi, Fidel Castro, or Mao Tsetung *now?* Is the liberation of India under Gandhi, of Cuba under Castro, of China under Mao theologically less significant than the *Exodus?* Does not the Spirit of God touch other people in *their* history to transform a certain moment from being part of mere *chronos* to become a significant *kairos?* Or, have we started from a false premise and reached a faulty conclusion limiting him who cannot and should not be limited? "A heathen asked Rabbi Joshua ben Kaska, 'Why did

God speak to Moses from the thorn bush?' Rabbi Joshua replied, 'If he had spoken from a carob tree or from a sycamore you would have asked me the same question! But so as not to dismiss you without an answer, God spoke from the thorn bush to teach you that there is no place where the Shekinah is not, not even a thorn bush'." [20]

4. The moment we talk about criteria to discern the activity of the Spirit we are in a dilemma. If "boundless freedom" is of the very essence of the Spirit, then to put any limits on the Spirit's activity is to negate that freedom. However, without some discernible "signs" to recognize the work of the Spirit we could be lost like a boat without a rudder in a sea of relativism. The Scriptures, the tradition of the church and our obedience to the living God *now* do give us some signs to recognize his continuing work. Spirit means *life,* not death, and so vitality, creativity, and growth. Spirit means *order,* not chaos, and so meaning, significance, and truth become important. Spirit means *community,* not separation, and so sharing, fellowship, bearing one another's burden is another mark. Wherever these marks are found—life, order, and community—there one should sense the work of the Spirit. But these cannot be too heavily drawn up or over-emphasized in structures because any orderly patterns can be broken up by the "boundless freedom" of that very Spirit who refuses to be organized and smothered by human limitations.

5. This leads us to the observation that, at this stage, to be sensitive to the contemporary working of the Holy Spirit might mean getting into areas which may as yet be unfamiliar to most of us and that, therefore, we should probably look for existential rather than conceptual criteria. This does not mean that theological imperatives are to be solely determined by the pressures of history. Neither does it mean that Chris-

tians should be theologically indifferent to their basic commitments. But it does mean that when existential involvement of Christians with people of living faiths and ideologies is taken seriously, older methods of theological approach will inevitably be affected. Life may be recognized to be larger than logic; love may take precedence over truth; the neighbor as a person may become more important than his belief. Reflection on the work of the Spirit may be subordinated to a readiness to be led by the Spirit together with the partners into the depths of God's mystery. Meeting urgent human needs of neighbors may suddenly become more important than prior theological discussion about basis, purpose, and motivations. I wish to illustrate this briefly first by referring to certain ongoing dialogues between Christians and people of living faiths and ideologies, and second by pointing to a contemporary situation in Britain itself.

It is striking that in our recent dialogues the question was mainly: How do we live together, how do we understand our relationship to each other and to God even though we are committed to particular faiths? This surely was not avoiding fundamental issues because such matters as revelation, truth, worship, mission, etc., have come up openly during discussions and these organized dialogues have by no means been without tensions. But these tensions were accepted within a milieu of freedom and friendliness, of confidence and trust where attempts were made to be open to God and to each other. At Ajaltoun, Lebanon, 1970, Christians, Muslims, Hindus, and Buddhists shared with each other their respective experience of dialogues in their particular countries. For the first time, an attempt was made to go beyond religious "ideas" and to open ourselves to the symbols of worship and devotion in a multi-religious context. The Spirit was not a topic for discussion but the milieu in which we met as persons and human beings. The Christian-Jewish meetings are continuing on a regular basis on the theme "The Search for World Community: Christian and Jewish Perspectives."[21] Significantly, the questions of "election," "people of God," "revelation," etc., have not come up prominently in the conversations. The Jews seem to be less keen on "election" at present than some of the "neo-elect" Christians! In July, 1972, a group of forty-six Christians and Muslims, almost equally divided between the two communities of faith, met at Broumana, Lebanon, to consider the theme "In Search of Understanding and Cooperation: Christian and Muslim Contributions."[22] In September, 1973, a consultation in Africa explored the theme: "The Wholeness of Human Life: Christian Involvement in Mankind's Inner Dialogue with Primal World-Views." A multi-religious dialogue on the theme "Towards World Community: Resources and Responsibilities for Living Together" is being prepared for 1974. This would bring together about fifty people from the Hindu, Buddhist, Jewish, Christian, and Muslim communities of faith. What is significant is perhaps not so much the topics discussed as the fact of their coming together and living together. It is the personal, living context and its inevitable consequences on the hearts and minds of people that must be taken seriously. This must increasingly provide us with the milieu in which the question of the continuing work of the Holy Spirit *now* must be experienced and pondered upon.

The second is an illustration taken from Britain itself. The reference is to the British Council of Churches' involvement with the question of the use of church properties for worship or other activities in multi-religious and multi-racial areas.[23] This has a bearing on our subject for several reasons. First, the theological question of what is holy and the work of the Holy Spirit is here discussed not in academic isolation, but

in response to actual and urgent human needs. People
—not just Christians, but Hindus, Buddhists, Muslims,
and Sikhs—are waiting. Second, not only a few theologians but committee members and congregations—
and in an indirect way, people of other faiths—are
already involved in the discussion. Clearly, existential
urgency has become influential in considering priorities.
Third, obviously the decisions taken will have consequences that will go far beyond the local context. This
seems to be one of the questions where theological
issues are inextricably bound up with political, economic, and sociological realities.

In the continuing debate, it was pointed out that the
majority of churches hold "the moderate view which
affirms *both* that Jesus Christ is unique *and* that God's
Spirit is and always has been at work in cultures and
faiths of men."[24] There is a certain impatience with
ponderous theological deliberations. "Are we in danger
of playing with the familiar game of discovering re-
spectable and weighty reasons for supporting disreput-
able positions? Is not the essence of the matter en-
shrined in the parable of the Good Samaritan crystal
clear?" "Let us not become Christian dogs in redundant
mangers."[25] In spite of this impatience, there is a considerable theological discussion on the question of what
is "holy," particularly in connection with church build-
ings once "consecrated," but later on not used by
Christians and now being asked for use by people of
other faiths for their worship. It is recognized that
"Asian Muslims living in our midst, far from being a
threat, may prove to be catalysts who will help English
Christians to rediscover the substance of the Gospel
(often obscured by the inherited cubic footage of redundant fabric).[26] This would apply not only to Muslims but also to Hindus, Buddhists, Sikhs, and others,
and may bring before Christians the question of the
larger work of the Holy Spirit in more urgent and con-

crete ways. Similar multi-religious and multi-racial situations are already developing in other parts of the world, particularly in Europe and America. Such situations are likely to raise perplexing issues to Christians unfamiliar with such experiences. Therefore, the issues raised and attitudes called for will be of considerable interest to others as well.

In many of the textbooks on theology, even in those devoted particularly to the work of the Holy Spirit, one looks in vain for a careful, sympathetic, and extended treatment of the work of the Spirit in relation to the life and thought of people of other faiths, cultures, and ideologies. It may be that one has looked at the wrong type of books but it looks as if, after a long period of neglect, the question of the Holy Spirit and people of other faiths is only now beginning to enter into the spiritual consciousness of people. However, it is yet to be taken seriously into the total spectrum of theological reflection in the church. And the question of the Holy Spirit must inevitably lead to the doctrine of God himself and of the Trinity in far more inclusive ways than Christian theology has ever done before. It must take into account the unknowability, the incomprehensibleness, and the mystery of God and the work of his Spirit among others no less than revelation in Jesus Christ through the Holy Spirit. Questions of peace and justice, of development and education, of dialogue and cooperation, of truth and love, and the almost desperate search for a quality of life that can sustain personal values in an age of technology—these are matters that bring together various people as they share a troubled past and look into a common future. The noise of old crusades, the shelter of ancient fortresses, and the spent bullets of theological armories of the past must be left behind. What we need today is a theology that is not less but more true to God by being generous and open, a theology not less but more loving toward the neighbor by being friendly and willing to listen, a theology that does not separate us from our fellow human beings but supports us in our common struggles and hopes. As we live together with our neighbors, what we need today is a theology that refuses to be impregnable, but which, in the spirit of Christ, is both ready and willing to be vulnerable.

Notes

1. S. J. Samartha, Editor, *Living Faiths and the Ecumenical Movement* (Geneva: World Council of Churches, 1971), p. 132.
2. Hendrikus Berkhof, *The Doctrine of the Holy Spirit* (Richmond, Va.: John Knox Press, 1964), p. 33.
3. *Ibid.,* p. 104.
4. See, for example, P. Evdokimov's paper on "Nature," presented to the Faith and Order Commission Meeting in Aarhus, 1964, published in *Verbum Caro,* 73, 1965. See also, *Mid-Stream,* Vol. X, No. 4, Summer 1971, pp. 6ff, for an article by Metropolitan Emilianos, "The Spirit Enlightens the Whole Mankind."
5. George S. Hendry, *The Holy Spirit in Christian Theology* (Philadelphia: Westminster Press, 1965), p. 29.
6. Augustine, *De Civ. dei,* VIII, 4.
7. Gregory Nazianzen, *OV*.31.5; P.G. 36, 137 B.C.
8. Irenaeus, *Adv. Haeres.,* III, 12:13.
9. Karl Barth, *Church Dogmatics,* Vol. 1 (Edinburgh: T & T Clark, 1955), "The Outpouring of the Holy Spirit," Sec. 2, pp. 103ff; and "The Revelation of God in the Abolition of Religion," Sec. 17, pp. 280ff.
10. *Ibid.,* p. 344.
11. *Ibid.,* p. 339.
12. *Ibid.,* p. 357.
13. S. J. Samartha, "Religious Pluralism and the Quest for World Community;" R. Robert Nelson and E. J. Brill, Editors, *No Man is Alien* (Leiden: E.J. Brill, 1971), pp. 132ff.
14. *History and the Gods* (Lund, C.W.K., Gleerup, 1967), quoted in *Religion and Life,* p. 92 (see footnote 16).
15. J. Weiss, "History and the Gospel," *Novum Testamentum,* 10, 1968, pp. 81-94.
16. For an excellent summary of recent debate on the whole question, see: James T. Clemons, "Critics and Criticism of Salvation History," *Religion in Life,* Vol. XLI, Spring, 1972, pp. 89-100.
17. Samartha, "Living Faiths and the Ecumenical Movement," *op. cit.,* p. 136.

18. Murray Rogers, "The Spirit: The Milieu of Inter-Faith Dialogue," *End and Odds,* Jerusalem, No. 7, 1972, pp. 1ff.
19. John S. Mbiti, "Spiritual Beings, Spirits, and the Living Dead," *African Religions and Philosophy* (London: Heinemann, 1969), pp. 75ff.
20. C. G. Montefiore and H. Loewe, *A Rabbinical Anthology* New York: Macmillan, 1938), p. 13.
21. *Ecumenical Review,* Vol. XXV, No. 2.
22. *Study Encounter,* Vol. VIII, No. 3, 1972, SE/31. The papers presented at the meeting in Broumana, Lebanon, will be available before long.
23. See, *The Use of Church Properties for Community Activities—An Interim Report,* British Council of Churches, Sept., 1972; esp., the theological section by John Picket under the appropriate title, "Let These Stones Live," appendix G.; and *The Use of Church Properties for Community Activities in Multi-Racial Areas: Memorandum of Comment,* Report by the Standing Committee, January 11, 1973, W. D. Pattison, Secretary General.
24. *Ibid.,* p. 33.
25. *Ibid.,* p. 13.
26. *Ibid.,* p. 39.

The Holy Spirit and Liberation Movements:

The Response of the Church

Richard Tholin

Introduction

The purpose of this chapter is to examine the Christian experience of the Holy Spirit in the context of contemporary liberation movements. This is not what I anticipated would become the focus when I began preparation for writing. At that time, my perception of the Spirit was influenced by the revival of Pentecostalism and I tended to view the work of the Spirit as subjective, charismatic, and often ecstatic. As a result, I expected to examine the ways in which the Holy Spirit might be seen as the dynamic element that enables creative change in established, static institutions (in a version of the church-sect tension). But the more I explored the biblical experience of the Spirit the more my purpose had to change. The perception of the Spirit as a source of radical social change persisted, but it became both broader and more precise—broader by moving beyond the church as a self-contained institution to the church as a part of world history, and more precise by focusing on the specific issue of oppression.

As a result, we will examine the biblical experience of the Spirit and its relationship to liberation movements among blacks fighting systems of white racism in the United States and southern Africa, among women resisting the cultural and economic oppression of male-dominated societies and, particularly, among the peoples of the Third World struggling against economic and political exploitation by the developed nations and their agents.

When I reached the decision to deal with liberation, I became acutely aware of my own identity. I am a white, male, affluent American Christian. I have had just enough experience with liberation movements to know that for me to assume the role of interpreter of these movements would be foolhardy. They rightly insist on speaking for themselves. What one in my position can do, however, is to listen and respond out of who one is and to assume responsibility in the light of that which comes from the Spirit and the liberation movements.

I cite this personal position not simply as a catharsis or a predelivery defense mechanism but because, for a long time, this is where the dominant leadership of the churches has been. Despite the beginnings of change, quota systems and all, the church, including Methodist segments of it around the world, has been led predominantly by white, male, middle-aged, relatively affluent Americans or Europeans. We will attempt a response to the Spirit and to movements for liberation from within the church, a church too often part of the systems of oppression that dehumanize blacks, women, the poor, and many others.

Let us begin with a biblical exploration of the work of the Spirit. The biblical word provides the norm for all Christian analysis. But it is particularly important for any analysis of the Holy Spirit. Not all spirits are the Holy Spirit, nor is all enthusiasm the work of the Spirit, as Wesley was quick to point out to his followers. Only those experiences which are in continuity with the biblical record as it comes to focus in the person and work of Jesus Christ are of the Holy Spirit. Further, if the church is to be freed from participation in established systems of oppression, then its resolve must be steeled by the most fundamental sources of its faith. For those in the Wesleyan tradition, the test of

the Spirit and the primary source of the radically converting word is the Bible, as it centers in Jesus Christ.*

* In the delivery of this material as a lecture, adaptations were made
which copyright rules make very difficult in the published version.

One form of oppression is found in language, in this case, the use
of the masculine for all generic terms. Much of the quoted material
in this paper uses male generic language. In the lecture form that
language was changed to more inclusive terms. Readers might well
attempt the same discipline.

In addition, where the pronoun is used for the Holy Spirit the
spoken version used "she." While not making an extended defense
here, there are some hotly debated linguistic arguments for this
usage. In any event, use of the female pronoun for the Spirit can
be a constructive way to move beyond exclusively male designations
for the triune God.

I. The Spirit in the Biblical Witness

A. In the Old Testament

In the Old Testament, the Spirit is *ruach,* the breath
of God. That breath filled inanimate matter and created human life (Genesis 2:7). But contrary to domes-
ticated images of the Spirit, as the gentle breeze com-
forting the weary or inspiring the poet, *ruach* is that
wind of God, out of the desert like Israel itself, that
dried up Noah's flood, held back the waters of the Red
Sea,[1] and devours and withers sinful people like grass.
(Isaiah 40:7, 59:19)

In the early history of Israel, the powerful wind of
God raised up charismatic leaders in the early judges
and kings. (cf. Judges 3:10, 6:34; 1 Samuel 11:6,
16:13) The Spirit was restless and unpredictable, often
creating ecstatic experiences, not unlike similar ecsta-
sies in other Semitic religions. But in the encounter of
Israel with Jahweh the power of the Spirit began to
take a particular form, one that set it completely apart
from interpretations of Spirit-possession in other religions.

The major prophets took the spirit-concept out of these
surroundings, and transformed the divine spirit from
something religiously and ethically neutral into the concept of the purposeful and deliberate operation of God's
personal power . . . in history and creation.[2]

This historicized, Hebraic view of the Spirit is in sharp contrast to all concepts of the Spirit as *mana,* the divine power existing in various forms of nature.[8]

As a result, in the mainstream of Old Testament literature, the Spirit is the source of the prophetic Word, the power of God entering human history through the judgments and actions of God's chosen spokesmen. That Word of the Spirit was not simply words. It was power, the power of God working through both *theoria* and *praxia.* Spirit-filled prophecy included both insight into underlying reality and action based on that insight.[1] As a result, the prophetic word of the Spirit became event. The inspired prophetic insight into God's ultimate purposes and immediate demands created encounters and happenings that shaped the flow of history—as the fear of prophetic proclamation by political leaders made abundantly clear.

But not every claim of prophetic inspiration comes from the Spirit of God. Ecstasy and visions can be claimed by anyone, including the false prophets. (cf. Jeremiah 5:12-13, 14:14, 23:16-22) The true mark of the Spirit is a particular content and concern, a content and concern that flow out of the compassion and commitment of God. Here the prophetic oracles must be allowed to speak for themselves, beginning with one of the most familiar messianic passages of the Old Testament. (Isaiah 11:1-9)

> There shall come forth a shoot from the stump
>   of Jesse and a branch shall grow out of his
>   roots.
> And the Spirit of the Lord shall rest upon him,
>   the spirit of wisdom and understanding,
>   the spirit of counsel and might,
>   the spirit of knowledge and the fear of the Lord.
>   (verses 1-2, RSV)

And what does the king who has the Spirit do?

> He will not judge by appearances,
>   nor decide by hearsay,
> but act with justice to the helpless,
>   and decide fairly for the humble.

> He will strike down the ruthless with his verdicts,
>> and slay the unjust with his sentences.
> Justice shall gird him for action,
>> he shall be belted with trustworthiness.
>> (verses 3b-5, Moffatt)

Only after such judgments is the vision of peace possible where the "wolf shall dwell with the lamb" (verse 6), and "they shall not hurt or destroy in all my holy mountain" (verse 9).

It is crucial to recognize the basic concerns that are linked inseparably to the gift of the Spirit. The Spirit brings justice, not the legalities of clever courtroom argument and external appearances, but the justice of one who loves the poor and helpless, who is consistently biased toward the humble and oppressed. And Spirit-inspired justice includes striking down the power of the ruthless oppressor, a justice that is enacted, not just proclaimed. Then comes the possibility of a land full of peace. (For similar passages in Isaiah, see 2:4, 9:7, and 32:15-18, all of which deal with the Spirit in the context of justice, concern for the oppressed, and the messianic vision of peace.)

The same dynamics can be seen in Micah. In the third chapter, the prophet speaks out against the rulers of Israel, "who hate the good and love the evil . . . who eat the flesh of my people." (verses 1-3) He then attacks the false prophets—". . . the seers shall be disgraced, and the diviners put to shame . . . for there is no answer from God." (verse 7) Then comes the true word of the Spirit.

> But as for me, I am filled with power,
>> with the Spirit of the Lord,
>> and with justice and might,
> to declare to Jacob his transgression
>> and to Israel his sin.
> Hear this, you heads of the house of Jacob
>> and rulers of the house of Israel,
> who abhor justice
>> and pervert all equity,
> who build Zion with blood
>> and Jerusalem with wrong . . .

> Therefore because of you
> Zion shall be plowed as a field . . . .
> (verses 8-10, 12, RSV)

As these and similar passages demonstrate, the Spirit
was given to the prophets to speak the word of the
Lord with a power far beyond their own. And why
did the Lord give this power? Was it to give the Spirit-
possessed the glow of mystical experience, the excite-
ment of ecstasy, the calm assurance of the redeemed?
Hardly. For the prophet, the Spirit was a burning fire
in the bones, a living word that could not be held in,
yet, when spoken, led to pain and alienation from his
own people. (cf. Jeremiah 20:7-18) Why did the
Spirit give prophetic power? Only because the Lord's
commitment to justice and the humanity of the oppressed demanded it. Paul Tillich summarized the
identifying mark of the Spirit in Old Testament literature.

> In all its parts the Old Testament follows this line. There
> is no Spiritual Presence where there is no humanity and
> justice. Without them—and this is the judgment of the
> prophets against their own religion—there is demonized
> or profanized Spiritual Presence.[5]

B. The Spirit in the Gospels

Of all the Gospel writers, Luke is most aware of the
activity of the Spirit and its primary role in providing
the power and authority of Jesus' ministry. It is only
consistent with the Old Testament then that Luke,
more than the other Gospel accounts, also presents
Jesus as the fulfillment of the prophetic stream of
Israel. G.W.H. Lampe describes Luke's basic perspective.

> Yet, although he excels the ancient prophets (by his
> steady, rather than intermittent, union with the Spirit),
> Jesus is nevertheless himself a prophet for whom they
> had prepared the way; his person and office, as described
> by St. Luke, recall many features of the character and
> work of the most outstanding figures among them; and
> he is presented to the readers of this Gospel and Acts as
> the fulfillment of the prophecy of Deuteronomy 18:15:

"The Lord thy God will raise up unto thee a prophet
. . . like unto me (Moses): unto him shall ye hearken."
(cf. Acts 3:22-23, 7:37)[6]

The Spirit-inspired, prophetic view of Jesus is set
firmly in a messianic context. In inter-Testamental
times, it was believed that the prophetic gift had ended
at the close of the Old Testament period. Since "the
Holy Spirit was primarily the spirit of prophecy," this
meant that the Holy Spirit was also absent. When
prophecy by the Spirit broke out again it would signal
the start of the messianic era.[7] Luke describes the
annunciation and birth of John and Jesus as just such
a new and powerful pouring out of the Spirit, seen
primarily in the oracles of the primary figures, including, Mary, Zechariah, and Simeon. But most of all, it
was the prophetic figure of John, striding out of the
wilderness, preaching the judgments of God upon his
generation, who was seen as the forerunner of the one
who would fulfill the messianic visions of the prophets.
Whatever else Jesus' baptism meant, it certainly identified him with the prophetic purpose and preaching of
John. It is hardly accidental that it was in the midst
of a prophetic movement, not in the official precincts
of the Temple or the neighborly circle of the synagogue,
that the Spirit descended on Jesus.

Thus, in Luke, the renewed activity of the Spirit is
linked with prophetic proclamation and the messianic
role of Jesus. But it is not just a proof-texting use of
the prophetic predictions without any concern for the
content of prophetic preaching. Mixed through these
events was the continuing concern of God for justice
and the cause of the oppressed. The core of the oracle
of Mary echoes with the words of Amos and Micah, a
fact not missed by the socialist Anglo-Catholic rector
of Thaxted, Conrad Noel, when the statue of the Virgin
and child in his church carried the words:

He has shown strength with his arm,
he has scattered the proud in the imaginations
    of their hearts,
he has put down the mighty from their thrones,
and exalted those of low degree;
he has filled the hungry with good things,
and the rich he has sent empty away.
(Luke 1:51-53, RSV)

The basic concern for justice and the poor also broke through John's preaching of repentance. When his hearers were stricken and asked what they should do, John translated the basic prophetic concerns into specific instructions that fit the situations of the penitents. This contrasts to so much of our generalized, spiritualized, and sanitized preaching. The multitude was to give priority to the needs of the poor: "He who has two coats, let him share with him who has none; and he who has food, let him do likewise." Tax-collectors were to behave justly: "Collect no more than is appointed you." And most importantly, soldiers, who enforced the power of the state, were not only to be just but were to get off the backs of the oppressed: "Rob no one by violence or by false accusation, and be content with your wages." (Luke 3:10-14) While on first reading these would seem mild enough, to carry through such acts of repentance would have been revolutionary for the social order of the time, just as they would be in legislative budget committees, offices of multi-national corporations, the White House, and urban police headquarters today.

When Jesus returned from his baptism he "was led by the Spirit" into the wilderness, very much in keeping with the biographies of earlier prophets. There he went through the struggle that prepared him for the messianic crisis he was to initiate. The relevance of this struggle for Jesus' later ministry has been interpreted many ways. But James H. Cone, writing from within a black community sensitized by struggle against white oppression, presents an understanding of this passage that fits the prophetic nature of Jesus' mission more closely than other interpretations.

> The Tempter's concern is to divert Jesus from the reality of his mission with the poor. Jesus' refusal to turn the stone into bread, or to worship the Tempter, or to throw himself from the pinnacle of the Temple (Luke 4:3-12) may be interpreted as his refusal to identify himself with any of the available modes of oppressive or self-glorifying power. His being in the world is as one of the humiliated, suffering poor.[8]

All of this comes to sharpest focus in Jesus' announcement of his mission in Nazareth. Here the work of the Spirit, the commitment of the Old Testament prophets to justice and the poor, and the dawn of the messianic era, are all fused in one powerful purpose expressed in the classic messianic passage from Isaiah 61.

> The Spirit of the Lord is upon me, because he has anointed me to preach good news to the poor. He has sent me to proclaim release to the captives and recovering of sight to the blind, to set at liberty those who are oppressed, to proclaim the acceptable year of the Lord.
> (Luke 4:18-19, RSV)

With this passage the basic relationship of the Spirit to the ministry of Jesus is set. Subsequently, Luke does not deal so explicitly with the Spirit. Instead, he describes the results of the Spirit's prophetic work in Jesus' preaching of the Kingdom of God with authority and power[9] and in his continual identification of God's redemptive activity with the poor and the oppressed.

Jesus' bias toward the poor comes as a shock to affluent Christians. But it pervades his teaching and action so completely that it can be denied only by evasion. The Sermon on the Plain in Luke is explicit.

> Blessed are you poor, for yours is the kingdom of God.
> Blessed are you that hunger now, for you shall be satisfied.
> Blessed are you that weep now, for you shall laugh.
> Blessed are you when men hate you, and when they exclude you and revile you, and cast out your name as evil, on account of the Son of Man! Rejoice in that day, and leap for joy, for behold, your reward is great in heaven; for so their fathers did to the prophets.
> (Luke 6:20b-23, RSV)

It is important to note how Luke differs from Matthew. Matthew uses the phrases "poor in spirit" and "hunger and thirst after righteousness;" Luke uses only the words "the poor" and "hunger." And in case the point is missed, the Lucan version describes the other half of the great reversal of the Kingdom.

> But woe to you that are rich, for you have received your consolation.
> Woe to you that are full now, for you shall hunger.
> Woe to you that laugh now, for you shall mourn and weep.
> Woe to you, when all men speak well of you, for so their fathers did to the false prophets.
> (Luke 6:24-26, RSV)

And this pervades Jesus' teaching. Two of his most powerful parables—the rich fool (Luke 12:13-21) and Dives and Lazarus (Luke 16:19-31)—dramatize the judgment of God on the uncaring rich. The pointed reply to the rich man, when he pleads to send a messenger to warn his family, is, "They have Moses and the prophets; let them hear them." (Luke 16:29)

Like the prophets, Jesus did not limit his pedagogy to words. The prophetic praxis was at work in his actions, including probably the most dramatic of his public confrontations. Jesus' cleansing of the Temple, following hard on the symbolic actions of his entry into Jerusalem, is now widely interpreted as a demonstration of messianic authority, not simply a puritan campaign against selling in sacred precincts or cheating on ecclesiastical exchange rates. But the prophetic content, i.e., God's concern for justice and the oppressed, is not so commonly seen in the midst of the messianic symbolism. And yet the Synoptic accounts of Jesus' brief words of explanation point in precisely that direction. Through the short-hand of referring to well-known Old Testament passages by citing a very familiar phrase from them, Jesus evokes—with "my house shall be a house of prayer for all nations"—a high point of prophetic universalism in Isaiah 56:1-8; and—with "you have made it a den of robbers"—the great Temple address of Jeremiah 7. The Isaiah passage speaks some of the strongest yet most tender words of inclusion for the rejected and despised found in biblical literature— in this case for eunuchs and foreigners. The Jeremiah passage derides all attempts to buy God's protection from the beseiging Babylonians with Temple litanies and demands; instead, it proclaims that they will be saved only if they "truly execute justice one with another . . . do not oppress the alien, the fatherless or the widow, or shed innocent blood . . . ." (Jeremiah 7:5) The Gospel accounts do not make clear the specific abuses Jesus was protesting. He could well have been taking action against the oppression of alien converts and women who may have been virtually excluded from Temple worship by relegation to areas not only on the margins of the Temple but also pre-empted for Temple profit-making. But whatever the specific abuses in the Temple or social order, the prophetic roots of Jesus' pedagogical action were clear. True worship demands participation in God's commitment to justice and inclusiveness, with special concern for the oppressed and excluded.

Finally, Jesus' active identification with the poor meant his life took the form of the Suffering Servant. This, too, continues the prophetic purpose. Lampe points out the connections.

> The Servant is pre-eminently a prophet, one in whom God had put his Spirit. (Isaiah 42:1) He is in some respects a new Moses . . . . His office, like that of Moses, is to release men from bondage and darkness by the power of the Lord . . . . (Isaiah 42:7)[10]

The whole series of events leading to Jesus' death— trials before the powerful authorities of Temple religion and Roman imperialism, torture by the soldiers, and execution among thieves—dramatized that the redemption brought by Jesus came not through participation in the forces of oppression but through identification with those condemned by established and quite legal authority. Like the Servant, "he was numbered with the lawless." (Luke 22:37; Isaiah 53:12) When God authored the triumph of the Resurrection, he set an ultimate contradiction in human history. His saving action came through self-sacrifice and suffering, through identification with the powerless and the outcast. The power of the oppressors, even when allied with death itself, is not final. The Servant becomes the judge, the Lord of history. The small community of Christians soon began to sing, "at the name of Jesus every knee should bow, in heaven and on earth and under the earth, and every tongue confess that Jesus Christ is Lord . . . ." (Philippians 2:10-11)

C. The Spirit in the New Testament Church

The work of the Spirit in the mission of the church is in continuity with the work of the Spirit in the life of Jesus, a continuity made clear by the unity of Luke-Acts. But the context changed in the early church. First, the scope of its work broadened. This can be seen in the new understanding of the kingdom of God that dawned on the disciples. "What the nature of that kingdom was to be they began to discover after the Resurrection. It turned out to be, not a restoration of the kingdom to Israel, but a mission to the world.[11] And God's Spirit was to fuel that mission.

> But you shall receive power when the Holy Spirit has come upon you; and you shall be my witnesses in Jerusalem and in all Judea and Samaria and to the end of the earth. (Acts 1:8)

Both the continuity and the changing context of the work of the Spirit can be seen in the account of Pentecost. In the Lucan account, prophesying, i.e., preaching, is still "the central and decisive activity of the Spirit,"[12] as it was in the Old Testament and with Jesus. But the context has become the world, not Israel. The crucial result of the gift of the Spirit at Pentecost is not ecstatic experience for its own sake but as a missional gift, i.e., the power to preach to all nations. As a result, it is possible to interpret the account of speaking in tongues as "a proleptic summary of the missionary story which is to be unfolded in the whole of the subsequent record in Acts."[13] The basic interpretation of what is happening comes from Joel, in which Luke underlines the way the Spirit means prophecy. Finally, the climactic event of the coming of the Spirit is Peter's kerygmatic preaching and the great ingathering of converts.

Second, the time span of the mission is seen as very short. The Gospel must be spread throughout the world before the return of the Lord. Therefore, the gift of the Spirit "inaugurates an intermediate period in the history of God's redemptive purposes," one which fulfills the prophetic expectation of the outpouring of the Spirit envisioned in Joel and "the ground of a new hope that Jesus will come again."[14] The strategy of the Spirit flows out of this shortened time span, a strategy that soon focused on missionary preaching to all peoples. Eduard Schweitzer points out how this basic perspective on the work of the Spirit permeates all the major New Testament letters, not just Luke's account in Acts.

> In this way, in John as in Paul, the Jewish answer is given a new twist: the Spirit is the Spirit of prophecy; but this is not a phenomenon of remote ages, but is the power of God now present in the preaching of the church, moulding the life of the Last-Age people of God and so challenging and judging the world.[15]

The continuities in method and content with Jesus' preaching of the kingdom of God and with the Israelite prophets need to be seen. The preaching of both Old Testament prophets and the New Testament church is a radical confrontation with human sin, a crisis that demands decision. Both insist on the necessity of conversion, that is, a turning away from sin in repentance and a turning toward God and divine love. And in both, the preached word is not just words, but the action of God that creates a new history for those it confronts.

The experience of the Spirit in the New Testament church also has some connections to the priority given by Jesus and the prophets to the poor. The gift of the Spirit created a new kind of corporate life, what Paul called "the fellowship of the Holy Spirit." The most obvious result at the time of Pentecost was a combination of intimate fellowship in worship and a radical communal sharing of goods. Dodd points out that each of the two accounts (in Acts 2 and 4) of such radical sharing, "which are thought to emanate from separate sources, is given as the immediate sequel to an account of the descent of the Holy Spirit."[16]

The most important connection, however, is the eschatalogical faith of the early church that saw Jesus as Lord over all principalities and powers. (cf. Colossians 1:16) That faith enabled Christians to stand against political and religious authorities, when necessary, in order to proclaim the Word, a power of contradiction that the Spirit gave both the Old Testament prophets and the followers of Jesus.

> And when they bring you before the synagogues and the rulers and the authorities, do not be anxious how or what you are to answer or what you are to say, for the Holy Spirit will teach you in that very hour what you ought to say. (Luke 12:11-12, RSV)

The record of Acts is that neither Temple authorities (Acts 4) nor Roman governors (Acts 24-26) could silence that powerful word. This Spirit-filled power of contradiction made the early church suspect in centers of established power and gave even simple Christians the confidence that they would triumph while the massive power of Rome would fall. An apocryphal story recounts the answer of a second century martyr to the taunt, "And what is your carpenter of Nazareth doing now?" as, "He is building coffins for Rome."

But the difference also must be recognized. As the church moved out of the people of Israel into the more diverse and individualistic Greco-Roman world, the concern for justice in political and economic structures found in the Hebrew prophets faded into the shadows of the consciousness of the church. And the commitment to the poor and oppressed was translated into communal sharing within the church, a sharing that in the early period of charismatic enthusiasm was radical but as the church grew soon became charity for the poor rather than socialization of all resources. In this sense, the prophetic Spirit of the Old Testament and Jesus was narrowed by the early church to the personal confrontation of individuals with the kerygmatic message and to the internal life of the church.

In another sense, the social consequences of the Spirit, working through prophetic proclamation, were broadened as the church broke out of the confines of Israel and undertook a worldwide mission. The potential power for radical political and economic change was submerged under individual and church consciousness which hardened over the centuries into heavy layers of institutional structure and political establishment. At the same time, the prophetic message of God's commitment to justice remained alive in segments of the church's life, waiting to be activated by the Spirit when historical situations sensitized Christians to hear the Word again. The Old Testament remained part of the canon and the Jesus of the Gospels, speaking through his dramatic parables and actions, led some Christians of all eras to stand with the poor and oppressed as an act of discipleship. The contradiction of human power made possible by the eschatological faith in Jesus as Lord and empowered by the Spirit steeled disciples to stand against the powers of this world. The evangelical preaching of the church called for radical repentance and conversion that, even when it was individualized and privatized in its concepts of sin, still challenged the values and orders of the world. When human history did not end in one generation, when Christians began to assume responsibility for government and the use of economic power, then these submerged forces again became appropriate for those who took seriously the Lordship of Jesus Christ, just as they had for the prophets and for Jesus in bringing the prophetic word to the nation of Israel.

II. The Church, the Spirit and Contemporary Liberation Movements

If at the heart of the work of the Spirit in the biblical record is action "to proclaim release to the captives . . ., to set at liberty those who are oppressed," (Isaiah 61:1-2, Luke 4:18) it should come as no surprise that Christians are confronted with the possibility that the Spirit is at work in the midst of movements for human liberation. In our time, many Christians, speaking from within oppressed communities which seek liberation, are insisting that such is precisely the case—James Cone, for instance.

> The Holy Spirit is the Spirit of the Father and the Son at work in the forces of human liberation in our society today. In America, the Holy Spirit is black people making decisions about their togetherness, which means making preparation for an encounter with white people.[17]

What follows is an attempt to see how the biblical view of the Spirit, the contemporary mission of the church, and a particular liberation movement interact in our moment of history. It will focus on only one liberation movement—that found in South America— and two spokesmen: Paulo Freire as the primary one, whose *Pedagogy of the Oppressed* "is rooted in concrete situations" and 'grows out of his identification with the peasants of northeastern Brazil through a liberation movement combining literacy training and political action;[18] and Rubem Alves, as the secondary source, who, in *A Theology of Human Hope,*[19] does theology in the context of the political humanism of revolutionary movements in South America. Given the limits of time, choosing one movement is the only way to make it possible for a liberation movement to speak even minimally for itself.

Freire has written his book for "radicals" (which I presume can be a legitimate description of a prophetic people possessed by the Spirit). As a result, he is "certain that Christians and Marxists, though they may disagree with me . . . will continue reading to the end."[20] Out of his reflection on his experience, he draws a sharp distinction between radicalization and sectarianism. "Sectarianism makes myths and thereby alienates; radicalization is critical and thereby liberates." Sectarianism can be of the Right, which treats the past as "something given and immutable;" or of the Left, in which " 'tomorrow' is decreed beforehand, is inexorably preordained." Both types of sectarianism are reactionary. Both types, "treating history in an equally proprietary fashion, end up without the people —which is another way of being against them."[21]

> The radical, committed to human liberation, does not become the prisoner of a "circle of certainty" within which he also imprisons reality. On the contrary, the more radical he is, the more fully he enters into reality so that, knowing it better, he can better transform it. He is not afraid to confront, to listen, to see the world unveiled. He is not afraid to meet the people or to enter into dialogue with them. He does not consider himself the proprietor of history or of men, or the liberator of the oppressed; but he does commit himself, within history, to fight at their side."[22]

For Freire and Alves, the core of liberation movements is not programs of economic welfare or even of political power, essential as these may be. The heart of the liberation movement is a vision of what it means to be human and a commitment to a process of humanization. According to Alves,

> Humanization, therefore, is not created by economic panaceas. It exists to the extent to which man, as free subject, creates his future, the future which liberates him from the passivity under which the master keeps him. "Man is only truly man," observes Paul VI in *Populorum Progressio,* "in as far as master of his own acts and judge of their worth, he is author of his own advancement."[23]

Oppression is everything that dehumanizes persons by dominating and controlling them, by treating them as powerless Objects. Liberation is setting the oppressed free to be Subjects, to find power to create their own unique history. Oppressive dehumanization and liberating humanization exist in contradiction.

> But while both humanization and dehumanization are real alternatives, only the first is man's vocation. This vocation is constantly negated, yet it is affirmed by that very negation. It is thwarted by injustice, exploitation, oppression, and the violence of the oppressors; it is affirmed by the yearning of the oppressed for freedom and justice and by their struggle to recover their lost humanity."[24]

The tool that the oppressed use for their liberation, in Freire's analysis, is conscientization (more familiar to some as "consciousness-raising"[25]). Conscientization includes four elements, integrated into one process. First, there is the growing awareness of basic contradictions between what the oppressed can be and what the oppressive system allows them to be, an awareness of their special human gifts and calling and of the forces of oppression that block the full realization of their humanity. Second, such a new consciousness is not a result of abstract analysis but of a combination of reflection and action. It is praxis, i.e., "action and reflection of men upon their world in order to reform it."[26] In an oppressive system praxis includes resistance, the negating of the oppressors' negation of their humanity. Third, a new consciousness brought alive in praxis is always corporate; it is impossible apart from

solidarity among the oppressed as they develop power
to break out of the grip of the oppressor. Finally, the
basic dynamic is liberation, one that stands both at
the end of the process and inside it, one that finally
frees the oppressor as well as the oppressed. "This,
then, is the great humanistic and historical task of the
oppressed: to liberate themselves and their oppressors,
as well."[27] For those on top in an unjust society, who
see the latter element as "humane" use of their power
to "help" the oppressed, a further word must be heard.

> The oppressors, who oppress, exploit, and rape by virtue
> of their power, cannot find in this power the strength to
> liberate either the oppressed or themselves. Only power
> that springs from the weakness of the oppressed will be
> sufficiently strong to free both.[28]

How does the church, sometimes a direct supporter
of oppression and often integrated into the established
order that benefits from exploitation of the powerless,
respond to such movements of liberation? Particularly,
is there any affinity between the biblical experience of
the Spirit and the process by which a church dominated
by white, male, middle-aged, affluent American and
European leadership responds to movements of liberation among blacks, women, the young, the poor and
the Third World? The process of conscientization can
provide a useful framework for such an exploration.

A. Developing an Awareness of the Contradictions Between Liberation and Oppression

The first requirement of Christians who hold power
in our society is to listen. This has always been the first
task of any Spirit-inspired, prophetic community, as
John Taylor insists.

> What turned a man into a prophet was not eloquence
> but vision, not getting the message across but getting the
> message. Prophecy is essentially an act of recognition by
> which one sees the significance of an event as a revela-
> tion that must be passed on.[29]

That moment of vision always comes as a gift, not a
product of our skill and effort. But we can be sensi-

tized to the possibility of new vision by recollection of the way the Spirit has worked in the biblical community and by listening with anticipation to the oppressed themselves.

Confronting the biblical experience has been the aim of the first half of this chapter. Some of that analysis has direct connections to the process of a new awareness of the contradictions of oppression. First, in the Old Testament and in Jesus, the Spirit is the source of passionate commitment to justice, of clear bias toward the poor, the excluded, and the oppressed, and of judgment upon the oppressors. But the identification with the oppressed goes deeper than words. In the Incarnation, Jesus becomes one with the poor and powerless, finally taking the form of the Servant who is crucified as a criminal. And he says we continue to meet him in the hungry and imprisoned. (Matthew 25:31-46) In the light of this, when the church is inescapably involved in the historical issues of its world, it will share the prophetic commitment to the powerless and expect the vision of the Spirit to come from the poor and oppressed more than from the oppressors.

Second, the Spirit inspired the eschatological vision of the people of God, both in the Old and New Testaments, a vision that always provided a vivid contrast between the way things are and the way God intends them to be. John Taylor again puts it well.

This unique and authentic opening of the eyes by the Spirit of creativity within the heart of all things produces that double exposure by which what is and what might be are seen in a single vision. The fire with which he burns is the fire of judgment precisely because it is the fire of creation. Possessed by such a Spirit, the prophet is bound to criticize and protest.[30]

Third, the Spirit has been the power that breaks through the thick barriers of prejudice and exclusion so that dialogue can take place. Peter's experience, as the Spirit dragged him out of the confines of superiority into an encounter with Cornelius, was such an event.

His radical new insight, "Truly, I perceive that God shows no partiality, but in every nation any one who fears him and does what is right is acceptable to him," (Acts 10:34-35) helped to enable Jews and Gentiles to meet each other as equals in genuine dialogue, not as superiors and inferiors. That same Spirit freed the church to recognize that there is "neither slave nor free, neither male nor female for you are all one in Christ Jesus." (Galatians 3:28) As a result, it should surprise no one if the Spirit calls those with power to listen to the oppressed, including fellow Christians, as equals. In many situations of oppression, it is precisely the ability to enter into such dialogue that can be the beginning of liberation for both the oppressed and the oppressors.[81]

All this leads to the conviction that the Spirit does not speak *about* the oppressed so much as the Spirit speaks *through* the oppressed. I would judge that most of us have had experiences that bear this out. Those of us for whom a social system works well find it almost impossible to break through the network of myths that every system develops, not only to explain but to justify, the vast inequities between rich nations and poor nations, between black and white.[82] And even when uncomfortable perceptions slip through the grid, they are too weak to overcome the inertia of familiar and comfortable patterns of life. Those among the oppressed who have to deal with leaders of established churches are quite clear about this. James Cone says it for blacks.

> White theologians, not having felt the sting of oppression, will find it most difficult to criticize this nation, for the condemnation of America means a condemnation of self.
>
> The true black thinker is in a different position. He cannot be *black* and be identified with the powers that be. To be black is to be committed to destroying everything this country loves and adores. Creativity and passion are possible when one stands where the black man stands, a

creature who has visions of the future because the present is unbearable.[33]

The oppressed are the only ones who can make clear, without either hardhearted evasion or sentimentality, what an oppressive system is doing to their humanity. Even more, once those on top begin to listen, the oppressed are the ones who can communicate contradictions and protective myths of the whole system. Often this must come through painful confrontation and acts of resistance that force the attention of the powerful, even practicing Christians among them. At other times, the demythologizing comes through humor, which requires a double vision of what is and what is pretended to be and recognizes that what society considers ultimate is not so profoundly serious as it pretends—a double vision with marked similarities to Christian eschatology.[34] As a result, the shafts of humor that suddenly reveal the truth of a system usually come from those who know oppression first hand. A personal experience can illustrate this. In the mid-1960's, we saw James Baldwin's play, *Blues for Mister Charlie,* in a predominantly black audience in New York. At one point in the play, the hero, a black musician, after ten years in the North, returns to his home town in the deep South and reports to his family.

> Edna . . . she said it wasn't as tight for a black man up there as it was down here. Well, that's a crock, Grandmama, believe me when I tell you. At first I thought it was true, hell, I was just a green country boy and they ain't got no signs up, dig, saying you can't go here—or you can't go there. No, you got to find that out all by your lonesome.

We smiled, but the rest of the audience exploded. And the experience became a sharp knife that punctured the pretense that hid the depths of oppression in our "liberal" world.

B. Conversion and Praxis

Freire describes a basic dynamic of conscientization that forms a second link to the experience of the Spirit.

Liberation is thus a childbirth, and a painful one. The man who emerges is a new man, viable only as the oppressor-oppressed contradiction is superseded by the humanization of all men. Or to put it another way, the solution of this contradiction is born in the labor which brings this new man into the world: no longer oppressor or oppressed, but man in the process of achieving freedom.[35]

For the oppressed, according to Freire, part of the pain in the birth of freedom is the risk of making choices, of challenging overwhelming power, of becoming a threat to oppressed comrades who are fearful of still greater oppression if they stand up to the powers that control them.

When we turn to the oppressors, the required transformation is even more radical. "Conversion to the people requires a profound rebirth. Those who undergo it must take on a new form of existence; they can no longer remain as they were."[36] Nor is this a matter of rhetoric or feeling. It requires radical action that links one's future to the oppressed.

Discovering himself to be an oppressor may cause considerable anguish, but it does not necessarily lead to solidarity with the oppressed. Rationalizing his guilt through paternalistic treatment of the oppressed, all the while holding them fast in a position of dependence, will not do. Solidarity requires that one enter into the situation of those with whom one is identifying; it is a radical posture.[37]

The biblical experience of the Spirit introduced a similar crisis of decision that could lead to a radical change, to a turning around, to conversion. To the prophets, use of power to exploit the helpless came under God's judgment. Only if one repented and then acted with justice could God's salvation come. Otherwise, one could repeat the magic words, "The Temple of the Lord," all day and offer sacrifices of ritual penitence forever and God's righteous anger would not be assuaged. (Jeremiah 7) Jesus' preaching of the Kingdom and his authoritative actions required a similar kind of radical decision. Nor did Jesus settle for token repentance or easy charity while keeping one's basic source of power intact. The rich young ruler was confronted with a decision, not about charitable tithes, but about his capital and identification with the powerlessness of Jesus' disciples.

Conversion has, over the centuries, often been so privatized or sacramentalized by the churches that it loses much of its impact. Yet, it retains in its Gospel form a power that has sometimes reached those who exercise or share in the benefits of exploitive power. Roman Catholic leaders in the Third World, sensitized by liberation movements and their faith, have recognized the power of conversion, as expressed in "Gospel and Revolution: Pastoral Letter from the Third World," written under the direction of Dom Helder Camera, Archbishop of Recife, August 15, 1967.

> From the doctrinal point of view, the church knows that the gospel demands the first and the most radical revolution—conversion, total transformation from sin to grace, from selfishness to love, from pride to humble service. And this conversion not only is inner and spiritual but is addressed to the whole man, the physical and social creature as well as the unique spiritual person.[38]

For many of us in the Wesleyan tradition the last ten years of confrontation by movements for liberation have brought the beginnings of a similar realization, cast in terms of our particular historical experience. A personal experience, one similar to what many of you have experienced, can illustrate the process. In 1963 some of us were confronted with a call for support from a group of black students who, with a few whites, had been arrested when attempting quietly to worship in a prestigious white Methodist church (ironically on Worldwide Communion Sunday). So early one Saturday evening three of us white pastors from a distant state found ourselves sitting on the floor of a crowded room with black students, singing, sharing experiences, laughing. But overarching everything was a sense of tension, the tension that grips you when you know that hard decisions must soon be made. Those decisions would lead to action, action that meant standing together publicly in a society dominated by whites and heavy with violence. And if we were to take that stand it meant taking orders from blacks, following their strategy completely, not knowing what to expect, not able to control the results. And suddenly I was back in a small Evangelical United Brethren church during evangelistic services, where there was lively singing, shared testimonies, laughter and, at the same time, the steady tension of knowing that an altar call was coming, that one must face a decision that could lead to action, first by taking a public stand at the altar and then by open Christian witnessing among one's friends. The future it would lead to was uncertain. In both situations, the dynamics were remarkably alike. And the response, the taking of a stand and the joy that swept around us afterwards in the living fellowship of those who shared a common commitment, was the same. The difference was that in one the Spirit confronted me with a decision about personal salvation and in the other, with a decision about standing with those seeking liberation. Such a short-term involvement is only a taste of the long-term commitments involved in genuine conversion or solidarity. In both there was an authentic biblical content and the dynamics of the Spirit. Together they provide some awareness of the radical range of conversion to which the Spirit calls, in experience consistent with our Wesleyan heritage.

C. Solidarity with the Oppressed

If those who benefit from oppression repent, if they turn around and act differently, they will not overcome the dichotomy between oppressor and oppressed by just any actions. The action that is required is solidarity with the oppressed. Freire makes clear the way action and solidarity are intertwined.

> . . . true solidarity with the oppressed means fighting at
> their side to transform the objective reality which has
> made them these "beings for another." The oppressor
> shows solidarity with the oppressed only . . . when he
> stops making pious, sentimental, and individualistic ges-
> tures and risks an act of love. True solidarity is found
> only in the plenitude of this act of love, in its existen-
> tiality, in its praxis. It is farce to affirm that men are
> people and thus should be free, yet to do nothing tangi-
> ble to make this affirmation a reality.[39]

But even when those who have been part of the
controlling strata align themselves with the oppressed,
there remains a distinct possibility that the spirit of
their identification can destroy its value. The danger is
to assume that they are to lead the oppressed or to
speak for them rather than to join them. Something
of this can be seen in the response of one Christian
thinker.

> We must demand entrance to the powerful because, in
> virtue of representing the poor, we are ambassadors of
> Christ. I hold that in every situation of injustice and op-
> pression, the Christian—who cannot deal with it by vio-
> lence—must make himself completely a part of it *as
> representatives of the victims* . . . . (stress in original)[40]

In contrast, Freire warns of the dangers of a conversion that retains the paternalistic position of the con-
vert.

> . . . certain members of the oppressor class join the
> oppressed in their struggle for liberation, thus moving
> from one pole of the contradiction to the other. Theirs is
> a fundamental role and has been throughout the history
> of the struggle. It happens, however, that as they cease
> to be exploiters or indifferent spectators or simply the
> heirs of exploitation and move to the side of the ex-
> ploited, they almost always bring with them the marks
> of their origin: their prejudices and their deformations,
> which include a lack of confidence in the people's ability
> to think, to want, and to know. Accordingly, these ad-
> herents to the people's cause constantly run the risk of
> falling into a type of generosity as harmful as that of the
> oppressors . . . because of their background they believe
> that they must be the executors of the transformation.
> They talk about the people, but they do not trust them;
> and trusting the people is the indispensable precondition
> for revolutionary change. A real humanist can be identi-
> fied more by his trust in the people, which engages him

in their struggle, than by a thousand actions in their favour without that trust.[41]

The perspective of this extended quotation is crucial for the leadership of the church if it is to work for authentic liberation. The objective of liberation is not simply political and economic programs but humanization. It aims to enable all persons to become Subjects, to create their own unique history. Control by the sympathetic and benevolent is still control.

One of the major functions of the Spirit has been to create solidarity among those who are converted. In Tillich's terms:

> The divine Spirit's invasion of the human spirit does not occur in isolated individuals but in social groups, since all the functions of the human spirit—moral self-integration, cultural self-creation, and religious self-transcendence—are conditioned by the social context of the ego-thou encounter.[42]

The experience of the early church is a good bit more graphic. As we have seen, the coming of the Spirit created a radical new community, one in which each person gave up the security of individual possessions and became solidly a part of the new community, a solidarity so powerful that to betray it—to "lie to the Holy Spirit"—was a life and death matter. (Acts 5:1-11)

The commitment to solidarity is particularly important for those of us in Methodist churches. With the discipline and group support of the class meeting far in the past, we often are surfeited with individualism and private pietism. As a result, the work of the Spirit is seen almost entirely as a source of inner, personal experience and seldom as the creator of a powerful new community. If we are to appropriate the meaning of the Spirit in our age, we need to open ourselves to a converting power that drives us into solidarity with all those who do God's work among the peoples of the world.

But the solidarity Freire calls for is solidarity with

the oppressed. And it must be a solidarity that trusts the people and supports their liberated potential. At this point, we must turn again to the prophetic identification with the poor, made visible in Jesus, who took upon himself the life of the poor and mixed with society's outcasts, not in condescension but in joy. He did not talk so much about lifting up the poor as joining them—"for every one who exalts himself will be humbled, but he who humbles himself will be exalted." He did not organize programs of charitable good works but dignified and accepted thankfully the gifts of those whom society ignored or despised (cf. the woman who anointed his feet or the widow dropping her coins in the Temple chest).

Where solidarity with the oppressed will lead varies with the situation and the range of options open. In some cases, where all options for peaceful protest and change are closed, some Christians, like Camillo Torres, may join the guerillas.[48] Others, like Archbishop Camera, may stay in high office in the church, live a simple life and use their position to challenge the violent injustice of the established order and to amplify the voice of the powerless. In other situations, those with power in the church, including the power of position and budget, will give up that power when powerless groups raise their voice, not as an act of paternalistic charity but as the result of honest dialogue and negotiation among equals. Churches with political and economic influence in developed countries will press for policies that enable equity and self-determination for the Third World. At a minimum, Christians will not oppose forces which make them their wealth and power. The pastoral letter from the Third World pleads for at least that much sensitivity to the Spirit.

> Even if we have not been able to (share all that we have) voluntarily through love, let us know at least how

to recognize the hand of God, correcting us like children
through the events that compel us to make this sacri-
fice.[44]

In all of these ways, and many others, the key question
will be solidarity. If the church's commitments are
clear, if it stays in direct and constant communication
with the oppressed, if it is willing to be a servant, not
a master, then ways will be found to support genuine
liberations.

The same must be said for the issue of violence.
Some Christians argue that they cannot support, much
less commit themselves to, movements of liberation
because they entail violence. But the prior question is,
"Which side are you on?" If one is a pacifist and is in
solidarity with the oppressed, then he or she will be
keenly aware of the official and legal violence that
maintains systems of exploitation and suppression. For
such persons, there is much useful work to be done in
calling attention to and acting against, through non-
violent means, the violence of the oppressors, as Christians with some status are doing in South Africa or
Mozambique. But, of course, when Christians in dominant strata publicly side with the oppressed they must
be ready to take the consequences. They become highly
suspect, even traitorous, because they break through
the moral pretensions and seeming unanimity that
unjust systems use to legitimate their oppression. As a
result, solidarity with the oppressed through non-violent
action usually leads to the deeper solidarity with the
oppressed through shared suffering.

But other Christians are not opposed to the use of
force against unjust powers, such as Nazism. Such
Christians must accept a wider range of options in
support of liberation movements, including violent
revolution when all other effective avenues for justice
are closed in situations of great oppression. Such Christians cannot easily require non-violent methods only of
liberation movements. As Helmut Gollwitzer puts it,

"anyone who uses pacifist arguments on the question of revolution but not on questions of the army, reveals his argument as the ideology of the ruling class."[45] But whether one is committed to pacifism or to the just use of force, the first question is the question of solidarity with the oppressed.

Other Christians hold back from commitment to the oppressed because they see the oppressed sometimes turning into oppressors when they gain power. Freire is well aware of the danger.

> However, the moment the new regime hardens into a dominating "bureaucracy" the humanist dimension of the struggle is lost and it is no longer possible to speak of liberation.[46]

But this realization is hardly an excuse for evasion of the biblical commitment of the Spirit to the poor and powerless. Rather, it keeps us aware that the church's work is never done, that if a revolution by the oppressed leads to new forms of oppression, then the church is on the side of the newly oppressed. One must be clear, that when former oppressors say they are now "oppressed" because they no longer have the power to exploit and the way of life exploitation makes possible, this is not true oppression.[47]

D. Liberation as a Process

The changing face of some revolutionary movements and the continual need for new forms of liberation, easy to document in the twentieth century, make it clear that liberation is both a goal and a process and that the reality of our lives is shaped more by the process than by the final fulfillment of liberation. Freire's pedagogy is built on such a reality. The struggle for humanization, for the ability to make one's own history, is not established forever in one quick contest. Rather, those involved in liberation "perceive through their relations with reality that reality is really a *process,* undergoing constant transformation."[48] This means that even when revolutions liberate oppressed groups, the struggle to maintain genuine human freedom must continue. This calls for varying forms of revolutionary change. Richard Shaull proposes a concept of permanent revolution in the light of the virtual impossibility, in many situations, of revolutions that completely overturn the existing order in "one moment of total victory."

> Instead of *total* revolution in the sense of a headon assault on the total structure of the established order, we can work for *permanent* revolution, by which the entire structure is confronted with an increasing number of challenges at those points where changes are most imperative.[49]

These views of liberation as a process have an affinity for particular ways of thinking about God and our response to God's action in history. First, our understanding of God as a God of liberation must be shaped by dynamic, not static, images.

> God's grace, instead of making human creativity superfluous or impossible, is therefore the politics that makes it possible and necessary. This is so because in the context of the politics of human liberation man encounters a God who remains open, who has not yet arrived, who is determined and helped by human activity.[50]

The dynamic power of God working with persons in the midst of human history has always been at the heart of the definition of the Spirit. The more we understand God in terms of process, particularly historical processes of liberation, the more the doctrine and experience of the Spirit moves toward the center of our theological reflection.

Second, our understanding of God's relationship to the People of God and their relationship to history is shaped by understanding liberation as a process. In this view, the church must always be a people on the move through history, a people who are pioneers more than settlers. When the church has been actively expansionist, pushing through existing boundaries, the work of the Spirit has been an essential source of

leading and power. This was certainly true in the Acts
accounts of how the Spirit lured and prodded the early
church to new missionary ventures. (cf. Acts 8:29, ch.
10, 13:1-4)[51] One should not expect it to be different
when the boundaries through which the church breaks
are not geographic, but political and economic, not
boundaries but bondage.

Liberation as a process also can be seen in the way
the oppressed begin to set free their oppressors, both
from the slavery of dependence upon exploiting others
and from their own exploitation by oppressive systems.
One of the forces that enslaves oppressors in our society is the bondage to impersonal and materialistic
structures. Freire analyzes that enslavement and its
source.

> This climate (of a process of violence) creates in the
> oppressor a strongly possessive consciousness—posses-
> sive of the world of men . . . . The earth, property, pro-
> duction, the creations of man, men themselves, time—
> everything is reduced to the status of objects at its
> disposal . . . . For them *to be is to have* and to be of the
> "having" class . . . . They cannot see that, in the egoistic
> pursuit of *having* as a possessing class, they suffocate in
> their own possessions and no longer *are;* they merely
> *have*. (Stress in the original)[52]

There is the liberation of heightened consciousness in
Freire's words. But many of us have found similar
awareness sharpened even more directly in the praxis
of shared experience with liberation movements. It has
been from oppressed groups that many of us successful
in the institutional church, often closely tied in life-
style to the dominating strata of society, have found the
power of commitment, human solidarity, and joyous
celebration that has begun to crack open the impersonal
and bureaucratic systems that have impoverished our
lives. It has been those on the margins of society, oppressed or rejected, who have helped us recover some
of the vitality of risk-taking and personal encounter
in the midst of direct action against systems of oppres-

sion. They have begun to open our eyes to the contradictions of a materialistic culture, of a culture that can imprison us in comfortable cells full of entertaining gadgets, but cells nonetheless—cells which wall us off from the direct encounter that can create a history of human, not mechanical, richness. In this sense, the oppressed, once they have entered into a process of their own liberation, have done the work of the Spirit for the oppressors, a work that helps us come alive again to Jesus' vision.

> . . . do not be anxious about your life, what you shall eat or what you shall drink, nor about your body, what you shall put on . . . . Look at the birds of the air! . . . Consider the lilies of the field, . . . do not be anxious, . . . But seek first his kingdom and his righteousness, and all these things shall be yours as well. (Matthew 6:25-33, RSV)

Finally, liberation as a process is not a hard and joyless building of perfect societies in the political sense, or the rigid pursuit of heaven when happiness can finally be allowed in the religious sense. Rather, it is living the future now, made possible because the power of the Spirit is at work in and beyond us. Alves catches that joyous reality of fulfillment in the midst of the process of liberation.

> The community of faith, however, does not find the erotic sense of life at the end of the praxis of liberation, but rather in the midst of it . . . . On the way toward the promised land man learned that there is a time to stop, to abdicate all attempts to build the future, to remain in pure receptivity and in a total abandonment of calculation. His today was God's gift. He could rest because the politics of liberation was not carried on by the power of man alone, but rather by the passion and activity of God.[53]

That "passion and activity of God" is the Holy Spirit, working to liberate both the oppressed and the oppressor from those principalities and powers, those systems of oppression, that destroy the basic humanity of both, and to enable both to "obtain the glorious liberty of the children of God." (Romans 8:21)

Notes

1. Cf. John V. Taylor, *The Go-Between God: The Holy Spirit and the Christian Mission* (London: SCM Press, 1972), p. 49.
2. Eduard Schweitzer and others, *Spirit of God* (from Gerhard Kittel, *Theologisches Worterbuch Zum Neuen Testament*) trans. by A. E. Harvey (London: Adam & Charles Black, 1960), p. 5.
3. *Ibid.,* p. 2.
4. Cf. Paul Tillich, *Systematic Theology,* Vol. III (Chicago: Univ. of Chicago Press, 1963), pp. 148-49.
5. *Ibid.,* p. 153. See also Schweitzer, *op. cit.,* p. 2: ". . .the Spirit of God is power, power with a moral emphasis. It is active power, that is to say, it is the personal activity of God's will, achieving a moral and religious object. It impinges on Israel as the power of history . . . ."
6. G. W. H. Lampe, "The Holy Spirit in the Writings of Luke," in D. E. Nineham, edit., *Studies in the Gospels* (Oxford: Basil Blackwell, 1955), pp. 172-173, and pp. 172-177, for a detailed exposition. See also A. Hastings, *Prophet and Witness in Jerusalem* (London, 1958), pp. 50-75.
7. Cf. E. Earle Ellis, *The Gospel of Luke,* New Century Bible Series (London: Thomas Nelson & Sons, 1966), pp. 28-29, 69.
8. James H. Cone, *A Black Theology of Liberation* (Philadelphia: J. B. Lippincott Co., 1970), p. 206.
9. Lampe, *op. cit.,* p. 184. "The connection between the Kingdom and the Spirit appears in the fact that the risen Lord's command to his disciples to await the promise of the Spirit-baptism seems to form part of a discourse about 'the things concerning the Kingdom of God,' and that the apostle's reception of the power of the Spirit constitutes the answer to their question concerning the restoration of the kingdom of Israel." Lampe also cites the Lucan interpretation of the phrase, "Thy Kingdom come" in the Lord's Prayer and the way Luke speaks of the Kingdom as "coming upon" persons.
10. *Ibid.,* p. 177.
11. *Ibid.,* p. 192.
12. Schweitzer, *op. cit.,* p. 43.
13. Lampe, *op. cit.,* p. 193.
14. *Ibid.,* p. 193.
15. Schweitzer, *op. cit.,* p. 97.
16. C. H. Dodd, *The Apostolic Preaching* (London: Hodder & Stoughton, 1936), p. 137.
17. Cone, *op. cit.,* p. 122.
18. Paulo Freire, *Pedagogy of the Oppressed* (Middlesex, England and Baltimore, Md.: Penguin Books, 1972), p. 16.

19. Rubem Alves, *A Theology of Human Hope* (New York: Corpus Books, 1969).
20. Freire, *op. cit.*, p. 17.
21. *Ibid.*, p. 18.
22. *Ibid.*, pp. 18-19.
23. *Ibid.*, p. 15. The quotation is from *Populorum Progressio* (Boston: St. Paul edition, 1967), no. 34.
24. Freire, *op. cit.*, p. 20.
25. Cf. Letty M. Russell, "Human Liberation in a Feminine Perspective," *Study Encounter* (World Council of Churches), Vol. VIII, No. 1, 1972, pp. 7-10.
26. Freire, *op. cit.*, p. 52.
27. *Ibid.*, p. 21.
28. *Ibid.*, p. 21.
29. Taylor, *op. cit.*, p. 69.
30. *Ibid.*, p. 21.
31. Cf. Freire, *op. cit.*, p. 82, for a description of the need for full participation of the oppressed in conscientization, and Russell, *op. cit.*, p. 11, on the need for honest dialogue between women and men. In places of political and economic oppression, e.g., among blacks in Mississippi or Chicago or among farm laborers in California and Texas, the basic struggle has been over the possibility of genuine negotiation between those in power and representatives chosen *from and by* the oppressed.
32. Cf. Freire, *op. cit.*, pp. 109-10, for an analysis of many such myths used by those in power and often internalized by the oppressed, to perpetuate an exploitative system.
33. Cone, *op. cit.*, p. 49.
34. For a sociological and theological analysis—and demonstration—of the central role of the comic in Christian faith, see Peter Berger, *The Precarious Vision* (New York: Doubleday, 1961).
35. Freire, *op. cit.*, p. 25.
36. *Ibid.*, p. 37.
37. *Ibid.*, p. 26.
38. (on p. 14) "Gospel and Revolution: Pastoral Letter from the Third World." in John Gerassi, edit., *Camillo Torres: Revolutionary Priest* (Middlesex, England: Pelican Books, 1973), p. 430.
39. Freire, *op. cit.*, p. 26.
40. Jacques Ellul, *Violence* (London: SCM Press, 1970), pp. 151-52, quoted in Taylor, *op. cit.*, p. 55.
41. Freire, *op. cit.*, p. 36.
42. Tillich, *op. cit.*, p. 148.
43. Cf. Gerassi, *op. cit.*, for a biography and complete edition of the works of Camillo Torres and pp. 40-44, for an account of the response of other South American priests.
44. "Pastoral Letter from the Third World," in *Ibid.*, p. 432.
45. Quoted in Jürgen Moltmann, "Racism and the Right to

Resist," *Study Encounter* (World Council of Churches), Vol. VIII, No. 1, 1972, p. 4.
46. Freire, *op. cit.*, p. 33.
47. Cf. *Ibid.*, p. 33.
48. *Ibid.*, p. 48.
49. Richard Shaull, "Revolution: Heritage and Contemporary Option" in Carl Oglesby and Richard Shaull, *Containment and Change* (New York: Macmillan, 1967), p. 238.
50. Alves, *op. cit.*, p. 136.
51. Cf. Schweitzer, *op. cit.*, p. 42.
52. Freire, *op. cit.*, pp. 34-35.
53. Alves, *op. cit.*, p. 156.

The Holy Spirit, As God

John Meyendorff

In contemporary Western Christian thought, a theology of the Spirit is most frequently expressed in the context of a new search for religious freedom. The Spirit is seen as justifying either institutional change, or a religion of personal experience, or spiritual phenomena known as "pentecostal." Unfortunately, traditional Western systematic theology, medieval or reformed, provides little material or context for an organic and integrated theology of the Spirit. It remains rather speculative as to the identity of the "Giver" and, therefore, its interpretation of "gifts" is frequently quite arbitrary. Here perhaps lies one of the reasons for contemporary theological *desarroi*.

In the Christian East, the theology of the Spirit has also found little systematic development. However, some basic points of reference are found in the great trinitarian disputes of the fourth century which lead to the affirmation of the Spirit's *divinity,* as the third *Person* of the Trinity, and also in the interpretation of human salvation and ultimate destiny in terms of *deification*. These points of reference are therefore of central importance for the Orthodox interpretation of both scriptural and traditional data on the Holy Spirit, as they are expressed in the liturgy of the church, the experiences of the saints, and the life of the Christian community.

In short compass, it would obviously be impossible for me to attempt a truly systematic presentation of pneumatology. I will limit myself to the basic trinitarian and anthropological frames of reference, which lead to my understanding of the Spirit as God, and then draw some theological implications for our own concerns today.

I. The Trinitarian Dimension

It has been often noted that East and West differ in their approach to the mystery of the divine Trinity. The West takes for granted God's unity and approaches his "trinity" as a matter of speculation, while the East starts with a living experience of the *three* and then moves to affirm their equal divinity, and therefore, their unity. Thus, the Greek Cappadocian fathers of the fourth century were accused of tri-theism, because "the groundwork of (their) thought lay in the triplicity of equal hypostases (persons), and the identity of the divine *ousia* (substance) came second in order of prominence to their minds."[1]

This difference of approach to the trinitarian mystery is not a philosophical one. It is based on a fundamental interpretation of the New Testament by the Greek Fathers who understood the Christian faith itself as primarily a revelation of divine *persons*. The Christian faith for them is first of all an answer to Jesus' question, "Whom say ye that I am? ... The Son of the living God." (Matthew 16:15-16) The authority and effectiveness of Jesus' actions, as well as of his teachings, depend upon his personal identity. Only God himself can be the *Savior,* only God overcomes death and forgives sins, only God can communicate divine life to humankind. And the same approach is valid for their interpretation of Jesus' sending of "another" comforter from the Father—the Spirit. The primarily personal revelation of God is discovered by the early Greek Fathers not only in the classical trinitarial formula— the baptismal formula of Matthew 28:19, or the three gifts personally qualified in 2 Corinthians 13:14 ("the grace of our Lord Jesus Christ, and the love of God the Father, and the communion κοινωνία of the Holy Spirit") but also in the Spirit speaking personally to Philip, (Acts 8:29) to Peter, (Acts 10:19; 11:12) to the Church of Antioch, (Acts 13:12) to the apostolic

council of Jerusalem ("it seemed good to the Holy
Spirit and to us"). (Acts 15:25) The Spirit is understood here as a presence, distinct from that of Jesus,
but possessing the same divine sovereignty.

It is therefore understandable that the insistence by
the Cappadocian Fathers on this personal (hypostatic)
distinctiveness could lead them to a trinitarian system
in which their enemies saw tri-theism. They were ready
to run that risk in order to preserve the biblical understanding of a living and acting God, fully independent
from the impersonal idealism of Greek philosophy.
Even the Nicaean formulation of "consubstantiality"
was long suspect in the East—and not only among the
Arians—of being both unbiblical and too philosophical.
It was finally accepted, but only in combination with
the traditional (origenistic) reaffirmation of the three
distinct *hypostaseis* in God.

The struggle against Arius, who accepted the distinction but not the substantial co-equality and co-sover-
eignty of the divine persons, was about the nature of
salvation. This is particularly evident in the writing of
Athanasius. It immediately and necessarily involved
not only the person of Jesus Christ, but also that of the
Spirit through whom the Son of God became man in
the bosom of Mary, and through whom also, until the
parousia, he is present in his body, the church. It is in
writings by Athanasius—his *Letters to Serapion*—that
one finds the first elaborate patristic argument defend-
ing the divinity of the Spirit. It is the same soteriological approach that one finds in the other major fourth
century treatise on the same subject: the *De Spiritu
Sancto* of St. Basil of Caesarea. Both Athanasius and
Basil consider the saving activity of the Spirit accessible
to the Christian experience, as being necessarily effected
by God himself. Since the *personal* character of the
Spirit is taken for granted, the evidence of the Spirit's
divinity is there to see.

The divine identity of the "Comforter" is, therefore, a basic coordinate of the Christian idea of salvation. It is reflected not only in the theological tradition of the Christian East, but also, very prominently, in its liturgy. A prayer addressed personally to the Spirit, "O Heavenly King," is the initial act of *every* liturgical action in the Orthodox Church. The sacraments and, more particularly, the sacrament of the Christian *koinonia* itself, i.e., the Eucharist, culminate in an invocation of the Spirit. Hymnology, especially that of the feast of Pentecost, proclaims the same relationship between the Spirit's acts and his divine identity:

> The Spirit bestows all things: it appoints prophets; it consecrates priests; it gives wisdom to the simple; it turned fishermen into theologians; it gathers together the whole assembly of the Church; O Comforter, consubstantial and co-reigning with the Father and the Son, glory to Thee.
> We have seen the true light; we have received the heavenly Spirit; we have found the true faith, worshiping the undivided Trinity, who has saved us.

In the text of the Nicaean Creed, in fact the Creed adopted at the Council of Constantinople in 381, the divine identity of the Spirit was defined in terms of his "procession from the Father." This definition is in accordance with the theology of the Cappadocian Fathers who saw in the *person* of God, the Father, the very "origin of the Godhead." It is precisely as God that the Spirit "proceeds from the Father" directly, while creatures are not direct products from the Father, but come into being through the operation and mediation of the Logos. Thus, the proclamation of the Spirit's "procession from the Father" is equivalent to the proclamation of his pre-eternal divinity.

At this point, it is easy to discern the difference of approach to the mystery of the Trinity between the Greek Fathers of the fourth century and the Latin West. In trying to define a doctrine of salvation, the Latin West became preoccupied with the issue of justification by faith, its relation to human "works" and produced systems explaining the very process of salvation, i.e., the Anselmian doctrine of satisfaction. The personal divine identity of Christ and the Spirit, though an intellectual necessity—"only God Himself can fully satisfy divine justice"—became in fact a peripheral issue, rather than a matter of direct Christian experience, grounded in the Gospel itself and providing the *starting point* of all theology. This development was itself based upon a doctrine of God which tended to relativize the *personal,* or trinitarian life of God, and approach him first as one single essence, while considering the persons as internal "relations." There is no doubt that this approach to God, popularized by St. Augustine, is, to a degree, responsible for the fact that so many Christians today are practical deists. Venerating God as a single "Heavenly Father," they tend to view trinitarianism as a mere speculation. In such a context, there is no real place for a theology of the Holy Spirit except in terms of "gifts," unrelated to the internal life of God.

These obvious differences of perspective between East and West constitute the background of the famous controversy on *Filioque.* As is well known, the "Nicaean" Creed, which was adopted as a solemn confession of faith by the universal church at its ecumenical councils of the fourth century, was interpolated locally in Spain (sixth century). The interpolated text was adopted throughout Carolingian Europe (eighth through ninth centuries) and, in spite of strong objections by contemporary Roman popes, it was transformed into a tool of anti-Greek polemics by Charlemagne. The interpolation consisted in an insertion of the words, "and from the Son" (Latin: *Filioque)* in the text of the creed, so that the paragraph which originally affirmed the procession of the Spirit "from the Father" (simply quoting John 15:26), now read: "(I believe) in the Holy Spirit, Lord, Giver of Life, who proceeds from the Father and the Son." Eventually, under German pressure, the church of Rome itself accepted the interpolation in spite of violent reactions by Greek theologians, particularly Photius (ninth century), who were not objecting against the idea that the gifts of the Spirit—in the "economy" of the Incarnation—were granted through Christ, i.e., through the Son, but against the Augustinian reduction of the hypostatic, personal life of the three Divine Persons, to mere "relations." Photius considered the Latin understanding of God as "modalistic" ("Sabellian," or "semi-Sabellian").

Contemporary Orthodox theologians, particularly Karsavin and Lossky, have expressed the opinion that the *Filioque* dispute is at the very root of ecclesiological differences between East and West. In Western "papal" ecclesiology the presence of the Spirit, i.e., a divine presence which restores and enhances a person's *free* response to God, is fully subordinated to the ecclesiastical institution, based upon a "vicar" of Christ. Whether or not one accepts this scheme, which may appear as somehow artificial, it is certainly true that essentialistic deism hardly allows for any real theology of the Spirit as an active, personal, and guiding presence in the church community and in the personal life of the Christian. The "gifts of the Spirit" tend to be understood within the framework of individual or group psychology, for which there can be no ecclesiological or theological framework.

In any case, in order to understand the Orthodox approach to pneumatology, one has to start with the divinity of the Spirit as that was established in the great anti-Arian controversies of the early church. Then one must accept a trinitarian theology which presupposes that the personal identity of the Spirit is understood absolutely, together, of course, with the doctrine of consubstantiality, preserving the essential unity of the Godhead.

II. The Anthropological Dimension

As we have noticed in the first part of this chapter the main patristic argument for the divinity of Christ and the Spirit was soteriological, because salvation itself was seen as "deification" *(theosis)*. Obviously only God can "deify." The argument is exemplified in the famous formulae found in almost identical words in Irenaeus ("The Word became man, so that men could become God," *Adversus Haereses,* V, *praef.*), and in Athanasius ("He was made that we might be made God," *De Incarn.* 54), which are applicable to both the "economy" of the Son and to that of the Spirit.

The patristic idea of deification was sometimes identified as pantheistic. It was assumed that it suppressed the necessary distinction and distance between God and creation, and that it reflected a spirituality which suppressed the integrity of the *humanum.* However, most contemporary partistic scholars would disagree with such an evaluation. The very word, deification *(theosis),* was used previously by Greek philosophers in a non-biblical and non-Christian context, but its use by the Greek Fathers and in the entire Orthodox tradition was based on the theology of the "image of God" within personality, and its various equivalents, i.e., upon a *theocentric* idea of humanity which cannot be adequately expressed in Western categories of "nature" and "grace."

Using a terminology very closely connected with St. Paul's, Irenaeus considers an individual to be "composed of a body taken from the earth, and a soul which receives the Spirit from God." *(Adv. Haer.* 3, 22, 2) "If the Spirit is wanting to the soul," he continues, "man is being left carnal, shall be an imperfect being, possessing indeed the image of God in his formation, but not receiving the similitude through the Spirit." *(Ibid.,* 5, 9, 1) Not only is the Holy Spirit, paradoxically, considered as a component of true humanity, but

Irenaeus also very specifically connects the Spirit with the "similitude." He interprets the similitude both as distinct from the "image," and as the "perfection of the individual, granted through the Spirit, provided one presents a free response to God's calling and presence. The individual is not a static and "closed" being. One is given the free task of perfecting oneself, and the role of the Spirit is to "seal" and direct one's ascent to God, so that this ascent may be in conformity with the divine, unending, limitless aim which God has set as one's destiny. The Spirit is not the bestower of "supernatural" gifts—additions to an otherwise "natural" human existence. He not only grants forgiveness and justification, he makes one become fully human.

This theocentric anthropology, so clearly expressed already in Irenaus (second century), will always be taken for granted by Greek patristic writers. The term, "deification," which does not yet appear as such in Irenaeus, will later become standard; it will designate "communion" with God. That communion is one's destiny since the individual's creation is according to God's "image and likeness." That has been made impossible, however, because of sin and death which "reigned" (Romans 5:14) over humanity until the coming of Christ, but it is now made accessible again by the power of the Spirit sent by Christ from the Father. It will find ultimate fulfillment in the age to come.

This basic and central role of the Spirit in defining what the individual is, and how one participates in the saving act of God in Christ not only presupposes the divinity of the Spirit as third Person of the Trinity, but also has direct implications for spirituality and ecclesiology.

Since "deification" is not only a free gift of the Spirit, but also requires one's cooperation, it is inevitably a dynamic process. It implies graduation and

stages of communion with God. It implies a religion of
personal experience. The monastic literature of the
Christian East is particularly rich in its understanding
and description of the various degrees of spiritual progress. One of the classics of Eastern monastic spirituality, written by St. John, abbot of Sinai (seventh century), even bears the title of *Ladder of Divine Ascent.*
It is a systematic, spiritual, and psychological analysis
of one's road to the direct vision of God.

This monastic spirituality inevitably had close neo-
Platonic parallels. The risk of transforming Christianity
into a de-materializing and de-personalizing escapism
was a very real one. However, the most prominent
leaders of Eastern monasticism succeeded in providing
an antidote to the "platonizing" temptation. This antidote was found in a biblical theology of the body and
in sacramentalism. The condition and basis for an
authentic Christian experience was seen in baptism and
the eucharistic communion. The point is made with
particular clarity in the writings of an anonymous
fourth-century writer who uses the pseudonym of "St.
Macarius." It is interesting that his insistence on
defining the Christian faith in terms of *personal* experience of the Holy Spirit, and the explicitly biblical
character of his spirituality, endeared him to John
Wesley who translated his writings into English.[2] "Macarius" also ranks among the most popular spiritual
writers of the East and is noteworthy for his persistency
in defining the Christian experience in both sacramental
and pneumatological terms.

> By analogy of faith, the Divine Spirit, our Advocate, who
> was sent to the apostles and through them drawn down
> upon the only true Church of God at the moment of
> baptism, this Spirit in various manifold ways accompa-
> nies every man who comes to baptism in faith.[3]
> When God created Adam he did not give him bodily
> wings like the birds, but prepared for him in advance
> the wings of the Holy Spirit—the wings he desires to
> give him in the resurrection—to lift him up and carry him
> wherever the Spirit wishes. (*Hom.* 5:11)

> It is possible to taste in Christianity the grace of God:
> Taste and see that the Lord is sweet. (Psalms 34:8) This
> tasting is the dynamic power of the Spirit manifesting
> itself in full certitude in the heart. The sons of light,
> ministers of the New Covenant in the Holy Spirit have
> nothing to learn from men; they are "taught by God."
> (John 6:45) Grace itself engraves the laws of the Spirit
> on their hearts . . . . (*Hom.* 15:20)

The references to a conscious "certitude" of communion with the Spirit and the quotation from John 6:45 on the immediacy of the Spirit's teaching are very characteristic, not only for Macarius, but for the entire tradition of Eastern spirituality. St. Symeon, the New Theologian (eleventh century), will be one of the most explicit spokesmen of this "prophetism of holiness." Tasting, experiencing God in the Spirit, as light, as joy, as truth, is the personal goal of each Christian. This experience is *accessible* to one in this world as an anticipation of the Kingdom to come. Each Christian, therefore, has access to the fullness of revelation and knowledge. One does not have to "learn from men." One enjoys the gift of the Spirit which was given through baptism.

Whether one labels this understanding of the Christian gospel "mystical" (the Christian East is often called "mystical" but the word is misleading in its Western connotations) or "eschatological," it is clear that it has important *ecclesiological* implications.

It is a fact that the Orthodox East, while recognizing the teaching responsibility of the ordained ministry, particularly bishops, also admits the *saints* as authoritative witnesses of truth. Historical examples of doctrinal conflicts between bishops, on the one hand, and popular opinion, frequently led by monks, on the other, are quite numerous. The solitary struggle of St. Maximus the Confessor, a simple monk, against an almost universally recognized "monothelite" establishment (seventh century) is the best known. The episcopal ministry implies teaching responsibility, but all

forms of institutional *infallibility* are formally excluded.
The priestly and prophetic functions are both neces-
sary to the church. Both are maintained by the same
Spirit. The Spirit created the apostolic ministry at
Pentecost. The Spirit maintains the church through his-
tory and also grants gifts to the entire people of God,
to the saints and prophets, those living witnesses of
God's presence in the world.

The mystery of the church consists precisely in that
its various ministries find an ultimate unity in *the Spirit,
as God,* in whom all contradictions and tensions are
resolved, particularly the tension between freedom and
authority. Christian freedom is not reducible to a freedom of choice between good and evil, or between
various alternatives of earthly behavior. It is, first of
all, the possibility to be *fully human,* i.e., to be in full
possession of one's life and one's potentials, to be
liberated from the powers of mortality and evil. Now,
as we have seen in the theological anthropology of St.
Irenaeus—also shared by the later patristic tradition—
to be fully human means to be in communion with God,
or to have fully restored in oneself the third and highest
component of humanity, the presence of the Holy Spirit.
This is why Gregory of Nyssa (fourth century) identified the "image of God" in one with *freedom.* In fact,
he is in full agreement with Irenaeus on this point,
since "where the Spirit of the Lord is, there is freedom."
(2 Corinthians 3:17)

However, the freedom given to one by "the Spirit of
God" is not a freedom for anarchy. It is precisely when
discussing the gifts of the Spirit that St. Paul also warns:
"Let all things be done decently and in order." (1
Corinthians 14:40) The Spirit is the source of freedom
and the principle of order in the church. The same
Spirit inspires the prophets and guarantees the effectiveness and permanence of sacramental ministry. Thus,
the Montanists who considered the church was to be

led by prophets, ultimately became a sect. But, on the other hand, a human institution which becomes an end in itself and claims infallibility is nothing but the demonic temptation described by Dostoyevsky in his "Legend of the Grand Inquisitor."

The true, "catholic" tradition of Christianity is the one where institutional and charismatic leaderships are able *to recognize in each other the same Spirit*. This mutual recognition and authentication is not simple coexistence, or simply a "creative tension," as between the divided powers of a democratic society. It is a common belonging and a joint communion with the Spirit as God. Clearly, throughout history there were conflicts between priests and prophets. It is noteworthy, also, that the Orthodox East never lost the sense of their distinctiveness. For example, the monastic communities and their leaders have traditionally been recognized as having a non-institutional, but a real authority in the church at large. The numerous challenges presented by monks to contemporary church establishments during the early Christian and Byzantine periods, as well as the witness of the "holy elders" *(startsy)* in nineteenth century Russia, to quote a more recent example, are all signs of a continuous recognition in Eastern Christendom of a charismatic leadership. That leadership at no time challenges the episcopal authority founded in the sacramental nature of the church. Neither the gift of episcopal ministry, nor that of charismatic leadership, if authentic, are created or humanly devised gifts. They are founded in one's participation in the same divine Spirit granted to the church at Pentecost, distributed in baptism, and always working at the "building-up" of the Body of Christ.

Conclusion

If the divinity of the Spirit is the very foundation of trinitarian theology, and also of the Christian understanding of salvation, there are other particularities in his existence which remain largely undeveloped in theological books but which appear both in Scripture and in the life of the church. The "Spirit of God moved upon the face of the waters" (Genesis 1:2) at the very inception of creation.[4] The Word, however, was the One *by whom* all things were made. (John 1:3) The Word (not the Spirit) "became flesh," yet it is because the Holy Spirit came upon Mary, (Luke 1:35) which heralded the beginning of a "new creation." And it is again the Spirit who makes Christ present in the midst of his disciples until he comes again. Every baptism is "sealed" by the Spirit who is also invoked at the celebration of the Eucharist "to make" the bread and wine, body and blood of Christ.[5] The saints also, while they practice the permanent "Jesus prayer," define their life as a "collection of the Spirit."[6]

All these forms of the Spirit's presence and action follow the same pattern. The Spirit is inseparable from the Son, both preceding him and completing, or "sealing," the Son's action. But the Spirit never calls persons to himself, but to the Son, the God-man, the New Adam, the only One, in whom the "hypostatic union" took place—the full union of God and humanity. The role of the Spirit in salvation (and also in the internal life of God?) is "kenotic;" it is always directed to the Other. This "kenoticism" leads modern theologians to discern, in the Spirit, the feminine aspect of the "image of God" in personhood.[7] Providing one avoids anthropomorphism and unhealthy gnostic speculation, one can find here the true theological basis for the image of motherhood, also applied to the church as Temple of the Spirit, or to Mary as the mother of the New Adam, head of the Body.

Thus, authentic pneumatology is always both trinitarian and "churchly." Without this foundation, the theological justifications of the "gifts of the Spirit" risk becoming nothing more than rationalizations for passing fads.

Notes

1. G. L. Prestige, *God in Patristic Thought* (London: SPCK, 1952), pp. 242-3.

2. John Wesley, *A Christian Library*, I, Bristol, 1749. On Wesley's admiration for Macarius, see, Albert C. Outler, editor, *John Wesley* (New York: Oxford University Press, 1964), p. 9, note 26; and pp. 274-5.

3. W. Jaeger, editor, "The Great Letter," *Two Rediscovered Works of Ancient Christian Literature* (Leiden: E. J. Brill, 1954), p. 236.

4. The identification of the "Spirit of God" with the "Holy Spirit" is widespread in patristic exegesis.

5. Cf., text of the "epiclesis" in the Liturgy of St. John Chrysostom.

6. This was particularly the case of the celebrated St. Seraphim of Sarov (+1833).

7. Would this be supported by the fact that the Hebrew word for "Spirit" *(ruah)* is feminine?

The Holy Spirit and the Incarnation[1]

Maurice F. Wiles

"The Holy Spirit and the Incarnation" is a title which can be understood in various ways. The most obvious would be: What was the role of the Holy Spirit in relation to the incarnate life of Jesus? But that is not the question with which I shall primarily be concerned; and that for two reasons:

1. Professor Lampe has recently published an essay on "The Holy Spirit and the Person of Christ."[2] I am in substantial agreement with the way in which he deals with the question. There is not a great deal that I would want to add to what he has said.

2. More importantly, the question is essentially an exegetical and historical one, rather than a properly theological one. Before it could be satisfactorily tackled, it would need, I believe, to be rephrased in some such form as: What views of the role of the Holy Spirit in relation to the incarnate life of Jesus are to be found in the various New Testament writers and in the earliest Church Fathers? The evidence, particularly for the New Testament, is not only varied but highly complex, and I am not qualified to assess it with the degree of expert knowledge that would be required. I would feel more at home with the Fathers. But in any case, such an investigation would lead only to a number of differing historical answers. And I am doubtful whether as a contemporary theologian I would want to raise the issue in that particular form at all.

I propose therefore to approach my task in a somewhat different way. I shall understand my title to refer to the relation of the Spirit and the Incarnation in the broader sense: the relation between the continuing work of the Spirit in history and the particular datable occurrence, or set of occurrences, which we call the Incarn-

ation. This may eventually lead me back to some of
the issues that the question in its more directly Chris-
tological form would have raised. But they will appear
in a rather different context, and from a rather different
perspective.

Traditional teaching about the Incarnation affirms
that in the person of Jesus, the Word of God has not
simply found expression through words human; he
has become human and spoken to us as human. The
events of his life, death, and Resurrection are not
merely providentially guided events expressing and furthering the purposes of God in the world; they are, in
a direct sense, decisive acts of God himself. In Christ
what needed to be done for us has been done; it was
something which God alone could do. It neither need,
nor will, nor could be done again. All this, taken by
itself, would suggest that for all subsequent generations
Christian faith would inevitably be backward-looking
in character. The essential attitude of faith would be
looking back to hear what God has said to us, to recall
what God himself has done for us.

But of course such claims never have stood by themselves. They stand side by side with other affirmations
about the Spirit which are oriented toward the present
and the future. Nor does this second forward-looking
type of affirmation simply appear where the incarnational emphasis is weak. In the Fourth Gospel, for example, which is primarily responsible for the dominance
of the incarnational concept in later theology, there is
an equally marked emphasis on the continuing role of
the Spirit in the world and in the church. In the eyes of
the Fourth Evangelist it may have been blessed to have
seen and to have believed. But we do not need to pine
for the days of the Incarnation, for it is more blessed
not to have seen and yet to have believed. (John 20:29)
The works of Jesus were great enough to be evidence
of the presence of the Father in him and to be the

grounds for the disciples' believing in him, yet the disciples were to do even greater works in the future. (John 14:10-12) The words of Jesus may have been spirit and life, (John 6:63) but they were more than the immediate disciples could bear. It would need the future work of the Spirit to guide them into all the truth. (John 16:12-13)

Now, as is well known, the Fourth Gospel has a clearly drawn picture of the relationship between Jesus and the Spirit. The Spirit "was not" until Jesus had been glorified; Jesus goes away so that the Comforter may come. (John 7:39; 16:7) But this relationship is something deeper and more profound than mere temporal succession. We can best feel our way into a consideration of that deeper relationship by looking more carefully at the famous promise that the Spirit will guide the disciples into all the truth. The text has often been used by those who were anxious to find biblical support for their conviction that all true knowledge in art or science is God-given. But however true that conviction, it is not that with which the Johannine text is concerned. The text has to be understood in relation to the Fourth Gospel's specific understanding of truth, and in particular to the claim of Jesus a little earlier in the farewill discourses to be the truth. (John 14:6) Jesus embodies the truth in himself as a person, but the significance of that truth will only be grasped as it is disclosed by the Spirit in the later life of the church. That which the Spirit will disclose will be new, subjectively, in the apprehension of Christians. It will not be new absolutely, for it will already have been present and realized in Jesus. The Spirit will not be an independent source of truth; he will take the things of Jesus and declare them to the disciples. (John 16:14) Here then is a basic sketch or ground-plan of the relationship between the incarnate Christ and the subsequent work of the Spirit.

What the theologian has to do is to ask whether this sketch can be filled out in a way which does justice to our experience as Christians, and, if so, how? The issue concerns the practical life as well as the intellectual. But let us take as an example the question of the development of doctrine. In their treatment of that subject, some modern scholars have certainly used a model of precisely the kind with which we are concerned. DeLubac, for example, insists that both the starting point and the very substance of dogma are not so much a form of teaching as a person.[8] What exactly is implied by such an assertion?

It is certainly capable of varied understandings. Let me try to illustrate this by spelling out two possible meanings at different ends of the scale. The first would go something like this. By faith we know Jesus to be the incarnation of the divine Logos, the earthly embodiment of the very mind and wisdom of God, who is of one substance with the Father. Therefore all truth (and *a fortiori* all truth about God) must, by definition, be in him. It may not have been expressed by Jesus of Nazareth; it may not indeed have been consciously present to his mind or even available to his consciousness. But that is irrelevant. Any apparent challenge of that kind to our claim can be met by a kenotic theory of the Incarnation or some similar means. It would still be the case that all Christian apprehension of truth would be an unfolding of that which was already present among us in the person of the incarnate Logos. Now the difficulty of this kind of position will be obvious. What is believed on other grounds to be true is thereby believed to have been implicit in the person of the incarnate Logos, rather than the other way around. The claim that the Spirit does not speak on his own authority but declares the things of Jesus is made true by definition. But the link with Jesus offers no help with the vital task of discerning the spirits, of determining what is the leading of the Holy Spirit, and what is not.

At the other end of the scale, it could be argued that nothing should be claimed as a proper part of that truth into which the Spirit is to lead us unless it can be linked to the person of the historic Jesus, either as to what he explicitly taught or as to what is implied by his life and ministry as witnessed to in the gospels and by the earliest preaching about him. But there are serious difficulties here, too. It is questionable how far we can know what was explicitly taught by Jesus. Insofar as we can, it was taught within a first century setting and needs translation before it can be taken over as truth for us. And that applies, of course, not only to the actual teaching of Jesus himself, but to the whole pattern of first century witness to him. If we spell out the relationship along these lines, then the truth into which the Spirit leads us is liable to prove far more restricted in form and scope than we will feel able to accept.

The two examples I have given come, as I said, from differing ends of a spectrum. Nevertheless, I do not think there is any satisfactory escape from the dilemma that they suggest. I am not able to find any midway position, expressed in terms of this model of the relation between the Incarnation and the Spirit, which would escape the challenge either of vacuity on the one hand, or undue restriction on the other. I do not say it cannot be done, but my own failure to find such a position leads me to regard the picture presented by the Fourth Gospel as one that does not square readily with the actual practice and experience of Christians. This should not be cause either for surprise or for anxiety. Our whole understanding of history is involved, and that is surely very different from the understanding of history characteristic of the first centuries of our era. Nor are we absolutely bound to the categories of Scripture or of the early church tradition. Let us therefore seek to reflect more generally on the way in which Christians today interpret the event of Jesus and subsequent Christian history, without requiring any predetermined scheme of the relationship between the Incarnation and the Spirit as the framework within which to order the results of our reflections.

Jesus Christ is central to Christian faith. He is not simply the founder of the Christian church, not just the first in historical sequence. He is also the one to whom Christians look back and look up, the paradigm and the effective agent of our communion with God. The proper referent of such affirmations may not be simply the historical figure, Jesus of Nazareth, but neither is it simply a Christ concept or idea. The historical figure, Jesus, is certainly a part of the referent in any such claim. It is this fact that makes matters of history so central to Christian faith. If the Incarnation is to continue to play the central role it has traditionally played in Christian faith, we seem to require reliable knowledge about the man, Jesus. There would be something odd about a faith which emphasized the vital importance of a divine incarnation at a particular moment in history, but acknowledged at the same time substantial uncertainty about the actual form taken by that incarnate life. The availability of such reliable knowledge has been a central issue of theological concern at least since the time of Lessing. This is not the place to survey the vicissitudes of those debates over the last two hundred years. It is, however, necessary to attempt some reflection on their general implications. The difficulties to which such reflection points can, I think, be separated out into two kinds, one more practical, the other more theoretical.

The first difficulty, the more practical one, is the lack of any agreed results in the attempts of scholars to distinguish the individual contribution of Jesus from the continuing contribution of the church. In the attempt to draw such distinctions, New Testament scholars have sharpened their tools to an extreme degree of precision. By the standards to be expected in such historical detective work, it can properly be said that the evidence suggests a reasonable degree of reliability in the Gospel records. But by those standards one would not expect to be able to distinguish with precision between the role of the founding figure of the movement and the ways in which his person and his teaching have been developed in the continuing tradition. Certainly there are lunatic fringe interpretations which can be excluded. Moreover, one can reasonably ascribe differing measures of probability to differing interpretations. But there is still a wide range of possibilities which remain seriously and genuinely open ones. And these affect not just details of the teachings of Jesus, but fundamental issues concerning the nature of his mission and his own understanding of it. The "new quest" for the historical Jesus may have overcome some of the particular problems of the old quest; it has not escaped its fundamental difficulty. The nature of the material available to us simply does not allow us to isolate the distinctive teaching or character of Jesus with anything more than a relatively limited degree of probability.

But the difficulty is not simply a matter of contingent limitations in the particular sources available to us. It can be set out in a more theoretical way. "No man is an island." Yet where the Incarnation is treated as involving distinct affirmations about the individual, Jesus of Nazareth, it seems to be committed to isolating him from his immediate surroundings in just that kind of way. The point can perhaps usefully be made by the citation of five affirmations which Norman Pittenger sets out in his book, *Christology Reconsidered,* as the subsection headings in the chapter entitled, "The Location of the Incarnation" (pp. 70-81).

(a) No historical person can be understood in separation from the past history from which that person emerges and from the culture of which he or she is a part.

(b) No person can be understood save in one's relationship with those who were associated with and were influenced by the person, as well as influencing him or her.

(c) No person can be understood unless the consequences of his or her impact on history are taken very seriously into account.

(d) Every person must be seen as thus focusing one's past, his or her present relationships during a lifetime, and the results of one's appearance at some given time and place.

(e) Any interpretation of a historical figure must have regard for these factors; and if God's activity is seen in the individual, even in the most eminent sense, that activity must be taken as having occurred in and through the whole constellation of which the figure is the center; it must not be confined solely and exclusively to one as an individual person.

Now clearly this kind of emphasis can easily be overplayed. It would be absurd to suggest that there is no such thing as an individual person, or that individuals are incapable of playing a recognizable, creative role within the historical process. It is quite clear that at the very lowest estimate Jesus was such a creative individual, and we can know a certain amount about the kind of creative influence he exercised.

Nevertheless, these two difficulties raised by this historical debate are serious and their implications have to be taken seriously. Jesus, as man, was a part of a developing culture; he not only influenced but was influenced by those with whom he lived and worked. Whatever the nature of our knowledge, difficulties would arise in any attempt to identify accurately his unique contribution to the ideas and events of his time. But in view of the actual nature of the sources available to us, such difficulties are greatly enhanced. Jesus comes to us reflected through the prism of a variety of different responses to him.

What difference does all this make? It affects the
terms in which the problem of the relationship of the
Spirit and the Incarnation can properly be posed. There
is no separable person, the incarnate Jesus, whom we
can first know and then go on to relate to the subsequent events of Christian history. We know him as a
creative element within a developing religious history.
We know him as those who stand within a subsequent
historical development and whose modes of apprehension are affected by the particular historical situation to which we belong.

To most of us all this will seem obvious enough. Am
I suggesting that Christian faith in Christ is simply a
matter of historical knowledge? Certainly not. But as I
said at the outset, the historical figure, Jesus, is certainly a part of the referent of Christian faith in Jesus
Christ. It is with the implications of that part of the
referent of our faith that I have so far been concerned.

If I am (whether rightly or wrongly) so sensitive to
the historical difficulties in relation to our secure
knowledge of Jesus, is it possible to compensate by
placing greater weight on the experience of the Spirit?
Paul Tillich is perhaps the supreme example of someone who has attempted to do just that. He claims that
"participation, not historical argument, guarantees the
reality of the event upon which Christianity is based.
It guarantees a personal life in which the New Being
has conquered the old being." Tillich goes on to say
that it is a consequence of historical method that it
cannot be guaranteed that the name of that person was
Jesus (however absurd that suggestion may be in
practice). But he concludes by insisting that "whatever
his name, the New Being was and is actual in this
man." *(Systematic Theology,* Vol. ii., p. 131.)

But despite the careful qualifications that Tillich
makes, I do not believe the approach that he pursues
can do the full job he wants it to do. Brian Hebble-

thwaite's essay, in the same volume as that of Professor
Lampe, to which I have already referred, entitled "The
Appeal to Experience in Christology," (pp. 263-278)
gives timely warning of the dangers and difficulties involved in any move of this sort. These are at the very
least as forbidding as those that beset a historical
approach to the understanding of the Incarnation. If
historians speak with varied voices about Jesus, the
variety is nothing as compared with the voices of those
who claim to be declaring the direct promptings of the
Spirit. Descriptions of experience can sound remarkably
similar from within different religious traditions. By
chance, I received through the mail this very morning
on which I am writing, a popular magazine of Nichiren
Buddhism. With a slight change of terminology, the
correspondence columns of that magazine might well
have graced the pages of any evangelical Christian
journal of similar status. Yet in each case, no doubt,
very real and significant experiences are seen as con-
firmation of a very different set of religious beliefs.
The same is patently true within Christianity itself,
with the great variety of its pentecostal manifestations.

But here too, as with the historical problem, the
difficulty can be expressed in more theoretical terms.
It is not just a puzzling contingent fact that persons
interpret their experiences so differently. There is no
such thing as pure experience. All experience is experience from within a tradition with meanings and interpretations already inherent in it. What we experience
as the presence or the power of the Holy Spirit at work
will be made up of things that our tradition associates
with the Holy Spirit, or of things that we cannot readily
assimilate as part of the common-sense expectations of
our particular society. This is not to deny the reality
of the Holy Spirit's presence or power in the lives of
persons. It is to question the reliability of any claim
to be able, on the basis of experience, to define the

particular forms of his presence or the nature of his working. Anglicans, who are the guests of Methodists at the present stage of inter-church relations, should be especially more aware of the embarrassments that may be involved in ascribing to the leading of the Holy Spirit the particular aspirations or decisions of ecumenical growth or lack of it. Yet it would be equally embarrassing to maintain that the Holy Spirit was not involved at all.

Where then do these considerations lead us? The structure of Christian experience certainly requires at least these two reference points: a reference to that partly hidden but creative figure, Jesus, and the responses to him that characterized the earliest, formative years of the Christian community; and a reference to the immediate experience of grace, of a power greater than ourselves, which characterizes Christian experience today, both individually and corporately. The two cannot be wholly separated. But we need to emphasize now one, now the other aspect. Each may be for us the focusing point through which we may know and experience the presence of God in our lives. God is, of course, never at our disposal. No procedure can guarantee that what we claim to be knowledge of God really is such. We live by faith, not by sight. But it seems to me a part of a characteristically Christian position to insist that neither of these two forms of reference is dispensable. It is the interrelation between the two with which the Fourth Gospel is concerned in its paradigmatic account of the relation between Christ and the Spirit which I took as my starting point. Traditionally, this has been developed in terms of distinct persons of the Trinity. Christ is the incarnate Son, the embodiment of the second person of the Trinity. The experience of the believers and of the believing church is the sphere of the work of the Holy Spirit. The unity of the two is secured, because it is a coequal and coessential Trinity which Christians affirm. Thus, there can be no conceivable difference in context or character in that divinity with which we are involved in each case.

But this scheme of interpretation leaves two puzzling questions. The Son does not cease to be living and active when the incarnate life is over. The risen Christ continues to be with his disciples to the end of the world. Is this something to be distinguished from the presence of the Holy Spirit? And if so, how is the relation between the two to be understood? And similarly, despite the "Spirit was not" of John 7:39, the Holy Spirit did not begin his existence or his activity only at Pentecost. He was operative before that— including the life of Jesus, as accounts such as those of the annunciation and the baptism imply. But what then was his relationship to that of the incarnate Son?

Such problems, I want to suggest, are not insoluble merely for lack of evidence. They are insoluble because they are wrongly conceived and wrongly posed. It was for this reason that I did not interpret my title along those lines. I hope that the more general lines I have pursued do not appear to be an evasion. Let me now try to say something a bit more positive in answer to the question: How should we speak about the Incarnation? And, in particular, how should our understanding of the Incarnation be linked to the theme of the Spirit?

In the course of the article referred to at the beginning of this chapter, Professor Lampe lists three major considerations which deterred the early church from developing a Spirit Christology—i.e., a Christology whose fundamental category would be possession by the Spirit of God rather than the incarnation of the Word or Son of God. These three are: (i) suspicion "of any theory which might seem to imply that Jesus was a 'mere' man;" (ii) "orthodox fear of patripassianism;" (iii) the difficulty of distinguishing "as orthodox theology required, between God-in-Christ—the divine being who pre-existed, was incarnate and is exalted to the right hand of the Father—and God-in-Christ's-people—witnessing to the former and assuring them of sonship to the Father in him." (pp. 120-1)

I believe this to be a fair statement of the historical position. But I would like to suggest that in the light of the subsequent history of doctrine, these three considerations might well be considered not as deterrents against developing a Spirit Christology but as positive incentives for doing so.

I take the third consideration first. A central theme here has been the inextricable interconnectedness of our knowledge of God-in-Christ and our knowledge of God-in-Christ's-people. They are not necessarily identical, but our understanding of each is mutually dependent on our understanding of the other. There are, therefore, distinct advantages in trying to understand them with the aid of a paradigm which emphasizes their intimate interrelation. The position in relation to Professor Lampe's first consideration is very similar. What can be objected to as possibly implying "mere manhood" can also be acclaimed as expressing the archetypal role of Christ for Christian faith better than traditional incarnational concepts—despite all the sophisticated developments those concepts have undergone in the attempts to enable the incarnational idea to fulfill that role. Finally the second, patripassian objection can be briefly dealt with. Once the Word or Son was firmly asserted to be coequal and consubstantial with the Father, the same difficulty had to be met once more. In what sense could God in his full "godness" be understood to be involved in all the sufferings of the incarnate? Spirit Christology is hardly more vulnerable than a traditional incarnational theology on that score.

Language about the Holy Spirit as it comes to us

from Scripture and from traditional usage in our own time seems to me to express primarily two essential themes. It speaks of a communication between God and the person, a real presence of his grace and power in the lives of Christians individually and corporately. But in addition, it makes clear that such ideas are not to be understood in a purely emotional sense, in static terms of private experiences. They are to be seen in relation to a continuing purpose, the achievement of God's purposes within history. Now these are precisely the things we want to say about the Incarnation. Christ is for us the paradigm of human life in its fullest relationship to God; he is also the supreme case of the realization and furthering of God's purpose in the world. A Spirit-Christology, a picture of Jesus as the spirit-filled man, would be a highly appropriate way of expressing such convictions. This would not necessarily be in competition with an incarnational theology— though if it were taken with appropriate seriousness it would certainly modify the way in which incarnational theology is understood. We need, I believe, a variety of models in seeking to understand and to respond to that which God has done and continues to do for us through the person of Jesus. The Spirit blows when it wills and one cannot tell where it comes from or whither it goes. To believe it to be either possible or desirable to define the role of the Spirit in the Incarnation with any kind of precision would be to be untrue to that basic fact about the Spirit. But to speak of the person and work of Jesus quite freely in Spirit language may be a very valuable way of giving expression to the mysterious and creative character of that which God gives to us through him. We do not need to be anxious that they may weaken the sense of the specialness of the Incarnation. It will certainly need to be supplemented by other language and other imagery. But we should rather be concerned with its positive potential.

And that, I believe, might be to bring home to us more effectively than much traditional language the figure of Jesus as one in whom the transforming presence of God to the world is to be seen, and through whom his love and purposes can be made effective in our own lives.

Notes

1. The issues discussed in this paper are dealt with at greater length in my book, *The Remaking of Christian Doctrine* (S.C.M., 1974).
2. S. W. Sykes and J. P. Clayton, editors, *Christ, Faith, and History* (C.U.P., 1972), pp. 111-130.
3. "Le point de départ et le substance même du dogme est moins un enseignement qu'une personne" (*Le Problème du développement du dogme,* RSR XXV, 1948), p. 158.

The Spirit of God and the Human Spirit

André J. Pieters

"Spirit" belongs to the group of words which raise enormous semantic problems. (a) It is an old and practically universal word *(ruach, pneuma, Geist, Esprit,* Spirit). (b) Its meaning is not universally agreed upon. (c) Its contour is lacking in precision. What is to be included in, and what is to be excluded from it? (d) Even within the limits of one particular language, the word has undergone important changes of meaning (cf. the extreme case of the English language where *pneuma* or *spiritus* is translated either "spirit" or "mind"). (e) Finally, the word "spirit" has been discarded in scientific circles (cf. "soul;" psychology has become the science of the soul "without soul"). The word is hardly used outside the church, and even in the church it is used only in theological language.

Since the word "spirit" is extensively used within the Bible and in theology, we cannot discard it. Therefore, we must attempt a definition.

1. *The human spirit.* "Life" manifests itself in different dimensions: plant life, animal life, human life. By "spirit" we understand the dimension of life which differentiates human life from the other forms of life. It is this that thus constitutes its specific human dimension. (a) As such, it is a gift of God. (Genesis 2:7) When a person dies, the spirit returns to God. (Ecclesiastes 12:7, James 2:26) (b) In religious language, "spirit" is the center of life in which communion with the Spirit of God is lived. "It is the Spirit himself bearing witness with our spirit that we are children of God," (Romans 8:16 and many other references). (c) Human life always has two dimensions: *thought* and *action.* Both need a source of inspiration: *meaning* and *power.* Therefore, we define "spirit" as the *ruach,* the *pneuma,* "wind," the driving force which produces the "unity" of meaning and power.

2. *The Spirit of God*. If we are going to maintain the expression in our theological language, we must start from the Christian doctrine of the Trinity. What the doctrine of the Trinity is not: (a) This doctrine is not to be understood and explained in mathematical terms: three persons in one Godhead. "One is not three, and three are not one." (b) *Opera Trinitatis ad extra sunt indivisa.* When we speak of the Spirit of God, we speak of God himself. It is here that it becomes extremely difficult to use the term *persona* within the Trinity. If God is Spirit, and if we stress the word *persona* in its modern sense, then, in speaking about the Spirit of God, we speak about "the Spirit of the Spirit," which is nonsensical.

The doctrine of the Trinity attempts to express the fact that there is only one God; that God through the ages manifests the fullness of his being in such a way that we need complementary affirmations in order to speak about him as the one God. In the Old Testament he is Creator, God of the Covenant. In the New Testament, we are given a bridge over the gap between God and humanity. Whereas the presence on earth of Jesus Christ was limited in time and space (thirty-three years in the land of Israel), the doctrine of the Spirit affirms that this same presence of God is now permanent. The Holy Spirit continues the divine presence in the realm of human life which was inaugurated by Christ. How is this presence manifested? As the *sophia* and *dunamis* of God. It is in these terms that we find the point of connection, of possible relation between the Spirit of God and the spirit of the human being. As *sophia,* the Spirit of God brings meaning. As *dunamis,* the Spirit gives power, and unites them.

In all human discourse, it is extremely important to mark clearly one's reference point. This is important for one's own thought. It is important for the one who reads or listens. Above all, it is important in order to do justice to the subject. Our subject, "The Spirit of God and the Human Spirit," requires such clarification. Briefly stated, my position is as follows: The reality of the presence of the Spirit of God is of such a nature one can only hope to speak about it in an appropriate way if one participates in the reality about which he or she speaks, i.e., existentially.

We can only hope to perceive the new life by our fullest possible participation in its fullest manifestation. I quote John Oman from his book, *The Natural and the Supernatural.*

> If in this limited experience man perceives a higher reality "which is seeking to reveal itself through our whole experience in this present world then we must reach out after our farthest vision and follow even the dimly discerned beckoning of its requirements, as they speak to us of what is beyond demonstration and only discerned in moments of deeper insight and higher consecration.[1] "

Reality (witness of the Spirit of God to the spirit of the human) must be allowed to speak for itself, both in its actual manifestations and in its potential development, or to use a theological phrase, in its eschatological perspective.

We have made an important discovery. Knowledge of the relation between the Spirit of God and the human spirit requires a life in communion with the Spirit of God. We must not speak about this relationship in general, as though it were a universal experience. This is in flat contradiction with the Bible. Indeed, if we turn to the Bible, there is no reference pointing to this relationship in such universal terms. Ecclesiastes 12:7 points to no such universal relationship. In addition to my own Old Testament studies, I discussed this matter at length with Professor J. Schoneveld, Professor of Old Testament in Brussels. Every intervention of the Spirit of God occurs within the fellowship of God's own people. So it is in Isaiah 45:4: "For the sake of my servant Jacob, and Israel, my chosen, I

shall call you by your name." I have checked rather
carefully the New Testament references. There can be
no doubt. The manifestation of the Spirit of God is
limited to the fellowship of believers.

For our present purpose, it matters little whether
this manifestation is individual (the believer), or col-
lective (the church). But we should carefully notice
this biblical indication. The Spirit of God is "the Spirit
of Christ," (John 15:26, 16:14) and as the message
of Christ was received by some and not by all, likewise
the Spirit was received by some and not by all. Christ
made this distinction very clearly. "The Father will
give you . . . the Spirit of truth to be with you for
ever." (John 14:16) "You know him for he dwells
with you, and will be in you." (John 14:17) The
world, however, "cannot receive him, because it neither sees him nor knows him." (John 14:17) The Spirit
of God calls together the people of God. He is the
"Spirit of holiness," (Romans 1:4) "the Spirit of
revelation," (1 Corinthians 2:10) "the Spirit of grace"
(Hebrews 10:29) and "the Spirit of glory." (1 Peter
4:14)

It is said in the New Testament, and constantly repeated, that the "Holy Spirit dwells within us," (2
Timothy 1:14) but never is this affirmed of the non-
Christian believer. Quite the contrary is said: "worldly
people, devoid of the Spirit." (Jude 19)

It may well be that in this ecumenical and pluralistic
age, we shrink from repeating these biblical statements.
Indeed, they may sound like an expression of intoler-
able presumption on the part of the church. This,
unfortunately, has happened, but this need not be so,
for we must understand God's purpose. The Spirit has
not been given to the *koinonia* of the church in order
that the church might boast in his possession. The
Spirit of God has been given to the church for the sake

of humanity. The church is an instrument, not an end in itself!

The church is the first manifestation of a potentiality which seeks complete actualization in the whole of humankind. Pride and presumption are therefore excluded. If the presence of the Spirit is a privilege, it is also a responsibility.

The presence of the Spirit is not to be understood as a quantitative difference. The action of the Spirit of God manifests itself not only *to* the spirit of the individual but also *in* the person. One who has the Spirit has become a *pneumatikos* in opposition to the *sarkikos,* who does not possess the Spirit of God. That person has received something which the other has not received. First Corinthians 2:13 speaks about those who possess the Spirit of God and distinguishes them from those who have not received, i.e., do not possess, the Spirit.

It is important that we should beware of a mistake which unfortunately is often made, namely to understand this "possession" or this "absence" of the Spirit in terms of a quantitative differentiation. In other words, the possession of the Spirit of God is not an addition to human personality. It is not a new function which is added to the other functions of the mind. If we accept the traditional scheme which discerns three major functions in the human mind—intellect, will, and feeling—then we should never understand the "gift of the Spirit of God" as the addition of a fourth function, as if the difference between the *pneumatikos* and the *sarkikos* could be explained in terms of a greater or smaller number of mental functions.

This is a very common error, maybe not among trained theologians, but in what we may call popular piety. It may well result from the way in which the gospel is preached in mass evangelism. This type of gospel preaching follows a precise pattern: Its first

affirmation is that natural *anthropos* lacks something
—faith. The second step is that people need to receive
that which is lacking. Third, it proclaims that God offers to a person the faith which one cannot obtain
through one's own merits. And finally, when a person
accepts the gospel, one is said to have received the
faith. In the same line, we may replace the word "faith"
by the expression "the Spirit of God." The *sarkikos*
is one who does not possess the Spirit of God, and this
is understood as a great lack. This one is invited to
receive the Spirit of God, and if the person accepts
this offer, he or she is then said to possess the Spirit.
Thus, the difference between *pneumatikos* and the
sarkikos is a differerence between the "haves" and the
"have nots." In a certain sense, of course, this is true,
provided however that we do not interpret this difference mathematically, that is, quantitatively. The absence of the Spirit of God is no reduction of the number of functions of the human mind; it's no psychological lack. Nor is the gift of the Spirit of God the addition
of a new element to the human mind. All interpretations
of the presence of the Spirit of God in the human
spirit, in terms of "quantity" must be rigorously banned
from our understanding and language. The absence or
presence of the Spirit of God in the spirit of an
individual is not a psychological difference.

We have already indicated that the possession of the
Spirit of God is put in close relationship with knowledge, and we must now come back to this point in a
more detailed way. The Spirit of God is the Spirit of
knowledge and understanding. Once again, we refer to
the classical passage in 1 Corinthians 2:8-10, "None
of the rulers of this age understood this . . . . But, as
it is written, 'What no eye has seen, nor ear heard, nor
the heart of man conceived, what God has prepared
for those who love him,' God has revealed to us
through the Spirit."

Knowledge is a gift of the Spirit. I would like to add one or two biblical references. In 1 Corinthians 12:8, Paul says that knowledge is one of the many gifts of the Spirit of God to the body of the church for the common good: " . . . to another (is given) the utterance of knowledge according to the same Spirit . . . ." In Romans 15:14, the apostle expresses his joy because the Christians in Rome are "filled with all knowledge." I need not labor the point any further.

The words *Yada-ginoskein* constantly come back throughout the Bible. It is important, therefore, that we should understand as exactly as possible what is meant by *Yada-ginoskein,* and especially what is not meant by these words. There is a type of knowledge which is usually referred to as "scientific knowledge," that is, the objective knowledge of reality in its manifold manifestations. This, indeed, is the most common significance which we attribute to the word "knowledge." I am, of course, aware of the fact that *Yada-ginoskein* has another meaning which might be defined as "existential knowledge," or "knowledge by participation in the reality of the object of knowledge." To this latter, we shall return. At this time we are more concerned with the more "scientific" definition of knowledge.

The important fact which we should clearly keep in mind when we speak about the Spirit of God producing knowledge in the human spirit is that this should not be understood as if a person under the influence of the Spirit of God would arrive at some sort of knowledge reserved to the *pneumatikos* and which would not be accessible to other people. In the modern, scientific sense of the word, there is no such thing as "esoteric knowledge" which is the exclusive possession of those who have the Spirit of God.

Scientific knowledge has its boundaries which, of course, are being broadened every day as research progresses. What I am trying to say is that these boundaries of knowledge are identical for Christians and non-Christians alike. The amount of knowledge available to the human mind is the same for everyone. Faith does not subtract anything from it, nor does it add anything to it. A Christian doesn't know *more* than any other person when it comes to factual knowledge provided by scientific research.

Of course, some people possess greater knowledge than others. Some are more intelligent than others. Some are more interested than others. But these differences do not affect our main proposition: The scope of possible knowledge is identical for both the *pneumatikos* and the *sarkikos*. Whatever the Bible may say about a particular type of "knowledge" which is revealed by the Spirit of God to the human spirit, we should not interpret these biblical statements in a quantitative way of *more* or *less*.

We thus reach an important conclusion, both for the human being as knowing subject and for reality as the object of knowledge. The impact exercised by the Spirit of God upon the human spirit should never be interpreted in terms of a quantitative difference, neither in the psychological structuring of human personality nor in the area of objective knowledge. And yet, as we have seen, the Bible speaks repeatedly and clearly about "knowledge" as the gift of the Spirit. How, then, are we to understand the teaching of the Bible on this subject?

We come back to the other definition of knowledge, namely "existential knowledge," or "knowledge by participation." In what way is this type of knowledge different from objective knowledge? If the difference is not one of quantity or extension where does the difference lie? The difference resides in the fact that existential knowledge adds *meaning* to the object of knowledge.

Let me use an example. When I had completed high school I wasn't sure about my future. My wife and I had married early and three years after our wedding we had two girls. The babies made us very happy, of course, but caring for a family also meant quite a responsibility. For a while I seriously considered taking a position in business; one day I applied for a job in a carpet factory. Soon after I had sent in my application, I received a letter from the manager in which, among other things, I was asked to undergo an eye test to measure my color-sensitivity (which of course is very important in the manufacturing and sale of carpets!). Well, I submitted to this test and what happened? The doctor at the test center opened a little booklet, turned to page one, which had nothing but a number of colored dots neatly arranged in a circle. He asked: "What do you see?" Well, I saw a large number of dots, and that was all! He asked me: "Don't you see something else?" And I said, "No." Then he turned to page two. Here again, a great number of colored dots were printed on a surface limited by a circle, and again the man asked: "What do you see?" I looked more closely, trying to see something which obviously I was supposed to notice. But however hard I tried, I only saw dots! So, we went on to page three, and to page four, and then when he turned that page, I immediately said: "Five!" There it was! Only dots of course, but in such a combination of colors, that in the middle of those hundreds of dots, those in the center clearly fell together in the form of the figure five! Well, to complete the story, I further discovered the number eight, and that was all, with the result that I didn't get the job. A few months later I entered a theological college. So, you see, had it not been for a certain degree of color-blindness, I might not have entered the ministry.

But why do I tell you this story? I choose it because

it illustrates the point I am trying to make: Colored dots are just colored dots until, all at once, they acquire a new dimension, a new meaning. They become a number if the eye is sensitive to the interior disposal of the colors. Now this "additional dimension" is not the result of an increase in the number of dots, the *expansion of the object of knowledge,* as we tried to correct earlier, but the result of the *injection* into that given and unchanged field of observation of another element, which I call *meaning.*

My example is quite imperfect, of course, since it was taken from the physical world and therefore cannot be applied as such to the realm of the spirit. And yet, it helps us to understand the point with which we are concerned. Colored dots reveal figures to those eyes which have a high color sensitivity; likewise, reality. Both the knowing subject and the object of knowledge are loaded with particular meaning according to the existential insertion into reality of the inquiring mind. In the previous sentence I used the verb "load"—"to be loaded with." I chose this verb intentionally because "weight" is a good symbol for defining *meaning.* Indeed, "meaning" is the *weight* we attach to particular aspects of reality.

Summarizing our investigation, we could define the relation between the scientific knowledge and existential knowledge (that is, knowledge with the inclusion of meaning) in the following way. The human mind is constantly in search of reality. On the one hand, this means that we assemble all possible data of objective knowledge. As we have seen, in this search all people are in an equal position as knowing subjects. They are faced with an object of knowledge, the boundaries of which are identical for everyone, as the number and color of the dots in the color sensitivity book are the same for everyone. But the human mind, in raising the question, "What?", simultaneously raises the question of meaning, of "the weight of the what," of the importance of that which is perceived as objectively existing. The Spirit of God is not an addition to, but a transformation of the spirit of a person. The way in which we have conducted our inquiry thus far now allows us to unmask one of the most subtle errors which has beguiled Christian thinking. This error consists, as we have already indicated, in conceiving the possession of the Spirit of God as an addition to the human spirit. Now, what are the dangers of such an interpretation? They are twofold and, hopefully, I shall be able to demonstrate that they are corollary.

1. If the possession of the Spirit of God is an addition to the human spirit, then obviously the life of the Spirit is lived in a *vase-clos* (closed vessel), i.e., in a realm of its own, unrelated to the other dimensions of the knowing subject and of the object of knowledge, which remains apart from that dimension of life which thus becomes an artificially created "spiritual realm." This is the type of piety which we can describe in an appropriate way as "Sunday religion." Here, the inspiration of the Spirit of God and his injunctions are introducing one to an area which is totally unrelated to the day-by-day course of life on earth.

There are many examples of this type of religious life. There is the example of the scientist who works all day in the laboratory and who at 5:30 p.m. hangs her white jacket on a coatrack, then goes out to another form of life on the assumption that there is no common denominator between the laboratory and the church. Or, there is the example of the medical doctor who objects to the reference made to science by his pastor, claiming that he did not come to church to get another lecture on science but to get a "spiritual message" (should I call it a "spiritual kick"?). We could multiply the examples endlessly, but we need not do so. These examples, and others we could give, all point to the widespread tendency to separate the church and the world to the extent that they become two different worlds, it being understood, of course, that the "area of the Spirit" functions in its own right, quite independent from and unrelated to the other aspects of life.

2. The corollary error unavoidably claims the autonomy of the non-religious or non-spiritual realms of life. This claim of autonomy, uttered on behalf of any dimension of life, is just as devastating as the previous error. Having granted the influence of the Spirit of God in some remote corner of human life, the other functions of the human mind, whether intellect, will, or feeling, then claim their own autonomy. If for once we may use religious language, this may well be the most profound and therefore the most subtle manifestation of sin. It does at one and the same time pay tribute to God, after having localized him in an unimportant, remote corner of personality and reality, and also claims one's autonomy in the other areas of life which are, as we are aware, the only important ones which really matter in the long run. Now what the Bible teaches about the impact of the Spirit of God upon the human spirit is not an addition to it but its thorough-going and fundamental transformation. In Romans 12:2, Paul exhorts his readers: "Be transformed by the renewal of your mind."

In other words, God is after the transformation of our being *as it is* and in its totality. God wants us to be changed in our intellect, in our will, and in our feeling. He wants to radically change our values. As a matter of fact, the indwelling of the Spirit means nothing less than the radical reevaluation of all human values. There is not a single element in the human personality which remains unaffected by this renewing power of the Spirit of God. So, unless I am entirely mistaken in my interpretation, this is precisely what is meant by the

biblical message of repentance. Repentance is the discovery of the failure, the *échec,* of all I am and all I do
outside the determinative impact of the Spirit of God
on the human spirit. The message of the Bible is not
the announcement of the arrival of *Superman* upon the
stage of world history, that is, the natural person *plus*
something. It is the manifestation and realization of
the *new person,* psychologically identical to the old
person spiritually, but a new creation.

The gift of the Spirit of God adds not only meaning,
but also power to the human spirit. The relationship
between *meaning* and *power* is obvious. A simple
observation of human conduct reveals unmistakable
evidence that the absence of meaning always results in
a paralyzing lack of power. Let us take just one example. Two people are getting married, but they really
don't believe in the value of marriage. No sooner is
the wedding over than they are faced with the inherent
problems of sharing life together. They run into problems of communication, of sharing, of only doing for
the partner what is required. The number of problems
which they encounter is not greater than the number
of problems encountered by a couple who really believes in marriage. So what happens? Lacking the
understanding of the meaning of marriage, they simply
split up, whereas the other couples go on wrestling with
their problems. *The lack of meaning results in a lack
of power.*

On the contrary, the discovery of a new meaning
releases an unexpected and astonishing new energy.
The biblical example of this, of course, is Peter. Before
the outpouring of the Spirit of God, he was just a big
mouth, a braggart, full of noise, signifying nothing. At
the table of the Last Supper he cried out, "Lord, I am
ready to go with you to prison and to death." (Luke
22:33) Hardly a few hours later, he had denied Jesus
three times (Luke 22:54-62)—lack of meaning, lack

of faith. But then came Pentecost, the outpouring of
the Spirit of God in the spirit of Peter, and the weak
was made strong, the hesitant became steadfast, the
frightened became unafraid, the coward was turned
into the unwavering and the faithful follower of his
Lord. The Spirit which is meaning or wisdom, *sophia,*
is equally the Spirit of power, *dunamis.* These two
qualifications of the Spirit of God relate to each other
in an unbreakable unity.

The fact that the impact of the Spirit of God upon
the human spirit has to do with meaning, rather than
with the expansion of factual knowledge, produces a
strange and unexpected situation. Whereas, on first
thought we might be tempted to believe that the manifestation of a new meaning might result in the clarification of the ambiguity of human life, we soon discover that it rather adds a new element of ambiguity.

Meaninglessness may of course manifest itself for
what it is, namely, no meaning. It is obvious that this
is the problem with which many people are wrestling.
They are aware of a sort of vacuum in their lives.
Some seriously search for meaning; others have given
up the attempt and go on living in a kind of silent
desperation. Where no meaning is seen for what it is,
the situation is simple and unambiguous. The problem,
however, arises when the no meaning presents itself in
the disguise of meaning, or, to use a number of images, when emptiness pretends to be fullness, when
darkness takes the form of light, when the fake pretends
to be genuine.

Let us briefly turn to two passages in the Bible. In
John 8, we read the discussion between Jesus and the
Jews about freedom and bondage. Jesus says a shock-
ing thing. He tells the Jews they are slaves. This produces an immediate and violent reaction. "We are
descendants of Abraham, and have never been in
bondage to anyone." (v. 33) The situation of the

Jews, which in the "meaning framework" of Jesus, is seen as bondage, but is understood by those who are in that existential situation as freedom. This gives us a perfect example of what I have called ambiguity. It affects all situations where real freedom encounters not slavery-manifested-as-slavery, but slavery-experienced-and-understood-as-freedom. And then comes that statement of Jesus which throws full light on the ambiguity of the situation: "If the Son makes you free, you will be free indeed," (v. 36) that is, not a slave who kisses his chains and takes his bondage for freedom, but free *indeed,* really free, genuinely liberated.

For my second illustration, I refer to one of the words from the cross: "Father, forgive them; *for they know not what they do.* (Luke 23:34) These words should not be understood as a reference to objective, factual knowledge, because on that level they knew exactly what they were doing. They were putting a man to death by crucifixion. None of those who were playing a responsible part in that tragic event would have denied that; and yet, when we move into the realm of meaning, the words of Jesus unmask their so-called knowledge for what it really was, that is to say *ignorance.* They pretended to know what they were doing, and yet they did not know! Their ignorance had taken on the form of knowledge.

We do not invent meaning; we *discover* it. It is there; we have no power over it. What do we "grasp" or "discover" in reading the Gospel stories? Why is it people read the Gospel their life long and yet do not "know" Jesus Christ?

When, therefore, we speak of the impact of the Spirit of God on the human spirit as the introduction of a new meaning, we should, in the first place, study very carefully the way in which this new meaning tends to increase rather than to diminish the ambiguity. As I indicated above, the opposition may present itself in its true character, namely the opposition of good and evil-understood-as-evil; yet, this is rarely the case. Most of the time, the opposition is between good and evil-as-good; between light and darkness-as-light; between beauty and the ugly-as-beautiful; between knowledge and ignorance-as-knowledge.

In the second place, we should be constantly aware that in situations in which truth faces falsehood-as-truth, no real dialogue, no real communication, is possible. When a particular aspect about the reality of life is charged with a different meaning, then the conversation of two partners-in-dialogue is nothing else but a dialogue of sounds (a dialogue of deaf people). In the words of Luther, no talking, no preaching, no singing is of any avail. Communicating meaning, a new meaning, therefore, is beyond our human strength, as we all know from our Christian experience. We know that we must witness to the gospel, but we also know that nothing will get across to those to whom we bear the witness unless and until a power-other-than-ourselves will, as it were, fertilize our words, thus transforming that which is received as nothing more than a tale-told-by-a-fool into a meaning-giving and power-releasing creative word.

In all that we have said so far, we have done hardly more than break ground for our major thesis. We have tried to explain that the influence of the Spirit of God in the human spirit produces meaning and power. We have stated our conviction that it is only through existential participation that we can come to the understanding of this new meaning and power. We have seen that the possession of the Spirit of God by the human spirit is not an addition to human personality but its transformation, and we have noted how the emergence of a new meaning results in a new situation in which ambiguity is not removed, but rather increased. We must now raise the basic question: What is the content of this new meaning? If the Spirit of God inflates a new understanding, a new vision of life, what is its specific content?

My answer is not better than many other answers. I only hope that it will not be worse. I would put it like this. By the illumination of the Spirit of God, the human spirit understands life as diversified unity. The realization of this new reality was potentially accomplished by Jesus Christ, and it is at present activated by the Spirit of God.

That the life of the human race manifests a great diversity is so obvious that I need not labor the point. All men and women are vaguely or clearly aware of the interior diversity within their own personalities, and even if they cannot state it in precise words, they know that there is a difference between thinking and willing, and that feeling is still different from these two. There is also a great diversity from one individual to the other; there are men and women, there are artists, philosophers, and social reformers. There are practice-oriented people and there are theory-oriented people. There are black people and there are white people. Both individually and socially, we discern an immense variety in human life.

The description of human life in these terms allows us to offer a definition of sin. In the first place, sin is everything which threatens the diversified unity of life. It's the introduction of dissonance in the harmony that life is intended to be. The devastating influence of sin manifests itself in two ways. It may attack the unity, either of a person as an individual, or of humanity as a whole. In that case, it produces a style of life in which the different elements either follow separate courses (a double life!) or clash. This was the experience described by Paul in Romans 7:24. "I want . . ., but I do not! I do . . . what I hate. I will . . . but I cannot. I act . . . but I don't understand what I do." This agonizing antagonism brings him to the fringe of despair. "Who will deliver me from this body of death?"

Second, sin manifests itself in every negation of the rightful existence of the diversity. Sin occurs whereever diversity is ruled out. This happens when the white pretends that only his culture is valid and thus discards the culture of the black community. It happens when the people of the Northern Hemisphere discard African culture as unimportant, to be substituted as rapidly as possible by their culture. It happens when the male makes the female into an object of pleasure and thus deprives her of her most intimate personality.

Sin occurs when the musicians deny either the unity of the orchestra or the diversity of the instruments. In the latter, it is the violinist saying to the pianist, "Since you are not a violinist, you are not a musician and you don't belong to the orchestra." In the former, it's the violinist and the pianist and the flutist who all want to play their own piece of music. Both ignore the harmony of the orchestra, and what they produce is cacophony, not harmony.

In this distorted world, the reconciling work of Christ is the inauguration of a new reality, that is, a world in which things fall into their proper place, where unity is established and where the diverse elements are allowed to occupy their proper place. In Christ this new reality has been potentially established. Its actualization is the work of the Spirit of God. Its full realization still lies ahead, of course, so that at present we can neither fully grasp it nor completely realize it. Today we are living "between the times" of the potential and the actual.

We have not yet attained perfection, and the proof of the present state of imperfection is given by the life of the church itself, where these reality-threatening and destructive powers are still at work. Let me just indicate some of them.

1. Time and eternity constitute a diversified unity, but again and again, Christians either deny their unity or their diversity. Some Christians are so concerned with time they forget about eternity. Others are so concerned with eternity that they have written off the dimension of time as unimportant.

2. The social and the individual constitute a diversified unity, but some have become individualistic to the point that they could not care less about the social, while others are concentrating on the social to the extent of ignoring or rejecting the claims of the individual.

3. Praying and working constitute a diversified unity, but some Christians declare: "If you pray, don't work. If you take it into your own hands, you show a lack of confidence in the power of God." The others declare: "If I act, why should I pray?"

4. Mission and development constitute a diversified unity, but some want to be missionaries, preaching a spiritual gospel, baptizing converts and building churches. Others want to be volunteers in Third World development programs, use their technical skills and build factories and schools of agriculture.

But if we put ourselves at the highest possible spiritual level by an existential act of participation in the new life of the Spirit, we shall commit ourselves to the realization of the unity in diversity of the new reality. How this new life will be in its final completion, we don't know yet. In Paul's words, "We are still dependent on a mirror, and even so we look at a riddle." We know in part, but the fact that we do not yet know perfectly, nor are allowed to take the last step to that perfection when God will be all and in all, is neither important nor necessary, as long as we have found that manifestation of meaning for evaluating the immediate situation with which we are confronted here and now, and we receive that amount of power which is required for acting accordingly. This is what I understand by the

presence and prompting of the Spirit of God in the
human Spirit.

Notes

1. John Oman, *The Natural and the Supernatural* (Freeport,
    New York: BFL Communications Books for Libraries,
    1972), p. 109.

The Gifts of the Spirit in the Church

Peter Stephens

Had this Institute been held ten years ago it is unlikely that there would have been a paper on "The Gifts of the Spirit in the Church." It is the charismatic movement in the church that has brought this subject to the fore, and what I have to say will, I hope, lead into a discussion of that later. Nevertheless, my immediate concern is to focus attention on two or three critical chapters of the New Testament, chapters 12 and 14 (and to a lesser extent chapter 13) in the First Letter to the Corinthians. I want us to see them at first in their own light, rather than in the light of questions which you and I want to put to them.

I. Paul

Paul appears to face a situation in which some people have certain spiritual gifts *(pneumatika),* and moreover set a very high value on those gifts. It is in response to this situation in which he sees perils for the Corinthian church that Paul engages in his only sustained discussion of spiritual gifts. However, such gifts are not limited to Corinth, nor indeed to churches founded by Paul, nor to letters written by him. They exist in the church at Rome, which he did not found. (Romans 12) They are referred to in 1 Peter 4:10, which (I think we may still hold) he did not write.

It is important to note the words which Paul uses to describe these spiritual gifts. He begins by referring to *pneumatika,* which is probably the word used by the Corinthians. But he very quickly uses other words, in particular *charisma* (grace gift) and *diakonia* (service). Paul seems to be the one who introduces the word *charisma* into theology;[1] it shows at once the way he understands spiritual gifts. An instructive use of this same word is seen in Romans 6:23, where he says: "The wages of sin is death, but the *charisma* of God is eternal life in Christ Jesus our Lord." It is in the context of this *charisma* of God that we can understand the *charismatic* (grace gifts) of God. Moreover, the *charismata* are at once referred to as services or ministries, that is, ways in which people are served. Paul's change of word, however, must not be exaggerated. He does not abandon the word spiritual *(pneumatika),* but in 14:1 returns to use it.

Before we examine Paul's critical assessment of these gifts, we ought to consider some of the affirmations he makes about them. First, there is the assumption that all Christians, without exception, share in the Spirit. "For by one Spirit we were all baptized into one body . . . and all were made to drink of one Spirit." (12:13) That all share in the Spirit is a fundamental difference between the old covenant and the new. Indeed, not to share in the Spirit is not to be a Christian at all. It is almost impossible to overestimate the importance of this assumption that all Christians share in the Spirit.

Second, Christians do not share only in the Spirit, but they share also in the gifts of the Spirit. These gifts are not the privilege of the few, whether ordained or lay, but of all Christians. Only in Ephesians 4:7 ("grace was given to each of us") do we have the absolutely explicit statement that everyone has a gift. It is, however, implied in 1 Corinthians 12 and 14 by the use of "all" and "each," for example, "but all of them, in all men, are the work of the same God." (12:6; cf. 12:7, 14:26, 1 Peter 4:10) Each person, therefore, is expected to exercise his or her gift. Indeed, it is assumed that when they meet for worship "each one has a hymn, a lesson, a revelation, a tongue, or an interpretation." (14:26) The problem is not whether there are any gifts—they are superabundant—but how they can best be used for the good of all.

Third, not only do they all have some gift or gifts, but they should all desire gifts of the Spirit. That implies gifts they do not already have. The desire should be especially for prophecy: "earnestly desire the spiritual gifts, especially that you may prophesy." (14:1) But Paul can equally say, "Now I want you all to speak in tongues," even if he does add, "but even more to prophesy." (14:5) He is not concerned to limit the gifts of the Spirit, except in a very particular sense. He is concerned, rather, to increase the openness of Christians to the immense variety of gifts that the Spirit wills to give. Thus, he beseeches the Thessalonians, "Do not quench the Spirit." (1 Thessalonians 5:19)

Fourth, the earnest desire for particular gifts in no way places them at the Christian's disposal. They are always gifts given by God in his sovereign freedom. The Spirit "apportions to each one individually as he wills." (12:11)

Fifth, the context in which Paul sees the gifts, however, is not an individual one—which is the context in which we tend to view the gifts. They are given individually, but they are given in the church. Thus Paul prefaces his list of the gifts with the words, "God has appointed in the church." (12:28) Not only are they given to the church, but they are also given in such a way that they complement each other, thus binding each member to the others. Here Paul uses the analogy of the body, the body which is the body of Christ and which consists of many members. Each part of the body needs the rest, so that "the eye cannot say to the hand, 'I have no need of you.'" (12:21) Moreover, the absence of a particular gift in a particular member does not make it any less a member of the body. "And if the ear should say, 'Because I am not an eye, I do not belong to the body,' that would not make it any less a part of the body." (12:16) One practical way in which one person or gift needs or complements another may be seen in the way Paul could write, "I

planted, Apollos watered, but God gave the growth."
(1 Corinthians 3:5-6)

Sixth, the gifts of which Paul speaks are immensely
varied. The variety does not mean that some are of
the Spirit and some not. No, "there are varieties of
gifts, but the same Spirit." (12:4) Now let me say at
once that Paul does not at first indicate the extent of
the variety. The first examples he gives in 12:8-10
are all what we may loosely call supernatural gifts,
gifts like miracles, tongues, prophecy. Not until later
does he place alongside these a couple of natural gifts
—helping and administration. (12:28) Here, however, he almost certainly went far beyond the way the
Corinthians saw the gifts of the Spirit. They seemed
to regard the sensational, the obviously supernatural,
as an expression of the Spirit. Paul does not reject that,
but he regards the unsensational and ordinary as equally
being gifts of the Spirit. In other words, the term
"Spirit" does not necessarily refer to either the sensational or the supernatural.

Seventh, within this variety there seems to be a certain order or hierarchy. Apostles, prophets, and teachers
are put in the first three places. (12:28) This appears
to be an accepted order at least for apostles and
prophets. (cf. Ephesians 2:20) The other gifts seem
to be put in particular order. The various gifts fall into
three main groups: those concerned with preaching
(these seem to be primary), those concerned with service, and those concerned with leadership. In Ephesians,
however, only the first group is represented. Nevertheless, an order or hierarchy of gifts does not mean
that some in the church are superior and some inferior
in status. Such an idea is alien to Paul. Rather, "God
has so adjusted the body, giving the greater honor to
the inferior part, that there may be no discord in the
body . . . ." (12:24-25)

Now let us turn to the criteria as well as to the

safeguards and limitations that Paul offers in these chapters. Recall first that he is dealing with those who appear to set great store by the gift of tongues, perhaps because its obvious abnormality made it appear a particularly spiritual gift. It could even be that they preferred it to a gift like prophecy, which Paul especially affirms, because tongues, without interpretation, could boost one's pride, whereas prophecy would disclose the secrets of one's heart and one would be convicted. (14:24-25) Whatever may have been in the mind of the Corinthians, Paul offers certain criteria by which gifts may be judged. He suggests certain safeguards or limitations in their use.

The first criterion is the most important, though some would doubt if it is meant as a criterion. It is, "no one speaking by the Spirit of God ever says 'Jesus be cursed!' and no one can say 'Jesus is Lord' except by the Holy Spirit." (12:3) This is regarded by some interpreters simply as an example of the operation of the Holy Spirit rather than as a criterion. But, in effect, it seems reasonable to take it as a criterion. If we do, we have the contrast between mere spirit possession, which can be pagan, and possession by the Holy Spirit. Satan indeed can produce signs and wonders (see, for example, 2 Thessalonians 2:9; Mark 13:22), so that miracles or tongues are not in themselves necessarily actions of God. When they were pagans, the Corinthians might have been spirit-possessed, but then, to quote Paul, they "would be led astray and carried away to the dumb idols." (12:2) A sure indication that possession is by the Holy Spirit and not by some other spirit is shown when the person who is possessed says, "Jesus is Lord," because such a confession is possible only by the Holy Spirit.

It could be that the reference to "Jesus be cursed" is explained as by C. K. Barrett, who suggests (in this he follows Allo) that Paul is referring to the cries of

Christian ecstatics who were resisting the trance or ecstasy they felt coming upon them "in the manner of the Sibyl who foamed as she resisted the inspiration that was taking possession of her, or of Cassandra who curses Apollo in Aeschylus's *Agamemnon*."[2]

The statement, "Jesus is Lord," is an affirmation about Jesus (one might say the historical Jesus) and about God. It is not, however, simply a correct theological statement. It is a statement of discipleship, an affirmation of the lordship of Jesus over oneself. A sense of this can be seen in the way Augustine contrasts 1 Corinthians 12:3 wth Matthew 7:21, in his *De Trinitate*.[3] The importance of discipleship in this kind of context can be seen in Acts where Jewish exorcists tried to use the name of Jesus to cast out demons. (Acts 19:13-17) They used his name but they did not accept his lordship. They were not disciples. (Compare Simon Magus in Acts 8:18-19.)

If "Jesus is Lord" is Paul's first criterion, then it fits in with the Johannine tradition which sees the Spirit primarily as one who bears witness to Christ. It also shows the very close link in Paul's thinking between Christ and the Spirit, so that the Spirit is not thought of as going beyond Christ in some way. This is in keeping with the parallel drawn between the Spirit and Christ in verses 4 and 5: "varieties of gifts, but the same Spirit . . . varieties of service, but the same Lord."

The second criterion is the serving or building up of the church. Gifts are given, not for the sake of the individual, but "for the common good." (12:7) They are to build up the congregation, a statement that runs right through chapter 14. (See verses 3-5, 12, 17, and 26.) Here again the Spirit is seen in a distinctively Christian way. The work of the Spirit is to create unity in Christ, indeed "by one Spirit we were all baptized into one body—Jews or Greeks, slaves or free—and all were made to drink of one Spirit." (12:13) The gifts of the Spirit are likewise concerned with the building up of this body and not merely with the building up of one member of it. This notion of the gifts of the Spirit is seen equally in the Letter to the Romans where Paul writes, "I want to bring you some spiritual gift to make you strong." (1:11)

It is concern for the congregation that leads Paul to stress the need for intelligibility. Unless what is said can be understood by those who hear it, there is no building up of the congregation. The person who hears can make no response with his or her mind and, therefore, cannot say "Amen." (14:16) One can, in other words, not make a response with the whole of one's being. What applies to the worshipper applies in a not dissimilar way to the outsider who happens to come in. Tongues, unless interpreted, would be unintelligible to such a person. The visitor would simply feel that the speakers were mad, presumably in the sense of possessed. (14:23) If, however, someone prophesies, then the visitor will be convicted and brought to worship God, (14:24f) and so be built into the body of Christ. There is thus a missionary concern here as well. The gifts of the Spirit can therefore build people into the body of Christ as well as build up the body of Christ.

To ensure that they do in fact build up the congregation, Paul mentions safeguards or limitations in the use of gifts, particularly the gift of tongues. When people speak in tongues there are to be two or three at most. They are to speak in turn, and there is to be interpretation. (14:27) If there is no one to interpret, they are to keep silence in church, although they may use the gift privately. (14:28) Thus, the purpose for which the gift is given determines the use to which the gift is put. In this way the variety of gifts can be a variety of service or ministry. (12:5) What is said about tongues and prophecy in this context implies that they can be controlled to some extent.

A third criterion, linked to that of building up the church, is the criterion of love. This is expressed in a variety of ways. It must underlie every gift. Without love, none of the gifts is truly spiritual. A gift such as knowledge might puff up, whereas love builds up. (8:1) It is love, moreover, which makes the gift the possession not of one, but of all. Without love the gift of tongues, or prophecy, or liberality is nothing. (13:1-3) The Corinthians are to aim at love and this is more important than spiritual gifts, though it does not displace them. (12:31, 14:1) It is not an accident that the theme of love in Romans 12 and 1 Corinthians 13 is so closely linked with the discussion of the gifts of the Spirit.

Along with these criteria are important comments on who is to do the testing of the gifts. The testing is by the Spirit through the congregation or certain members of it. The Spirit gives to some "the ability to distinguish between spirits." (12:10) However, at one point Paul suggests that either the whole congregation or everyone who is a prophet is to do this work of distinguishing between what is from the Holy Spirit and what is from other spirits. "Let two or three prophets speak, and let the others weigh what is said." (14:29) If it is the congregation, then that is in keeping with what is said in 1 John where it is assumed that the whole congregation will test the spirits, (1 John 4:1) and in the Didache. (11:2-7) The congregation does not, without reason, accept something as from the Holy Spirit. It must be able to say, "Amen," and that involves giving assent to it as well as understanding it. As discernment is the control exercised over prophecy, so in a somewhat different way interpretation is the control exercised over tongues. Interpretation, like discernment, is a specific gift of the Spirit.

Before we look at other ways in which the gifts of the Spirit were experienced and assessed in the early church, we need to consider how far the gifts in Paul's writings were what may loosely be called natural or supernatural. The Corinthians seemed to think of them as supernatural, regarding such an apparently super-natural gift as tongues as a spiritual endowment. Paul seems to qualify this in a number of ways in light of his understanding of the Spirit as the Spirit of Christ. He does not regard extraordinariness as a sign that some-thing is a gift of the Spirit. It is not a gift of the Spirit unless it bears witness to Christ and builds up the body of Christ. Moreover, quite ordinary activities such as helping and administering, which to the pagan mind do not suggest any possession of the Spirit, can be described as gifts of God. Now there are non-Christian equivalents of administration, as there are non-Christian equivalents of miracles. They may, however, be seen as gifts of the Spirit by a number of tests, such as whether they build up the body of Christ.

But the question may still be asked whether they are seen by Paul as natural qualities which we have and which we put to good use, or whether they are specific gifts of the Spirit. I find the second more likely.

In this, a lot depends on how we understand 1 Corinthians, chapter seven. Some read this chapter, especially verses 7 and 17, as though being married or unmarried, enslaved or free, circumcised or uncircumcised, is a gift of God—at least if you accept it as such. I am not persuaded that this is what Paul means. In verse 7, Paul clearly accepts the idea that God gives some, but not others, a gift of celibacy. But this is not the same as saying that the state of celibacy or marriage is, in itself, a gift from God, or becomes so if we accept it as such. Certainly it does not follow without more ado that verse 7 controls the exegesis of verse 17, and that whatever state one is in is a gift of the Spirit (as Paul uses the term in chapter 12 and 14) as long as in that state one leads the life to which God has called one.

Paul appears to use the idea of the gifts of the Spirit for specific gifts to members of the church. They may be ordinary gifts that coincide with their natural qualities, or they may be extraordinary gifts that do not coincide with their natural qualities. The critical matter is not their ordinariness or their extraordinariness, but their being gifts of the Spirit. Being gifts of the Spirit stresses the fact that behind them lies the initiative of God, rather than human initiative. I should add that a very different view of 1 Corinthians, chapter seven, can be found in many writings.[4]

II. The Church After Paul

Let us now look briefly at the experience of the gifts of the Spirit in the early church and, in particular, at some of the criteria it applied for testing whether something was of the Spirit or not. Rightly or wrongly, all we shall do is focus on certain important points of comparison or contrast with what we find in Paul.

We turn first to 1 and 2 Timothy where there is an important contrast with 1 Corinthians. This lies in the understanding of the church and the ministry. Corinthians sets the gifts in the context of the body and its various members. There is a rich variety of gifts in which all share in different ways. There is no opposition between the ordained and the non-ordained; indeed, there is none who, in the normal sense of the term, is ordained. In the Pastorals, however, the word *charisma* is used twice only, and on both occasions of what can be called ordination. First, "Do not neglect the gift you have, which was given you by prophetic utterance when the elders laid their hands upon you." (1 Timothy 4:14) Second, "Hence I remind you to rekindle the gift of God that is within you through the laying on of my hands." (2 Timothy 1:6)

This linking of gifts with the ordained ministry finds further expression through the centuries in different ways, either in the insistence that those with the gifts should be ordained, or in the view that those who are ordained thereby receive a gift of the Spirit.

In 1 John, the Didache, and the Shepherd of Hermas, we find various criteria suggested or applied for testing the spirits. The criteria are to some extent determined by the situation for which they were written. Thus, in the situation in which 1 John was written, there were clearly prophets who had once been within the church. They spoke by inspiration, but the writer regards the inspiration as coming from antichrist, not from God. They are people who deny the Incarnation and who lack love, whatever else they may possess. In the face of such people who had been within the church and who were still regarded as being inspired, the writer offers a twofold test, a doctrinal one and a moral one. The doctrinal test is explicit. "Beloved, do not believe every spirit, but test the spirits to see whether they are of God; for many false prophets have gone out into the world. By this you know the Spirit of God: every spirit which confesses that Jesus Christ has come in the flesh is of God, and every spirit which does not confess Jesus is not of God." (1 John 4:1-3) The moral test, which is the test of love, is not explicit in the same way, but it runs through the whole letter. We should note, as well, that the author expects the whole congregation to be able to test the spirits.

In the Didache the concern is once more with prophets. They are now held in much greater awe than in Paul, perhaps because there are fewer of them. Thus we read: "Do not test or examine any prophet who speaks in a spirit, 'for every sin shall be forgiven, but this sin shall not be forgiven.'" (11:7) It is recognized, however, that there are false prophets, and the quotation continues: "But not everyone who speaks in a spirit is a prophet, except he have the behaviour of the Lord. From his behaviour, then, the false prophet and

the true prophet shall be known." (11:8) Examples of
such behavior are given: "And no prophet who orders
a meal in a spirit shall eat of it: otherwise he is a false
prophet. And every prophet who teaches the truth, if
he do not what he teaches, is a false prophet." (11:9-
10) The test of the prophets is essentially one of character. As in Matthew 7:16, they are to be known by
their fruits. The inadequacy of a mere moral test is
evident, but the important thing is that it may well have
been an adequate test in that situation.

The way in which the moral argument has constantly
been used in the church can be seen in our own day in
the Soviet Union in the division in the Baptist Church
between the Council of Churches and the All-Union
Council. Listen now to an extract from the "Message to
the Whole Brotherhood of Evangelical Christians and
Baptists in the USSR from Former Pastors of the Council of Churches" which declares: "For all those in doubt
about the activity of the AUCECB (All-Union Council), we declare that the work of God is being carried
on in the power of the Holy Spirit; this is testified to
by the good fruits of the Spirit in the life and ministry
of the united brotherhood."[5]

It is interesting to note that the Didache assumes
that the congregation has the ability to test the spirits.
"Let everyone who 'comes in the name of the Lord' be
received; but when you have tested him you shall
know him, for you shall have understanding of true and
false" (literally, "right and left understanding").
(12:1)

Hermas equally assumes that the congregation can
discern true prophets from false ones. The people are
told, "Test, then, from his life and deeds, the man who
says he is inspired." (Commandment XI:16) The criterion again is essentially moral. It is seen that even the
false prophet "also speaks some true words, for the
devil fills him with his spirit, to see if he can break any

of the righteous." (XI:3) The true prophet is "meek and gentle, and lowly-minded, and refrains from all wickedness and evil desire of this world, and makes himself poorer than all men, and gives no answers to anyone when he is consulted, nor does he speak by himself (for the Holy Spirit does not speak when a man wishes to speak), but he speaks at that time when God wishes him to speak." (XI:8) The false prophet "exalts himself and wishes to have the first place, and he is instantly impudent and shameless and talkative, and lives in great luxury and in many other deceits, and accepts rewards for his prophecy, and if he does not receive them he does not prophesy." (XI:12)

The primary test is moral, but there are two other elements worth noting. There is a test that has to do with the nature of prophecy—that is, the true prophet cannot speak in response to human requests, but only in response to the Spirit's initiative. There is also a test that has to do with the church itself.

The church is the place where the Spirit dwells and, therefore, when prophets are in its midst they are either inspired by the Spirit if true, or deserted by their evil spirit if false. "Therefore, when the man who has the Divine Spirit comes into a meeting of righteous men who have the faith of the Divine Spirit, and intercession is made to God from the assembly of those men, then the angel of the prophetic spirit rests on him and fills the man, and the man, being filled with the Holy Spirit, speaks to the congregation as the Lord wills." (XI:9) By contrast, a false prophet "does not come near to an assembly of righteous men, but shuns them." (XI:13) If he does come near, "the earthly spirit flees from him in fear, and that man is made dumb and is altogether broken up, being able to say nothing." (XI:14)

The second century sees the effective disappearance of many of the varied gifts of the Spirit, the rejection of Montanism being a kind of posthumous death blow.

In Montanism there was an outbreak of prophecy. Montanus and two companions, Priscilla and Maximilla, claimed they were inspired by the Spirit. They announced the coming of the Lord not far from the city of Philadelphia.

Eusebius refers to certain moral and doctrinal objections that were made against Montanism. Indeed, one quotation he makes has an almost contemporary ring in it when he writes: "But it is necessary to test all the fruits of a prophet. . . .Tell me, does a prophet dye his hair? Does he pencil his eyelids?"[6] Yet the attack was not altogether—some would say not at all—against its orthodoxy or its morality, for it was orthodox and intensely moral, but against the ecstatic nature of its prophecy. Listen to two quotations. "He began to be ecstatic and to speak and to talk strangely, prophesying contrary to the custom which belongs to the tradition and succession of the church from the beginning."[7] "But the false prophet speaks in ecstasy . . . . But they cannot show that any prophet, either of those in the Old Testament or of those in the New, was inspired in this way . . . ."[8] Thus, the ecstasy which Montanists regarded as evidence of the Spirit, as possibly the Corinthians did, is regarded as evidence the other way.

From this point, one could almost say that charismatic ministries were forced out of the church, at least out of its congregational life. Montanism displays a conflict between the charismatic ministries and the ordained hierarchical ministries which at many points had existed happily alongside each other, rather than in opposition to each other.

III. The Reformers

A summary glance at the reformers may take us a stage further in considering the gift of the Spirit and gifts of the Spirit. With the reformers the doctrine of the Spirit gains new prominence. There are many ways in which their understanding differs from that of the Roman Church. For the reformers, it is the Spirit who is the source of new life. The church does not possess the Spirit or have him at its disposal; rather does the Spirit possess and give life to the church. Nor is it only some in the church who are spiritual, such as priests and monks, but all Christians are spiritual, because they all have the Spirit. Moreover, because all Christians have the Spirit, they understand the things of the Spirit. Like the New Testament church, they are capable of judging what is true from what is false. Thus doctrinal disputations did not need to be referred to the pope or to the universities for their adjudication. This is particularly true of Zwingli in Zürich. For him it was sufficient to have an assembly of Christians before whom the Scriptures were opened.

All Christians may, in principle, engage in the ministry of the church, though in fact some hold office and some do not. In an emergency any Christian may properly minister to others. In Luther's words, "all Christians are truly of the spiritual estate, there is no difference among them, save of office alone."[9]

It is possible for the reformers to see that the gifts of the Spirit belong to the whole church and not just to those ordained. Thus Bucer, stating that the purpose of reading the Bible is edification, affirms, "Those who adhere to this purpose will appoint to interpret the Scriptures in the Church the person on whom the gift of interpretation has been bestowed, irrespective in the end of the position he occupies. This was still the practice in the days of Origen."[10]

The place at which the reformers differed among themselves was in how one received the Spirit. In this the sharpest contrast is seen between Luther and the so-called enthusiasts, although there were immense differences among those who are loosely classed enthusiasts. They range from the fundamentalism of the anabaptist, Grebel, who is shocked to find that Thomas Müntzer has the singing of hymns in his German mass, to the sublime freedom towards Scripture of Sebastian Franck. Thus Grebel's reaction to Müntzer's hymns was: "Whatever we are not taught by clear passages or examples (of Scripture) must be regarded as forbidden, just as if it were written: 'This do not, sing not.' "[11] Franck's response to Grebel would have been even stronger than his words about Luther when he wrote, ". . . thou shouldst not believe and accept something (merely) reported by Scripture—and feel that the God in thy heart must yield to Scripture."[12]

Consider with me for a moment how the reformers viewed the relation of Spirit and Word. For Luther, the Spirit was given in, with, and under the Word, both the audible word of proclamation and the visible words of the sacraments. This is central in his thinking, tied in with his whole theology of the cross—that is, that God makes himself known to us in a hidden way, in Christ. He opposed this to a theology of glory in which we seek to meet and see God as he is in himself. For Luther that belongs to the future, not to the present where we walk by faith and not by sight. Just as God used the flesh of Christ to meet us in the past, so now in the present he uses word and sacrament to come to us. There was not for Luther, as there was for the spiritualists, an opposition between the Spirit and what is physical or material. They belong together. Indeed, the Spirit does not come to us apart from what is outward. Luther can therefore speak of the word as "the door and window of the Holy Spirit. Windows are in the house, so that light may enter. If you wish to close them, God will not give you the proper Spirit. But he will use this door which is the word whether written or spoken . . . ."[13] For Luther, the devil misleads the enthusiasts. He uses the words Spirit, Spirit, Spirit to destroy the very bridge by which the Holy Spirit comes to the human spirit, that is word and sacrament, and teaches them not how the Spirit comes to them but how they come to the Spirit.[14]

At the opposite pole from Luther's view is that of a spiritualist like Sebastian Franck. For him, everything (word, sacraments, church) is like a doll that God gave the church in its infancy and has now taken away. What matters is the inward teaching of the Spirit, and that knows no bounds. Listen to what he says: "Consider as thy brothers all Turks and heathen, wherever they be, who fear God and work righteousness, instructed by God and inwardly drawn by him, even though they have never heard of baptism, indeed, of Christ himself, neither of his story or Scripture, but only of his power through the inner Word perceived within and made fruitful .... And therefore I hold that just as there are many Adams who do not know there was one Adam, so also there are many Christians who have never heard Christ's name."[15] Some may feel that the new theology of Geneva sounds uncommonly like the old theology of Sebastian Franck.

Standing between these two extremes of Luther and Franck we find the other reformers. Of them Zwingli stands farthest from Luther, but for reasons quite different from those of Franck. He is concerned above all to assert the sovereignty of God. This is a thread that runs through and holds together the whole of his theology. For him, to ascribe to the sacraments the power to convey the Spirit, as it were of their own accord, diminishes the sovereignty of God and puts the Spirit in some way at the individual's disposal. Zwingli uses a series of texts to sustain his case, texts such as, "It is the Spirit who gives life, the flesh is of no avail," to show that what is outward is not of itself effective; or texts like, "the Spirit blows where he wills," to demonstrate the sovereign freedom of the Spirit.

For Zwingli, Luther's position is too close to that of

the Roman Church which he believes leads to idolatry. He is opposed to putting confidence in what is created and not in the Creator—in the sacramental bread rather than in Christ, for example. This, for Zwingli, is a denial of the central doctrine of justification by faith.

In a sense it is Zwingli's reformation theology (his concern to affirm that salvation is God's gift in Christ) that leads him to a position other than Luther's, although a further factor is important. That factor is a somewhat negative and unbiblical way of looking at what is physical and material.

It is interesting to note that Bucer came to a position that held together the Lutheran insistence on the Word with the Zwinglian insistence on the sovereign freedom of the Spirit; the key to this was in his doctrine of election. The gift of the Spirit was tied closely to Christ. Thus God normally gives the Spirit and all his gifts *with* (but not *in*) the outward word and sacraments, although of course only the elect receive this gift; exceptionally God can act apart from the outward word. Indeed Bucer goes so far as to say that on the ground of their election there are among the pagans those who have received the Spirit, not simply the gifts of the Spirit which he believed the non-elect like Judas could receive, but also the Spirit of sonship. Bucer would regard the election of those pagans and the gift of the Spirit to them as being linked with Christ, but his position would here be unlike Luther's.[16]

Thus the characteristic theological understanding of each of the reformers, with their own particular theological stress, produced a striking diversity in their views of how and where the Spirit works, both in the world and in the church.

IV. The Church

The gifts of the Spirit are most naturally linked by us with a theology of the ordained ministry. Clearly in

Corinthians they are concerned not with the ministry of the few, but with the varied ministry of the whole people of God. The gifts of the Spirit show a church in which there is no division between the ordained and the non-ordained. There are no ordained ministers who are given a kind of unilateral or one-way ministry to the rest. Rather, within the body of Christ are multifarious ministries which enrich the common life and build up each other. Together all the members exercise ministry. It is noteworthy that Paul does not appeal to any leader, bishop or presbyter, to take a lead, for example, in improving the disorderly arrangements for the Lord's Supper or initiating the discipline of a member. Paul expects them together to make whatever decisions are to be made.

The Pauline picture of the church is seen most clearly when the church assembles for worship. There the Spirit who has bound the whole community together moves each person to share what he or she has been given with the rest of the congregation. Each one has a hymn, a prayer, a lesson, a revelation. The Corinthian Christian would certainly have a shock if he or she worshipped in almost any Christian congregation today, except among such as the Pentecostals, the center of whose worship is not in the priest or preacher, but in the people acting in response to the Spirit.

The chapters in Corinthians about the gifts of the Spirit are therefore a constant challenge to the church to ask whether it substitutes a doctrine of the ministry for a doctrine of the church.

Within the body the members have their varied gifts, gifts which are different rather than equal. To each is given a particular gift, which he or she is called to exercise. We are not called to do what others are doing, but only what we are given as a gift of the Spirit to do. The source of our action is in God's initiative in granting his gift and in addressing his call to us, not

in our own personal initiative. Our natural qualities are
not the basis of our service within the church, but the
gift and the calling of God are. Of course, our natural
abilities may be used, although even then they are not
the basis of our service.

The way people come to exercise their gifts may
imply something much less dramatic and personal than
our traditional Methodist sense of vocation. Not everyone goes along a Damascus road. Stephanas, for example, seems simply to have offered his services as one of
the first converts in Corinth. (1 Corinthians 16) By
contrast, in the Lukan tradition the deacons in Acts
were chosen by others when an emergency situation
arose, but they were chosen from those already full of
the Spirit.

Although the Pauline pattern is not limited to Corinth
or indeed to the Pauline churches, still it is not the only
pattern in the New Testament period. A system in which
presbyters or elders were appointed to a special ministry within the congregation existed from the start
alongside the Pauline pattern and gradually replaced
it in the Pauline churches themselves. It cannot be said
with certainty why the Pauline pattern disappeared,
although it was probably more dependent on the role
of an apostle than its present-day admirers allow.
After Paul's death the Pauline pattern was less able to
cope with the turmoils (doctrinal and ecclesiastical)
of the second century than was the pattern of elders
and the system that evolved from it. Nevertheless, the
presbyterial pattern is not necessarily in opposition
to the charismatic pattern. For some decades they
existed side by side in the same church. Hans von
Campenhausen, writing of the second century, could
say, "It is, therefore, not surprising that in addition to
the office-holders the old free men of the Spirit continue to play their part; and the Church is proud that
this should be so .... Not only do office-holders pos-

sess the Spirit, but the spirituals for their part, to the extent that they rightly belong to the Church, derive the power of their teaching from the traditional apostolic truth."[17]

There are even hints (if one-sided ones) of how these two patterns should exist today in our British ordination service, where the ordinands are asked: ". . . will you do all that in you lies to build up the Body of Christ, to persuade and encourage every member to exercise the gift of grace that is in him . . . ?" This question presupposes that each Christian has a gift of grace, but that without persuasion and encouragement they are not likely to exercise it. The question shows that the role of the minister as enabler is not new, but it also helps to explain why a charismatic movement has arisen inside and outside the historic churches.

Käsemann rightly poses the question "why . . . Protestantism itself . . . has never made a serious attempt to create a Church order which reflected the Pauline doctrine of *charisma,* but has left this to the sects." [18]

V. The Ordained Ministry

There are a number of ways in which the gifts of the Spirit are associated with an ordained ministry. There is in the Pastorals the idea that a gift of the Spirit is given in ordination itself. By contrast, there is the view that because one has the gift already, one should be ordained. Thus Origen held that "the one who is endowed with spiritual gifts should also be appointed to the corresponding position in the Church."[19] In fact, both views have prevailed in the church, the accent lying in some traditions on the first, and in others on the second. It is interesting to note that there was a period in the early church when, for example, a person with the gift of healing who clearly already had a special gift of the Holy Spirit (such as is given in ordination) was admitted without ordination to the ranks of the clergy. By the time of Cyprian this had changed, and such persons had to be ordained.

There are certain implications for an ordained ministry which can be drawn from the Pauline understanding of the gifts of the Spirit. The gifts of the Spirit are not at our disposal; they are always the gift of God. The church does not give, or command, or guarantee the equipment for a certain ministry, but prays God to grant it. The gift is God's, not the church's. This is precisely what is said in First and Second Timothy.

Moreover, people's claim to have a gift of the Spirit is not sufficient for their acceptance by the church. The church has to recognize whether it is a gift of God; moreover, it can recognize and test it only as it is used. According to the way one interprets the New Testament evidence, one will say either that natural qualities such as speech or leadership, if used in the service of God and in response to the Spirit, are the gifts of God, or that God's gift is something given more specifically and therefore may or may not coincide with natural qualities.

The traditional Methodist approach, with its emphasis on gifts and graces and the inward call of God, has stressed the second. Our more recent approach, with its stress on the dedication to God of natural qualities, has inclined to the first. The present emphasis, for example, on academic attainment by candidates for the ministry is always in danger of incurring Wesley's reproach to Dr. Lowth, the Bishop of London, when in 1780 he refused to ordain John Hoskins for America: ". . . your Lordship did see good to ordain and send into America other persons who knew something of Greek and Latin, but who knew no more of saving souls than of catching whales."[20] I do not raise the question as to whether we should ascribe the zeal for Latin and Greek in American seminaries today to the inspiration of Mr. Wesley or of Dr. Lowth.

Although Paul is not referring to what we would call ordained ministries, there is a further important implication for the ordained ministry in what he says about the gifts of the Spirit. It is that all the gifts are not given to one person. Our doctrine and practice have usually belied that in this country. We have often spoken of the minister as one in whom all the varied gifts of the Spirit (or at least the great majority of them) are focused. On that basis it could be said that the total ministry of the church is focused in the minister. I am not now concerned with whether the total ministry of the church is focused in the minister, only with the fact that this cannot be based on the assumption that he or she has received all the gifts of the Spirit. Rather, it is of fundamental importance to Paul's argument in First Corinthians that people have varied gifts and that each needs the other for this reason.

The true implication of this for the ministry (as Bucer saw in the sixteenth century) is that every minister is in some sense a specialist (with a gift of teaching or of pastoral care, for instance) and that he or she needs to be complemented by those with other gifts. Much of what is said about group or team ministry (perhaps especially when the team is made up of lay people as well as ordained ministers) has a solid basis in what Paul says about the gifts of the Spirit.

VI. Pentecostalism

We must be warned first against approaching Pentecostalism armed with a carefully prepared set of theological double standards. We accuse Pentecostalist Christians of divisiveness, individualism, irrationalism (as though Roman, radical, and reformed Christians had not their share of these qualities), or like the normally so perceptive Hans Küng, we lump them with spiritualists, Mormons, and Seventh Day Adventists (although he adds Congregationalists, Baptists, and

Quakers to the same happy band of enthusiasts).[21] No movement should be judged by its extremists or by its abuses, although they will throw some light on it.

There is not space here to do the Pentecostal tradition justice. I only hope that in making three critical comments I shall not do them a great injustice. First, they speak of a second gift of the Spirit, following and distinct from what they call conversion. This is how one Pentecostalist puts it: "The New Testament appears to indicate as an unmistakable historical fact that after the first entry of the Spirit in regeneration there can be and should be also a special personal reception by believers of the Holy Spirit in his original and unique person. This experience is called the 'baptism in the Holy Spirit'; its purpose is not to impart life, but to impart power. Its characteristic accompaniments are not fruits, but gifts."[22]

I do not want to comment on whether or not this is the way Pentecostalists experience this today. All I want to say is that this is not at all how Paul speaks of the gifts of the Spirit. He does not speak of some second reception of the Holy Spirit. Nor does the New Testament as a whole point in that direction. There is no such sharp distinction between receiving the fruit and receiving the gifts of the Spirit; no sense that there can anywhere be Christians who in fact have the fruit but do not have the gifts. Indeed the problem in the New Testament is rather that some claim the gifts but do not manifest the fruit. Moreover, the New Testament does not speak of the Spirit's coming in a distinctly different way, or in such a way that it is Christ who comes in conversion but the Spirit at this second point. Yet this is what R.M. Riggs affirms when he writes: "As the Spirit of Christ, He had come at conversion, imparting the Christ-life, revealing Christ, and making Him real. At the Baptism in the Spirit He Himself in His own person comes upon and fills the waiting believer. This experience is as distinct from conversion as the Holy Spirit is distinct from Christ. His coming to the believer at the Baptism (in the Holy Spirit) is the coming of the Third Person of the Trinity, in addition to the coming of Christ, which takes place at conversion."[28]

However, let me repeat that to say it is not true to the New Testament does not mean that it is not true to people's experience today.

Second, we turn to the gifts of the Spirit. It is held that the experience of the Spirit leads to "(1) the *indwelling* or infilling of the Spirit and hence, (2) *power* for service, with the equipment, usually, of (3) the *gifts* of the Spirit."[24] We shall in a moment consider the gift of tongues, but we need to see beforehand that Pentecostalists tend to the same emphasis as the Corinthians. Among the gifts, they stress the more sensational or supernatural. They ignore the more ordinary, more apparently natural gifts. They prefer 1 Corinthians 12:8-10 to Romans 12:6-8. They could, of course, legitimately reply that the rest of the church makes the opposite, and equally serious, mistake.

Still, for the moment we are looking at them and not at the rest of the church. It is right to see that the typically Methodist *charismata* of making tea and showing people to their place with a warm handshake would find a more natural place in a Pauline than in a Pentecostal theology. Behind this may lie the danger of making the Spirit too spiritual, with the result that one has no sense of the variety of the Spirit's gifts.

Third, let us consider the gift of tongues. Cultured and educated middle-class Christians have an extraordinary horror of tongues, although it is more often our good taste that is offended than our good theology. Needless to say, we see to it that our good taste is armed with all the weaponry of wise theological serpents. Paul, who knew far more about tongues than we,

and who had the bad taste to speak in them, was
fundamentally positive in what he said about them.

He urges the Thessalonians not to quench the Spirit.
He tells the Corinthians not to forbid tongues. Indeed,
he wants all the Corinthians to speak in tongues. He
even seems to link tongues with prophecy, which for
him is the supreme gift of the Spirit, as long as there is
an accompanying interpretation. Certainly tongues do
not build up the church if there is no one to interpret;
in that situation Paul forbids tongues in church, but not
in private. One may then speak to oneself (or it could
be for oneself, that is, for one's own advantage) and to
God. (1 Corinthians 14:28) It is needlessly subtle to
suggest as some do[25] that Paul does not explicitly tell
the Corinthians to seek tongues because love does not
seek its own and that to seek tongues if there is no one
to interpret is to seek what is for one's own benefit,
not the congregation's.

It is a piece of theological sophistry to suggest that
Christians may not, in principle, seek that which is for
their own benefit. It is manifestly contrary to Paul's
encouragement of people to exercise the gift of tongues
in private, which is a situation in which only the person
can benefit. The fact that it does not build up the body
is directly relevant as a criterion on those occasions
when the congregation meets for worship. It is only
indirectly relevant on other occasions. In any case there
is no necessary reason why tongues should not, in an
indirect way, benefit the body by directly benefiting one
member.

Pentecostalists go beyond Paul in regarding tongues
as initial evidence of baptism in the Spirit. There are
situations where Acts appears to take this step. But
Paul is much more cautious in his assessment of tongues. Far from being a necessary evidence of the Holy
Spirit, tongues can be an expression of demon possession.

VII. Further Comments on Criteria

In Mark 16:17-18, we read: "These signs will accompany those who believe: ... they will pick up serpents, and if they drink any deadly thing it will not hurt them." Some Christians, even Christians in the most highly developed society in the world today, have taken this to be an objective test of a person's faith and of possession by the Spirit. Let me read to you an excerpt from *The Times* correspondent in New York, July 4, 1973: "Mr. Murl Bass belongs to a church in the mountains of Tennessee which demands that its members test themselves with snakes, fire and poison .... Hundreds of worshippers had gathered at the Holiness Church of God in Jesus' Name to chant, sing, clap their hands and test the strength of their faith by passing round snakes, including an Indian cobra. However, a diamondback rattlesnake was obviously not impressed and Mr. Bass, although praising the Lord for some time after the attack, collapsed .... The pastor, whose brother died in April after taking strychnine during a prayer meeting, claimed that the snakes are as safe as worms if the handler is anointed with the Spirit. In the case of the rattlesnake, he admitted: 'We had a contentious spirit today.' "

The signs mentioned in the Markan passage (besides picking up serpents and drinking poison, they are exorcism, tongues, and healing) may well be signs that accompany those who believe, but they are not necessarily criteria by which one can discern those who believe from those who do not, nor those possessed by the Holy Spirit from those possessed by demons. The New Testament is fully aware that unbelievers can do all these things, and the criteria it offers are criteria that reflect its belief that the Spirit is the Spirit of Christ.

The Spirit is one who witnesses to Christ. The Spirit unites people in Christ's body, and conforms them to the image of Christ. Therefore, where faith and love, unity and mutual service are found, the Spirit of Christ is at work. Or perhaps one should say that where the Spirit of Christ is at work, there faith, love, unity, and mutual service are to be found—and one might add, prayer and praise, freedom and forgiveness, healing and reconciliation, and much else.

It is this basic criterion that the New Testament and the early church applied: whether the Spirit is the Spirit of Christ (this involved a test of faith in the fullest sense of the term—faith, for example, that "Jesus is Lord," and "Jesus Christ has come in the flesh"); a test of character or love; and a test of mutual service and upbuilding. The tests were applied according to the situation. Thus, for prophecy the first test would most naturally be one of doctrine, although later the test of character would be as important. Whereas for tongues which, unlike prophecy, would not be intelligible, the first test would most naturally be the building up of the community.

When the more dramatic gifts (such as tongues, prophecy, and healing) became infrequent, another test intruded, as it does today. It involved the manner of the gift, rather than the matter. Thus, for example, with Montanism the objection was to the ecstatic *manner* of the prophecy; something like ecstatic inspiration was a feature of some biblical prophecy, however. Despite the church's reaction to Montanism, and ours to Pentecostalism, it is doubtful whether there is any valid theological objection to ecstasy in itself. Even the argument that the Spirit does not suppress our freedom is a double-edged one. Moreover, however important the role of reason may be in the Christian faith, the gifts and insights of the Spirit do not all have to come that way, even if they need somehow to be tested by reason.

Although the New Testament may supply us with surprisingly adequate general criteria by which to judge the gifts of the Spirit, it does not supply us with exhaustive lists of the gifts. It is interesting to note how often new interpretations may be given to the New Testament gifts, or new gifts added to them. Take for example the gift of power *(dunameis)*. Bucer saw an example of this in the way Peter dealt with Ananias and Sapphira, and Paul with Elymas, the sorcerer. He can ask the question in his *Dialogi:* "The work of whose Spirit was it when St. Peter killed Ananias and his wife Sapphira ... and Paul made Elymas the sorcerer blind?"[26] In his day Bucer saw this apostolic gift expressed in the church through the exercise of church discipline. We need not accept his exegesis to realize that the Spirit may achieve his work in various ways. The Holy Spirit is not static and his gifts may increase in variety according to the situation.

Now if the test of the gifts is whether the work of the Spirit of Christ is done, it is at least arguable (I will not say more) that the episcopal and petrine ministry that we see in the Roman Catholic Church (and I am not referring to its abuses) is a gift of the Spirit that we should consider "taking into our system." I do not say that is what constitutes the church. It is the Spirit who constitutes the church, not some particular gift of his. For that reason we shall receive these gifts not in order to become one church, that is, as a necessary condition for being one, but in order to express within it a unity already given by the Spirit in the diversity of his gifts.

A hint of such openness to the gifts of the Spirit in others is found in the Decree on Ecumenism of Vatican II: "Nor must we disregard the contribution to our own edification which can be made by the effects of the Holy Spirit's grace in our separated brethren." (4:9) We might surprise our separated Roman brethren, and even more our unseparated Methodist ones, by our zeal to affirm that there are diversities of gifts by the same Spirit, diversities of ministry but the same Lord.

We may or may not admit the value of the apostolic office, whether of apostle or bishop, in safeguarding the apostolic faith and the church's unity—above all, in the early centuries. But undoubtedly the church needs to discover the twentieth-century forms of the *charismata* of word, of service, and of leadership which were manifested in Corinth and Rome.

We need to be open to the gifts that are finding expression in many groups (traditional and radical) both inside, and in some measure alongside, the church. They will suggest to us a style of church life and a pattern of Christian community much less formal, much less hierarchical, much less inhibited, much less religious than we see displayed at present. In this we need to begin with the gifts that are given, and then test them, rather than begin with a fixed idea of what the gifts may be and so inhibit or limit the sovereign freedom of the Spirit.

VIII. A Postscript

The stress in Protestant theology has been excessively on the Word as over against the Spirit. Where this has happened there has been less concern for the fruit and the gifts of the Spirit.

Luther was himself aware of the danger and complained of certain preachers: "They may be fine Easter preachers, but they are very poor Pentecost preachers, for they do not preach ... 'about the sanctification by the Holy Spirit,' but solely about the redemption of Jesus Christ, although Christ (whom they extoll so highly, and rightly so) is Christ, that is, he has purchased redemption from sin and death so that the Holy Spirit might transform us out of the old Adam into new men . . . . Christ did not only earn *gratia,* 'grace,' for us, but also *donum,* 'the gift of the Holy Spirit,' so that we might have not only forgiveness of, but also cessation of, sin."[27]

But Luther and his followers, for various reasons, did not preserve this balance and the result is that the charge Luther brings against others is the charge usually brought against him, and by people as different as Erasmus, Müntzer, and the anabaptists. It is perhaps significant that only Bucer of the reformers won back into the established church a large group of anabaptists. In his theology there was a particular stress on the Spirit as well as on the Word, on love as well as on faith.

Doctrine and life both go together and a stress on the doctrine of the Spirit goes with a stress on the life of love as the fruit of the Spirit, as our own Methodist heritage testifies.

What applies to the Spirit as sanctifier applies to the Spirit as the life-giver, whether we see this in the gift of faith or in the gifts of the Spirit. The natural Protestant emphasis on the Word focuses attention on the objective acts of God in Christ and has often led to a stress that is intellectual and verbal—intellectual in appeal and verbal in approach. The non-intellectual, the non-verbal is suspect. An appeal that touches our emotion and imagination is suspect just as is the appeal to what the Spirit has done in us as distinct from what was done in Christ. Yet for many these are the missing dimensions.

The appeal, for example, of music (and not only pop or folk music), with all its release of emotion, the appeal of Alcoholics Anonymous with its stress on personal testimony, the appeal of the occult and the mystical—all reflect some of the missing elements in contemporary Protestant Christianity. For all its imperfections, the charismatic tradition, inside the Pentecostal Church and outside it, makes this kind of appeal. It appeals to and releases the emotions; it expects changed lives and points to them; it believes in the supernatural and demonstrates it. It is one-sided, unbalanced in its teaching and therefore in its life, but the one-sidedness may well be what the great church needs if it is to manifest fully in our day the fellowship of the Spirit.

As we look at the pentecostal or charismatic tradition, or at the catholic or orthodox traditions, and see the diverse gifts of the Spirit which they have received, we would do well to sing with Charles Wesley, "The gift which He on one bestows, we all delight to prove."

Notes

1. Ernst Käsemann, *Essays on New Testament Themes* (London: S.C.M., 1964), p. 64.
2. C. K. Barrett, *The First Epistle to the Corinthians* (London: A. and C. Black, 1968), p. 280.
3. *Augustine: Later Works, Library of Christian Classics,* Vol. VIII (London: S.C.M., 1955), p. 67.
4. Käsemann, *op. cit.,* pp. 65, 69.
5. *Religion in Communist Lands* (34 Lubbock Road, Chislehurst, Kent, England: Center for the Study of Religion and Communism), Vol. 1, No. 2, p. 16.
6. Eusebius, *Ecclesiastical History,* Book V, xviii.
7. *Ibid.,* V, xvi.
8. *Ibid.,* V, xvii. Here Eusebius quotes Miltiades.
9. E. G. Rupp and Benjamin Drewery, *Martin Luther* (London: Edward Arnold, 1970), p. 43.
10. David F. Wright, *Common Places of Martin Bucer* (Abingdon: Sutton Courtenay, 1972), p. 223.
11. *Spiritual and Anabaptist Writers, Library of Christian Classics,* Vol. XXV (London: S.C.M., 1957), p. 75.
12. *Ibid.,* p. 159.
13. W. A., 20.451.7-10.
14. *Ibid.,* 18.137.5-16.
15. *Library of Christian Classics,* Vol. XXV, p. 156.
16. For a detailed treatment of Bucer, see W. P. Stephens, *The Holy Spirit in the Theology of Martin Bucer* (London: C.U.P., 1970), especially pages 168-169 and 185-189.
17. Hans von Campenhausen, *Ecclesiastical Authority and Spiritual Power in the Church of the First Three Centuries* (London: A. and C. Black, 1969), p. 178.
18. Käsemann, *op. cit.,* p. 93.
19. Campenhausen, *op cit.,* p. 250.
20. *The Letters of the Rev. John Wesley,* A.M., Vol. VII (London: Epworth, 1931), p. 31.
21. Hans Küng, *The Church* (London: Burns and Oates, 1968), p. 195.

22. For the translation of Donald M. Gee, *Die Früchte der Geistes*, p. 6, see Frederick Dale Bruner, *A Theology of the Holy Spirit* (London: Hodder and Stoughton, 1971), p. 75. The quotation is translated back into English from the German version given in an article by O. Eggenberger in *Theologische Zeitschrift*, II, 1955, p. 278. I have been unable to trace Gee's book.

23. Ralph M. Riggs, *The Spirit Himself* (Springfield, Mo.: Gospel Publishing House, 1949), pp. 79-80; cited in Bruner, *op. cit.*, p. 71. I have been unable to trace Riggs' book.

24. Frederick Dale Bruner, *A Theology of The Holy Spirit* (London: Hodder and Stoughton, 1971), p. 70.

25. *Ibid.*, p. 298.

26. Bucer, *Dialogi,* M.4.A.36-B.35.

27. W.A., 50.599. The translation follows that of *Luther's Works,* Vol. 41, *Church and Ministry* III (Philadelphia: Fortress, 1966), p. 114.

The Holy Spirit and the Ordained Ministry

Daniel C. Arichea, Jr.

There are three aspects to be considered in this chapter as suggested by the title itself: the Holy Spirit, the ministry, and ordination. The assumptions that can be deduced from the title, among other things, are (1) that there is a validity for an ordained ministry within the church; (2) that there is a vital relationship between this ordained ministry and the Holy Spirit; and (3) that there is a greater and wider ministry within the church, outside of and apart from the ordained.

In most of the churches today, the above are reflected in church order and in various rituals of ordination. But apart from the usual practices of the church, can the above assertions be maintained? Can their validity be proven historically, theologically, biblically?

It is our endeavor to discuss the church's ministry primarily from a biblical perspective. The choice of this particular approach can easily be justified. For one thing, the writer does not feel competent to discuss this subject from either the historical or the theological point of view. Moreover, it is the writer's conviction that the biblical record, primarily the New Testament, presents us with enough material for a serious and fruitful discussion of the ministry of the church, and for laying out principles with which to evaluate the whole question of ministry in our contemporary situation.

I. The Pauline Concept of the Ministry

Any discussion of the church's ministry of course has to start with the Apostle Paul. It is not simply that his letters are laden with insights on the ministry of the church; it is also a recognition of the fact that the churches reflected in Paul's letter belong to a lower strata in history. A study of them, therefore, would give us some clues as to how the church in its inception understood its own ministry in relation to its own life.

Of course, we recognize that Paul's ideas of the ministry have been interpreted and reinterpreted in different and sometimes contradictory ways, depending on the ecclesiastical persuasions and theological presuppositions of the interpreters. This chapter by no means poses to be an objective statement of the Pauline position; hopefully, however, one more personal interpretation would not do a great deal of harm.

A. The concept of charisma

The Pauline concept of ministry starts with the doctrine of *charisma*. "A charisma," Ernest Käsemann writes, "is the specific part which the individual has in the lordship and glory of Christ; and this specific part which the individual has in the Lord shows itself in a specific service and a specific vocation."[1] In short, *charisma* is a gift, a gift from God. Ministry, understood as *charisma*, simply means that it is not primarily an office, nor a function of a special group of people, but a gift from the Holy Spirit. That the Spirit is the source of *charisma* is clear from Paul's writing, particularly in his first letter to the Corinthians. In chapter twelve, he starts his first list of ministries with the words: "There are varieties of gifts, but the same Spirit . . . ."[2] His conclusion is even more positive: "All these are inspired by one and the same Spirit, who apportions to each one individually as he wills." This verse not only makes clear the source of *charisma*, but also that no Christian can choose one's own calling or one's own gifts; it is the Spirit who distributes *charismata* according to his will. And who are the recipients? Not a special group, not a select few, but the whole body of believers. Every believer, by virtue of his or her baptism, is a recipient of the Holy Spirit's *charisma,* and thereby is empowered to become a significant member of the fellowship. It is in this sense that Paul could speak of believers as "saints," as the "holy ones," for to him at least there is no segment of the church that is set aside as holy and dedicated to God, and there is no part of the world which is not touched by the act of God in Christ.

> The secular is no longer abandoned to demons and demonic energies. Grace pushes home its attack to the very heart of the world; it liberates it from the demons . . . . As nothing is *charisma* in itself, so nothing is secular in itself . . . . All things stand within the charismatic possibility and are holy to the extent to which the holy ones of God make use of them . . . . The field of the Church's operation must be the world in its totality, for nothing less can be the field of Christ the Cosmocreator.[3]

This means, further, that to Paul there is no division between the "clergy" and the "laity;" it is the total membership of the church who are recipients of *charisma,* and not a select few.

> *Charisma* is no longer the distinguishing mark of elect individuals but that which is the common endowment of all who call upon the name of the Lord . . . a demonstration of the fact that the Spirit of God has been poured out on all flesh.[4]

B. The place of the specialized ministry

The question is raised, however, if Paul regarded everyone in the community of faith as recipients of *charisma,* then does he deny a place for specially selected people within the fellowship to occupy positions of leadership? To answer this question necessitates a closer look at the evidence which Paul has left us.

Paul presents three listings of the church's ministries: one in Romans 12, and two in 1 Corinthians 12. A cursory glance at these lists reveals three things. First of all, Paul is talking primarily of functions to be performed rather than of offices to be filled. It is true that he mentions apostles, teachers, and prophets, but as John Knox has remarked: "For Paul there were teachers and prophets, but hardly the offices of teacher and prophet."[5] Knox continues:

> More obviously the healers, speakers in tongues, miracle workers were not "officials" of the church. Even the "bishops" and "deacons" of Philippians 1:1 are not to be thought of as officials.[6]

We can grant, of course, with J.K.S. Reid that ministry, even in Paul, partakes both of office and function.[7] Nevertheless, it is almost universally held that what is primary in Paul is not the office, but the task; not the form of the ministry, but its function. Robertson and Plummer, commenting on Romans 12, write:

> We are not dealing with classes of officials, each with definite functions; *munus* in the sense of *donum* has not yet passed into *munus* in the sense of *officium,* and the process of transition has scarcely begun. In correcting the errors into which the Corinthians had fallen, the apostle does not tell any officials to take action, but addresses the congregation as a whole. The inference is that although there were no officials in the ecclesiastical sense, although, as in every society, there were leading men.[8]

Secondly, Paul does present a hierarchy of *charisma.* In 1 Corinthians 12:28, he writes:

> God has appointed in the church first apostles, second prophets, third teachers, then workers of miracles, then healers, helpers, administrators, speakers of various kinds of tongues.

One notes right away that for Paul the primary functions or "offices," if we can call them that, are those of apostles, prophets, and teachers. One thing which all these have in common is that they all deal in one way or another with the proclamation and interpretation of the good news, the gospel of Jesus Christ. The apostles were witnesses to the Resurrection, and were concerned primarily with the proclamation of the message in a wide area; they were the itinerant, or traveling ministers. The prophets, on the other hand, were those endowed with ecstatic character, and enabled to interpret the meaning of sacred mysteries.[9] Finally, the teachers were concerned with defining for any local congregation the implications of the good news for its life and mission.[10]

As a final observation, the very fact that these lists do not correspond to one another reveals that, at that time, there was no definite church order, no well-defined offices. But there were functions to be performed, and these functions were carried on by members of the congregations who were all recipients of varied *charismata* appropriate for particular tasks. One seems to look in vain for any ceremony of setting aside any person or group for special tasks; one cannot discover any rite of ordination corresponding to that which we will discover later in the Pastoral Epistles or in the Book of Acts. Schweizer, commenting on 1 Corinthians 11:14, writes:

> Paul knows no one in Corinth to whom he could apply as a leader, to achieve an ordered observance of the Lord's Supper, for instance, or of worship; he can appeal only to the Church as a whole. Probably, however, the most important observation about this is that for Paul, an ordination, any explicit appointment on undertaking a form of service, is impossible.[11]

C. Summary

To sum up then, Paul pictures for us a church in which the Spirit plays a very active role. It is the Spirit who chooses ministers. It is he who equips men and women with *charisma,* it is he who enables them to become prophets and teachers, it is he who as the giver of *charisma* to every believer enables the church to be itself *charisma* for the world. Again, to quote Schweizer:

> The Spirit's authority is obeyed as it actually comes to be; this leads to an order that conforms itself afterwards to the "event" of the Spirit; and its only purpose is to make room for the Spirit to carry out his work of edifying the church with as little hindrance as possible . . . . All order is an "afterwards," an attempt to follow what God has already designed. It is not because a person has been chosen as prophet or presbyter that he may exercise this or that ministry, but on the contrary, because God

has given him the *charisma,* the possibility is given to him, through the Church order, of exercising it.[12]

II. The Pastorals

When one leaves Paul and goes into the Pastoral Epistles, one senses immediately that something new and different has happened to the church. Instead of the spontaneity and freedom that characterize the Pauline churches, there seem to be rigid rules and regulations governing church order. In place of the primacy of function in the ministry there is now an overarching emphasis on the importance of certain offices. Paul talks of *charisma* as an endowment for all Christians, the act of the Spirit to every believer at the time of baptism. The Pastorals talk of certain specific offices, the bearers of which are specially endowed with the gift of the Holy Spirit. The implication, of course, is that the whole church does not now receive *charisma;* only a few people within the fellowship are recipients of it. Käsemann writes:

An office which stands over against the rest of the community is now the real bearer of the Spirit; and the primitive Christian view, that every Christian receives the Spirit in his baptism, recedes into the background and indeed, for all practical purposes, disappears.[18]

The Spirit now becomes, not the Spirit for the church, but the "ministerial Spirit."[14] And so is born within the church an idea and a movement which could accurately be labeled as "clerical pentecostalism."

A. A new world view

A new world view undergirds all these developments. The Pauline world view is centered on the action of Christ for the whole world, and for all humanity, Christ reconciling everything and everyone to himself, Christ being all in all. Every Christian is a sanctified being, a holy one, a saint. There are no special groups within the church who are recipients of blessings they alone can receive, and for which they can claim greater

glory and blessedness. There are no persons set aside
for special, holy purposes. Everyone is holy and sanctified in the sight of God.

The development of the Pastorals is a reversion both
to the Jewish idea of sanctity and to the Gentile idea of
holiness. For Judaism and the mystery cults of the
Gentile world both participate in a common understanding of the world, namely, that part of it is mun-
dane and part of it is divine and sacred. Both systems
had their priests and priestesses who were guardians of
that which was holy. Both systems had their rites and
their sacrifices. The Christian faith, at its inception,
and as it was proclaimed by the apostle Paul, had finally removed the dichotomy between the sacred and
the secular, between the divine and the human, between heaven and earth. The Christian doctrine of the
Incarnation is the answer, the cue, the solution to the
malady of a split world.

But the Pastorals represent a return to a system
which the Incarnation already defeated. For within
their pages one can find once again the distinction
between clergy and laity.[15] And that distinction is
symptomatic of even a bigger rift, that of the church
and the world. Käsemann writes:

> The community of which the Pastorals are the mouth-
> piece is being heavily pressed back onto the defensive
> and its order represents something in the nature of a
> stockade erected against its assailants in a last despair-
> ing effort for survival. This order is chiefly designed
> simply to mark the frontiers which separate the Church
> and the world. For the Church is no longer . . . the
> world-wide body of Christ, the dominion of that grace
> which has invaded the world in its total being. Rather,
> it is the house of God, *familia Dei,* and as such exposed
> to attack from outside and in need of protection.[16]

Thus, instead of the Spirit of God being poured on all
flesh, it is now the Spirit of God being imparted to a
privileged few.

B. The threefold ministry

But there are other implications. A cursory look at the ministerial terms reveals that the Pauline functions of prophet, apostle, teacher, etc., have now been supplanted by a threefold ministry of bishop, elder, and deacon. To be sure, Paul already mentions "bishops" and "deacons" in his letters, (e.g., Philippians 1:1) but even here, as John Knox clearly points out, we are dealing not with formal offices, but with functions.[17] In the Pastorals, however, these terms are definitely technical designations, not simply of functions, but of clerical offices with definite functions and special qualifications of the office-bearers. How are these three offices related to each other? It seems that the elders were those entrusted with administering the affairs of the local church, taking upon themselves teaching and pastoral responsibilities, in much the same way that the elders of Judaism exercised supervision and responsibility over the Synagogue. (See 1 Timothy 5:17-22.) They ruled, they taught, preached, conducted worship, shepherded the flock. The deacons, on the other hand, were of a lower rank, assisting the elders in their work of supervision and administration.[18]

But what about the bishops? In many passages in the New Testament, it is made clear that the terms "bishop" and "elder" were two names for the same office-bearers.[19] In the Pastorals, however, the question has to be asked regarding the intended relationship between the officers mentioned and that of the recipients themselves. Take the case of Timothy. He was ordained by an elder by the laying on of hands. (1 Timothy 4:14) But he also is expected to ordain others through the laying on of hands,[20] and to have supervision over bishops and deacons. What then is his role and his office? And what of the writer of the epistles, using the pseudonym "Paul"? Price offers an answer:

> The status which is held by "Timothy" and "Titus" is
> superior to the "elders" whom they appoint, supervise,
> and discipline. If "Timothy" and "Titus" were (Monarch-
> ical) bishops, then it follows that the Pastor himself as-
> sumed prerogatives later held by archbishops or the
> metropolitans . . . ."[21]

If Price is correct in his analysis, then we see in the
Pastorals the beginnings of the system which came
down to us as monepiscopacy. Kee and Young describe
the development thus:

> In some of the communities, one of the presbyters began
> to emerge as head of the college of presbyters, and as
> head of the local church itself. The leader came to be
> known as *episcopos*, or bishop, to distinguish his office
> from that of presbyter.[22]

C. Ordination

A further development is the rite of ordination
whereby the Holy Spirit is imparted to the office-
bearers. As we have already seen, this was not present
in Paul, since there was no rite whereby persons were
set apart for some special task within the church. But
in the Pastorals, there are several passages which speak
of ordination through the laying on of hands. In 1
Timothy 4:14, Timothy is said to have been ordained
by a presbytery, and at the time of his ordination,
received a form of *charisma*. In 2 Timothy 1:6, it was
Paul who laid his hands on Timothy, and again, as a
result, Timothy was the recipient of *charisma*. And in
1 Timothy 5:22, Timothy is himself urged not to be
hasty in ordaining anyone.[23]

Perhaps a fuller discussion of the practice of the
laying on of hands will reveal how far the developments
within the church represented in the Pastorals have
gone, when compared with the practices of the apostolic
church. Judaism, of course, had it own practice of
ordination through the laying on of hands.

> Any rabbi could ordain one of his disciples and thus
> confer his own authority upon him; the laying on of
> hands is here a leaning, not a mere placing of the hands,
> on the head of the ordained, and "its object is the pour-

ing of the ordaining scholar's personality into the scholar to be ordained." [24]

The Old Testament knows of the practice of laying on of hands; it was a

> ritual gesture by which a man transmits his own characteristics, his personality, to an animal (cf. Leviticus 1:3-4; Exodus 29:10, etc.) or to certain men (the Levites, Numbers 8:10), so as to bring about a substitution of persons, i.e., to be validly represented in the cultus by such an animal sacrificed, or by the Levites in the service of the Temple.[25]

In the New Testament itself, the laying on of hands is used in healing [26] and baptizing.[27] In the Book of Acts, two passages stand out as paralleling those of the Pastorals, namely Acts 6:6 and 13:3. However, many scholars take these to be not ordination, but commissioning and consecration for a task.[28] It is most likely then that the passages in the book of Acts are not at all referring to an ordination, but to an installation service. If our contention is correct, then the only remaining references to the rite of ordination are those in the Pastorals which we have already mentioned.

Apart from the deductions at which we have arrived, namely, that there was ordination by a council of presbyters, that ordination was through the laying on of hands, and that the gift of the Spirit was received through ordination—what else does the presence of ordination in the Pastorals mean?

The issue here seems to be twofold; first, the relationship of the gift of the Spirit to the rite of ordination, and second, the doctrine of apostolic succession as having its basis in the Pastorals. Space does not allow us to discuss these at any length. It is enough to observe that the interpretations of these passages from the Pastorals have been very much influenced by the interpreters' own theological positions. For example, free church interpreters have tried to explain away the imparting of the gift through ordination by various ingenious ways.[29] It would be much more profitable to interpret the Pastorals in the light of their own situation, and to recognize that these passages do mean that there was a laying on of hands, and by this act, gifts were imparted. Ordination was a means of receiving the Spirit and his gifts. This ordination was believed to have originated from the apostles, in this particular instance, the apostle Paul, and the authority to ordain is handed down to the apostle's designated delegate.

D. Historical justification for the developments within the Pastorals

How does one regard these developments in the church as depicted in the Pastorals? The fact of the matter is, viewed from the historical situation, these developments could be understood as being expedient, or even necessary for the life and mission of the church at that time. What was the historical situation? Insofar as it can be ascertained, the church was faced with the problems of schism and heresy. Price notes that whereas unity was an assumed fact during the time of Paul, it was something to be striven for during the post-apostolic age.[30] One of the greatest sources of schism was the Pauline concept of *charisma,* where possession or the lack of it started to be definitive of Christian character and where, logically, the gifts in which the Spirit's enthusiasm is more outwardly displayed were preferred.[31] A form of this over-emphasis of enthusiasm is of course Gnosticism, with its appeal to Christian insight, to the working of the Spirit, and to Christian baptism. Gnosticism and similar movements, of course, disrupted the unity of the church which was assumed during the Pauline era, and challenged the spontaneity and looseness of church order and the ministries.

All the developments then can be traced as responses of the church to the crisis which it met. Richardson puts it clearly and accurately:

The historical truth is that monepiscopacy was an urgent practical necessity. . . . The setting up of one representative man, an archpoimen of the flock who should be the visible, personal guarantee of the unity and continuity of the apostolic fellowship and doctrine, could meet the need of the Church in an age in which schismatics and heretics of every kind threatened the very continuance of the church and the church's Gospel. The bishop became in his person . . . the embodiment of the Gospel of God, by which the church itself was called into being. The existence of the church is bound up with the church's unity and cannot be separated from it; this is the truth which brought the episcopate into being . . . and which monepiscopacy enshrines and defends.[32]

One can even go so far as to see the hand of God, or the movement of the Holy Spirit, in these developments.[33] For indeed, a case could be made for the relevance of these developments for the post-apostolic period, because of the problems that the church had to face, and because of the very nature of the organizations, both secular and sacred, which influenced it at that time. The difficulty, however, arises, and indeed has arisen, when these developments are viewed as normative, not only for the post-apostolic church, but for the church from post-apostolic times to the present; and when it is thought, therefore, that for the church to be the church it must reflect within its government and organization the same church order present in the post-apostolic church. A more profitable line of argument, in our opinion, is to take seriously the situation of the post-apostolic church, and evaluate the developments in the light of the specific historical situation. It is the genius of the early church that it understood the working of the Spirit as leading it to be effective in any situation, and that church order must be an instrument whereby the church's mission to the world can best be carried out. To draw out the developments of the post-apostolic period as permanent and as normative for church order for centuries to come is, of course, to ignore the historical context and therefore to misunderstand the reasons for these developments. The principle that must be reasserted is the primacy of the mission of the church, and the function of church order as that of organizing the church in order to fulfill its appointed task faithfully in every generation and in every historical situation.

III. The Book of Acts

But before we get carried away with drawing out the implications of our study for our own situation, let us first turn to one more biblical writing in order to discover another facet of the ministry which is relevant for our discussion.

A. The Book of Acts in relation to the Pastorals and Paul

The book of Acts bears some similarities with the Pastorals. In fact, at some points it represents a further development of the trends that are reflected in the Pastoral Epistles. Käsemann, for instance, goes through the Book of Acts, examining the activities of the apostles in Jerusalem, and comes to the conclusion that in the Book of Acts, "The *charisma* concept has now completely disappeared."[34] Furthermore, the Apostle now appears as the guarantor of the gospel tradition. For instance, Peter has to inspect the missionary movement in Judea and Samaria before the converts in these regions are incorporated into the Christian church.[35] Still further, despite all the gains of the Seven in Judea and Samaria, the Gentile mission has to be inaugurated by the conversion of Cornelius through Peter. (chapter 11) Finally, one should mention that it was perhaps the apostles who bestowed the office or commission to the Seven.[36] How does one explain these developments? Käsemann offers an answer:

The only possible interested party is a church which is under the necessity (in the context of its conflict with heresy) of demonstrating the legitimacy of its own position; and which does so by maintaining that this position is based on continuity with the original apostolate. Outside the boundaries of this church which has become a sacred area within the world and which bases itself on the sacred office and the sacred tradition of the original apostolate, there is no salvation and no possession of the Spirit. So far as we can see, then, it was Luke who was the first to propagate the theories of tradition and legitimate succession which mark the advent of early Catholicism.[37]

In another sense, however, the Book of Acts is very similar to Paul. The Holy Spirit is not understood as a ministerial Spirit, but as the Spirit which empowers all believers. It is true that the Spirit is promised only to the apostles on Ascension day, (Acts 1:6ff) but it is also true that on the day of the Pentecost, the Spirit falls not only on the apostles, but on all the believers.[38] The gift of the Spirit is promised to anyone who repents and receives baptism. (Acts 2:38) With some exception, the Spirit is imparted to those who believe, primarily through preaching, and not by the laying on of hands.[39]

B. The development of the ministry

But the unique contribution of the Book of Acts, at least for the topic under discussion, is the way the development of the ministry is presented.

The first group of ministers mentioned in the Book of Acts is, of course, the apostles, corresponding to the Twelve. There are various questions regarding the nature of the Twelve and of the office of an apostle, but these are not relevant to this study.[40] What concerns us here is that in the Book of Acts, the Twelve are the first ministers; they are called upon to perform a special task, namely, to proclaim the event of Christ as eyewitnesses of what actually happened. At the start of the church, they were the only ministers, the sole administrators: they taught, they witnessed, they baptized, they supervised. But this was only as the church remained a Jewish church. It is now an accepted fact that early in its history the Christian church did not dissociate itself from Judaism; in fact, in organization, it followed the same patterns as the Judaic religion. Its mission was to win Jews to faith in Jesus as Messiah and still remain within Judaism. Rightly understood, therefore, the church at its inception was a Jewish sect and nothing more. In this situation, the Twelve, who were all Jews, were the natural and logical ministers. They knew Aramaic, they were well versed in Jewish law, they were sensitive to Jewish culture. Therefore, they were suited by language, training, and disposition to be effective ministers to the Jews in Palestine. Luke profoundly informs us that not for one moment did the Twelve minister to Gentiles, the one exception being in chapter ten when Peter, through a vision, was led to visit the Roman, Cornelius, but even Cornelius was a God-fearing man, and therefore was not far from Judaism.

When, however, the witness of the church expanded beyond the sphere of Palestinian Judaism, and the gospel was proclaimed to the Jewish Diaspora, to Jews who were influenced by both Greek language and culture, then the role of the Twelve started to be minimized. Can one imagine Peter, the Galilean fisherman, with his Galilean accent, becoming a minister to an educated and sophisticated Greek congregation? Of course not. Therefore a new understanding of mission demanded a new office and a new kind of minister, one who by disposition, training, and language, can be an effective witness to people other than Palestinian or Orthodox Jews. And thus, as we read in the sixth chapter of Acts, the office of the Seven was created.

Who were these Seven? One notices that they all bear Greek names. It is as if the community decided that since the aggrieved party were the Grecian Jews, they should elect from them those who were to supervise the distribution of food. The passage further mentions that these men were full of wisdom and of the Spirit. In short, the picture which is given to us by

Luke is that of a group who by training, dedication, and disposition were fully adequate to be ministers to a different group of people. Surely, the Galilean fisherman who spoke broken Greek would not be sufficient for an effective ministry to Greek-speaking Jews.

The Seven opened up the church from a Jewish sect into what it really ought to be: a faith for all humanity. The message of Stephen in chapter seven is a poignant attack on the Jews for their rejection of the gospel, rooting their rebellion in their very history; the golden calf at the foot of Mt. Sinai is the beginning of a history of idolatry and infidelity to God. And this infidelity, Stephen asserts, finds its climax in the erection of the Temple in Jerusalem. Here we find the key to Stephen's polemic against the Jews. While they considered the Temple as the center of their life and worship, Stephen characterized it as a symbol of Jewish idolatry. For Stephen, it was never God's will that the Jews should build a Temple, for indeed it is a symbol of stagnation and immobility. And while Stephen's preaching led to his stoning and death, it also led the church away from Jerusalem into other areas of Palestine and of the Greek and Roman worlds.

The church in Antioch is a case in point. Luke makes it very clear that the believers were first called Christians in Antioch. (Acts 11:26) But Luke also specially mentions the fact that the church in Antioch started as a result of the death of Stephen and the persecution which ensued. (Acts 11:19)

The success of the mission to Greeks started at Antioch necessitated a rethinking of the ministry, and a further development of church order. For now the church saw before itself the enormous possibilities and challenges of witness before vast numbers of people in centers of civilization, in the important cities of the Roman empire. And so there arose the office of the church missionary, and appropriately enough, it was the church at Antioch that started the whole development. In chapter thirteen, we get a picture of the church at worship, during which time it received a command from the Holy Spirit: "Set apart for me Barnabas and Saul for the work to which I have called them." (Acts 13:2) Saul, or Paul, is no stranger to us. A Pharisee, a Hebrew, a learned Jewish scholar, and yet a Roman citizen, born in Tarsus, one of the thriving Greek cities: this man who is very Jew, and very Greek, and very Roman, is now set aside for mission to the great world of the Roman empire, preaching to both Jews and Greeks, using both the Hebrew and Greek languages, and quoting as freely from Greek literature as he does from the Hebrew scriptures.

IV. Implications

In the light of the above discussion, what implications can we draw for our present understanding of the ministry and its relationship to the Spirit?

A. Ministry and servanthood

A valid implication of the Pauline concept of *charisma* is the understanding of the ministry as servanthood. The New Testament word for ministry is *diakonia,* the verb form of which means "to serve at table," and the noun form meaning "service," in a generic sense. In the midst of modern day circumstances where ministers are understood (or misunderstood) as leaders and rulers, as those who demand and expect service, rather than as servants, it is well to be reminded that for the New Testament church, the ministry was primarily understood as service to others. For the ministry should be understood in the light of the very nature and mission of the church. As Simpson puts it, church order is dependent on ecclesiology.[41]

When one asks seriously the question, "What really is the church for?" or, "What is the call of the church?", I think the answer which comes closest to the truth is that the church is called to be faithful and obedient to its head, Jesus Christ. Our concept of the church's mission is therefore totally dependent on our concept of Jesus. In much the same way that church order is dependent on ecclesiology, so ecclesiology is dependent on Christology.

A second question would of course arise: "Who is this Jesus?" Or, putting it another way, what aspect of Jesus would one emphasize as a model for the church's obedience? How indeed did the early church understand the life of Jesus? What to them is the core, the basic aspect of Jesus' earthly life? These questions, of course, can only be answered by a serious study not only of the Gospels but of the whole New Testament. I venture an answer: A primary aspect of Jesus' life and ministry which the early church emphasized and which it adopted as a model for its own life and mission is that of servanthood. It is now debated whether Jesus identified himself with the suffering servant of Deutero-Isaiah; what cannot be denied, however, is that the Gospels are full of allusions to the fact that the early church understood Jesus as being profoundly influenced by the servant songs of Deutero-Isaiah and as fulfilling the servant's destiny. Paul himself preserves for us an early Christian hymn on the servanthood of Jesus.

New Testament faith is centered on this guiltless, sinless man who dies on a cross, this innocent one who suffers for the guilty, this sinless man who dies for the sinful. But because this is so, then the church as his body, must do likewise. The church therefore performs a role in the fulfillment of the servant motif in Deutero-Isaiah. The Servant Lord has committed his vocation to his servant people, the church. It is this Christ, now risen, who commissions his church to be like he is, namely, a servant for the world. Elmer Homrighausen writes:

The very essence of the church, the body of Christ, is the spirit of the servant . . . . As the individual is saved by losing himself for the sake of Christ, so the Church is saved by losing itself in the service which Jesus Christ started and which is continuing through the power of the Holy Spirit . . . . Conscious of its mission, it (the church) lays aside its outer garments, pours water into a basin, girds itself with a towel, and washes the dirty accumulations which men pick up on life's pilgrim way.[42]

One of the main expressions of the servant-role of the church is of course its ministry. When Paul uses the term *doulos* to describe himself, it could be that he was referring to the idea of a slave in the Roman system; it is more likely, however, that what he has in mind is the servant concept as found in Deutero-Isaiah; for him, *doulos* is a translation of *ebed*. And if one takes into account the fact that three more letters start with the same formula, (James, 2 Peter, Jude) then one can safely conclude that the ministry was indeed identified as a fulfillment of the servant concept of the Old Testament. Even Peter's commission in the sixteenth chapter of Matthew is misinterpreted if it is understood as a passage bestowing authority on the disciples apart from their roles as servants. Whatever interpretation one gives to the binding and loosing functions, it is wrong to take the passage and separate it from its immediate context, which is Jesus' first saying regarding his suffering in Jerusalem.

From that time Jesus began to show his disciples that he must go to Jerusalem and suffer many things from the elders and chief priests and scribes, and be killed, and on the third day be raised. And Peter took him aside and began to rebuke him, saying, "God forbid, Lord. This shall never happen to you." But he turned and said to Peter, "Get behind me, Satan! You are a hindrance to me; for you are not on the side of God but of men." (Matthew 16:21ff)

The roles of binding and loosing, whatever they imply, are in the context of suffering, and cannot be understood apart from the disciples' role as followers of the suffering Lord.

Suffering in the biblical sense is the selfless giving

of oneself in joyful and unselfish service to others. Paul reminds us that *charisma* is given primarily for this purpose: "To each is given the manifestation of the Spirit for the common good." (1 Corinthians 12:7) The epistle to the Ephesians also echoes the same spirit when it affirms that the gifts of ministry are "for the equipment of the saints, for the work of ministry, for building up the body of Christ." (Ephesians 4:12) As John Knox very well puts it:

> *Diakonos* denotes not primarily a status . . . but a function of a useful service. A minister of Christ is useful to Christ, assisting in the fulfillment of Christ's purposes in the world. A minister of the church is useful to the church, serving its members in all possible ways and contributing to the gospel, making known the good news of what God has done in Christ so that the gospel may reach those for whom it is intended and may have its true fruits.[43]

B. Ministry and the mission of the church

A second point, which is related to and is an expansion of the first, is that not only the ministry but all church order is dependent on the mission of the church.

The church in every age and generation is called upon to fulfill a mission which in some way is unique to that period of history. The mission remains the same. It is the proclamation of the good news of Jesus Christ, drawing out its implications and living according to its precepts. But the ways of proclamation and of living the good news vary from one age to another, and from one cultural setting to another. It is perhaps a theological truism to affirm that the Spirit empowers the church in any setting to be sufficient for any task. He does this precisely through *charisma,* the gifts he bestows on the church, generally to the total membership, and in a more specialized manner to its ministry. Nonetheless, if the church is sensitive and obedient to the bidding of the Spirit, it must ask seriously what its mission is in light of its own unique historical and cul-

tural situation. For the mission of the church dictates
its structure. It determines which offices are necessary
and which are not. The varied responses to mission in
the New Testament, as we have seen, all point to one
principle: Obedience demands spontaneity and sensitivity to what is going on. If the New Testament
church is any model at all, it is not in its structures to
be followed, nor in its indispensable offices to be
maintained regardless of the historical situation. In the
midst of changing situations, conflicts, and confusion,
the guidance of the Spirit must be sought after and
realized. The Lordship of the risen Christ, which is
not only over the church but over the world as well,
must be proclaimed, recognized, and reaffirmed. Perhaps Ernst Käsemann has a valid point in these words:

> No romantic postulate, however enveloped it may be in
> the cloak of salvation history, can be permitted to weaken
> the sober observation that the historian is unable to speak
> of an unbroken unity in New Testament ecclesiology.
> In that field he becomes aware of our own situation in
> microcosm—difference, difficulties, contradictions, at best
> an ancient ecumenical federation without an ecumenical
> council. The tensions between Jewish and Gentile Chris-
> tian churches, between Paul and the Corinthian enthu-
> siasts, between John and early catholicism, are as great as
> those of our own day. One-sided emphases, fossilized atti-
> tudes, fabrications, and contradictory opposites in doc-
> trine, organization and devotional practice are to be
> found in the ecclesiology of the New Testament no less
> than among ourselves. To recognize this is even a great
> comfort and, so far as ecumenical work today is con-
> cerned, a theological gain. For, in so doing, we come to
> see that our own history is one with that of primitive
> Christianity. Today, too, God's Spirit hovers over the
> waters of chaos out of which divine creation is to take
> shape. So it is right to emphasize yet again at this point
> that Jesus' proclamation of the dawning of God's kingly
> rule may have conjured up many ecclesiologies, but it
> remains strangely transcendent over them all and is by
> them all at best brokenly reflected and not seldom totally
> distorted.[44]

Is it not imperative then for the church to ask once
again what its main task is, and then allow its structures to be instruments in such a task? What can we

say about the world as we know it, and the mission of the church in this kind of a world? To put it another way, in what areas should the church recognize the bidding of the Holy Spirit particularly with regard to the church's ministry? The challenges of the modern world demand a widening of our concepts of ministry, recognizing not simply the traditional ministry for the parish or for the organized church, but a ministry for a non-church society. To effect relevance, the Pauline model of flexibility, spontaneity, and freedom must once again become indispensable standards for ministerial office and education, and for all other aspects of church order.

What about ministry to women? It is unfortunate that the creation story which predominated in the church (and in the whole of the New Testament) is that of the second and third chapters of Genesis. Those chapters depict woman as a creation from man. All the sins of the world are portrayed as stemming from the disobedience of that first woman who could not have known about the forbidden fruit since the command not to touch it was given before she was created. A more realistic story, and theologically more pregnant with possibilities, is that of the first chapter of Genesis where God does not create one but two: a man and a woman together, at the same time, and both in God's image.

It is to the credit of Paul, however, that despite his adherence to the second chapter of Genesis and his belief in the inferiority of women, he could still come out with a doctrine of redemption in Christ which would restore woman, as it were, into her rightful place in creation and in the church. One can only rejoice at the fact that there were no female leaders in the church of Galatia who could be blamed for foolishness and apostasy. Paul was free to include in his Galatian letter a comprehensive statement on Christ's work of redemption in overcoming the rift effected by the fall. Henceforth, in Christ, men and women have equal status in the sight of God. There is, therefore, no impediment to the full participation of women in the ministry of the church in the light of Galatians 3.

Be that as it may, we return to our main contention, and that is, mission is primary and structures secondary. For me at least, there are no indispensable offices. Where any office or any structure no longer makes the church effective in fulfilling its mission, then such structures, no matter how historically rooted they are, no matter how indispensable they seem to be, should go, and quickly. Where offices and structures are found to be effective instruments for the fulfillment of the mission of the church, then by all means they should be introduced, strengthened, and maintained. But they should not be regarded as the final answers to the church's needs. Structures are at their best when they are temporary rather than permanent, when they are regarded as functional rather than as sacrosanct.

C. Varied understandings of the ministry

This brings us to a third point at which we have already hinted: There is no New Testament model for one exclusive concept of the ordained ministry. This means, then, there is no one ministry that is acceptable to God and through which the Holy Spirit carries out his task in the church and the world. To claim, even in a single instance, that the ministry of any church is *the* valid ministry, sanctioned by the Holy Spirit, is to claim that the Spirit blesses and sanctifies a certain system which creates disorder and disunity within the body of Christ. We do not have to be reminded that one of the greatest, if not the greatest, deterrent to Christian unity in this supra-ecumenical age is the doctrine of the ministry. Can we assert with a clear conscience that the Spirit has sanctioned this situation?

Is the Spirit the Spirit of disunity? Is the ministry of the church still a ministry resting on the Holy Spirit when it becomes an instrument for fragmentation of the body of Christ? Do we still have the courage to claim the Spirit's presence in the rite of ordination when in that rite itself we put ourselves over against other Christians?

Apostolic succession, assert the free churches, has no basis in the New Testament. The ministries in the free churches, assert the apostolic successionists, have no basis either from the New Testament or from tradition. What are we to believe?

One has to awaken to the fact that ordination as an act of the Holy Spirit is still an act of faith, whether one believes in apostolic succession or not. The problem then is not in these systems, but in people's attitudes toward them. The absolutizing of these systems is the root of endless, futile, and destructive debates within the church. For here system, and not the Lordship of Christ, has become primary! The mission of the church has been relegated to the background in favor of church order and polity. In fact, church order and polity now are determinative of the nature of the church itself! In the midst of all these comes the New Testament verdict that, indeed, there are no set structures and no set offices. Apostolic succession can be proven from the New Testament by those who so choose; it can, likewise, be easily disproven. The threefold ministry of bishops, elders, and deacons is well documented from the Pastorals. The free church idea of a non-ordained ministry is equally well documented by Paul's letters, especially by his doctrine of the *charisma,* as we have seen.

Where do we go from here? It is simply to recognize that the New Testament presents different church orders, each one as valid as the other. The validity of any church order depends on the historical and cultural situation of the church, for in the end, as we have already asserted, the mission of the church dictates the order of the church! For me, therefore, it is not a matter of proving the validity either of apostolic succession or of non-apostolic succession. It is recognizing that the insistence of those who belong to apostolic succession, on the sole validity of their order, and the intolerant attitude toward other systems as portrayed by the sects and others belonging to the free church tradition, are doing great damage to the life of the church, dividing members in their worship, in their ministry, and even in the training of ministers! Perhaps we can and should affirm that the Holy Spirit is leading us to accept varied theological understandings of the ministry, and to recognize that all these systems rest on faith and not on sight.

D. The ministry and the Holy Spirit

And finally, we do well to affirm that in all of this, the ministry still belongs to the Holy Spirit. He can and still does initiate new offices. It is still within his power to bestow *charisma* to all the faithful, or to a special part of the church, according to his will and purpose.

> There must be no church order—even in obedience to the apostle himself—through which a meeting with the living Lord is avoided . . . . An obedience that conforms to the law, to the regulations laid down by some authority—whether a bishop or the majority of the voters—is no obedience without a perception that the required action is a necessity derived from the gospel. What was shown in Jesus' own life is also true here: faith is genuine only where the distress, difficulty, and tribulation of a direct meeting with God himself, as he comes to us in Jesus Christ, are not avoided. No law and no legally interpreted authority must excuse the believer from asking what is God's will and from subordinating himself to the Holy Spirit and the risen Lord.[45]

We should not, therefore, in any way, either by legislation or scriptural validation, impair the freedom of the Holy Spirit to act within the church. The ministry's effectiveness, in the long run, will depend on its dedication and obedience to the Holy Spirit in order to effect changes in its order and in its ministry.[46]

The words of Käsemann seem to be a good quotation with which to end.

> The direct legacy of all past time to us can only be the questions and the needs of bygone ages and the various ways in which men have attempted to deal with them. But perhaps that sharpens not only our insight but also our conscience and tells us that no age is exempt from the necessity of beginning all over again, of testing, critically and yet humbly, the spirits of the ages that have gone before, because we, too, are called to decision. Perhaps, as we learn this, we are brought to acknowledge that the church can only exist as the community of Christ insofar as grace repeatedly lays hold on us and re-creates us as instruments of his service; and that we must leave him to care for the continuity of the church, who alone is able to ensure the continuance of grace.[47]

Notes

1. Ernst Käsemann, "Ministry and Community in the New Testament," *Essays in New Testament Themes* (London: SCM Press, 1964), pp. 63-94; p. 65.
2. 1 Corinthians 12:4. If verses 4 through 6 are quoted, they show how Paul attributes *charisma* not only to the Holy Spirit, but to the Trinity. The passage uses Trinitarian language: Spirit, Lord, God.
3. Käsemann, *op. cit.*, p. 72.
4. *Ibid.*, pp. 73ff.
5. "The Ministry in the Primitive Church," in *The Ministry in Historical Perspectives,* ed. Richard H. Niebuhr and Daniel D. Williams (New York: Harper and Brothers, 1956), p. 18.
6. *Ibid.*, pp. 18ff.
7. "The Biblical Doctrine of the Ministry," as referred to in Harry G. Goodykoontz, *The Minister in the Reformation Tradition* (National Council of Churches of Christ in the USA, 1952), pp. 22ff. Goodykoontz is able to find in Paul a much greater emphasis on the office of the minister, simply by accepting Ephesians as a genuine Pauline letter.
8. Archibald Robertson and Alfred Plummer, *A Critical and Exegetical Commentary on the First Epistle of St. Paul to the Corinthians* (Edinburgh: T and T Clark, 1914), p. 284. See further C.K. Barrett, *A Commentary on the Epistle to the Romans* (New York: Harper and Brothers, 1957), pp. 238ff.
9. It will do well, in the light of this definition of the prophet in Paul, to take heed to Richardson's warning against justifying the prophetic ministry of the church by

means of the New Testament concept of the prophetic office; see Alan Richardson, *An Introduction to the Theology of the New Testament* (New York: Harper and Brothers, 1958), p. 336.

10. John Knox, *op. cit.,* p. 14: "The word 'teacher' suggests instruction in the more ordinary sense, a setting forth, perhaps in somewhat objective fashion, of the facts of the tradition and the truth of the gospel, the inculcation of true beliefs, the encouraging of appropriate ethical impulses and conduct." Knox further warns against drawing too rigid a line between the prophet and the teacher in the primitive church: "Both were inspired by the same Spirit and both were concerned only with the truth and relevance of the gospel."

11. Eduard Schweizer, *Church Order in the New Testament* (London: SCM Press, 1961), p. 101.

12. *Ibid.,* p. 102.

13. Käsemann, *op. cit.,* p. 87.

14. *Ibid.*

15. Robert A. Spivey and D. Moody Smith, Jr., *Anatomy of the New Testament* (London: Macmillan Company, 1969), p. 368; also Käsemann, *op. cit.,* p. 88: "The distinction between clerics and laymen is now in being, in practice if not in theory."

16. Käsemann, *op. cit.,* p. 85.

17. Knox, *op. cit.,* pp. 10ff. Knox continues: "Indeed the 'deacons' and 'bishops' of Philippians are almost certainly to be identified with the 'helpers' and 'administrators' of 1 Corinthians 12:28 and with the helpers of several kinds and the 'presidents' who are mentioned in Romans 12:6-8."

18. 1 Timothy 3:8-13. It is doubtful whether one should regard Acts 6:1-6 as the establishment of the office of deacon, for the simple reason that the noun, *diakonos,* is not used by Luke in that passage, but simply the verb, *diakoneo,* which implies much more of a function than an office. For further discussion of this point, see Ernst Haenchen, *The Acts of the Apostles, A Commentary* (Philadelphia: Westminster Press, 1971), pp. 260ff.

19. See Acts 20:17 and 20:28; 1 Peter 5:2; Titus 1:5 and 1:7-9.

20. 1 Timothy 5:22. Note, however, that this verse is sometimes taken to refer not to ordination, but to the act of readmitting a sinner into the fellowship; see Schweizer, *op. cit.,* p. 207.

21. James L. Price, *Interpreting the New Testament* (New York: Holt, Rinehart and Winston, 1961), pp. 474ff. See also Käsemann, *op cit.,* p. 87: "The apostolic delegate is regarded in the Pastorals as the connecting link between apostle and monarchical bishop who under the guise of the apostolic delegate, is being addressed and reminded of his duties."

22. Howard Clark Kee and Franklin W. Young, *Understanding the New Testament* (Englewood Cliffs, N.J.: Prentice-Hall, Inc., 1957), p. 362. They further write: "It has been said in jest that at the end of the apostolic age the church was like a locomotive going into a dark tunnel and that it emerged in the post-apostolic period with bishops on its cow-catcher." *Ibid.*, p. 363. Richardson observes that the monepiscopacy remained the universal form of church government until the time of the Reformation, *op. cit.*, p. 326.

23. To be sure, there are some who interpret the passages as referring to baptism, *e.g.*, Schweizer, *op. cit.*, pp. 210ff.

24. Richardson, *op. cit.*, p. 330.

25. Goodykoontz, *op. cit.*, p. 25.

26. Mark 5:23, 6:5; 7:32, 8:23, 24; 16:18; (Acts 1:12, 17), 28:8.

27. Mark 10:16, Acts 8:17-19; 19:5ff.; Hebrews 6:2.

28. *E.g.*, Schweizer, *op. cit.*, p. 280, where he describes the rite as an installation, "a placing in a particular sphere of service which differs in some respects from that previously occupied." One should also note that in Acts 13, Paul is already included under the designation of "prophets and teachers," and therefore is already a recognized leader in the church. A further note on Acts 6: there is a great deal of uncertainty as to who did the laying on of hands—the apostles or the members of the congregation. Most translations leave the rendering ambiguous; some, however, have made it definite that it was the apostles who did the action, *e.g.*, TEV, NEB, etc. Here is one place where the interpreter can do anything he wants with the text, without any fear of being unfaithful to it.

29. *E.g.*, Ervin Peter Yount Simpson, *Ordination and Christian Unity* (Valley Forge: The Judson Press, 1966), p. 119: "we must not imagine that the laying on of hands, in itself, was significant. It was merely a physical part of a solemn prayer that divine equipping might be conferred upon the young men. It was not the means of conferring this divine gift, but rather the moment when God answered the solemn prayers which were being offered."

30. Price, *op. cit.*, p. 458: "Ideally the Church is one, but instead of a conviction of its reality writers of this time yearned for unity." Price mentions the Gospel of John, Ephesians, and of course the Pastorals, as included in the writings where this lack of unity is displayed.

31. One already sees this development even during Paul's time, among the Corinthians, *e.g.*, in 1 Corinthians 14.

32. Richardson, *op. cit.*, p. 328.

33. This position is apparent in Kee and Young, *op. cit.*, p. 365, and Richardson, *op. cit.*, p. 328. A rather negative evaluation of these developments is found in Käsemann, *op. cit.*, pp. 87ff. and Simpson, *op. cit.*, pp. 101ff.

34. Käsemann, *op. cit.*, p. 89.

35. See esp., Acts 8:14-16. It is rather unusual that here the Holy Spirit can only be bestowed by Peter and John, and not by Philip, a member of the Seven, when in fact Philip would of course be full of the Holy Spirit. See Acts 6:3.
36. Acts 6:6, but see previous note 18.
37. Käsemann, *op. cit.,* p. 91.
38. Acts 2:1. The "they" here most probably refers to the one hundred and twenty in 1:15. How all of them could be accommodated in one room is of course a problem, but was no concern to Luke.
39. *E.g.,* Acts 10:44ff. The exceptions are Acts 9:17-18, where Paul receives the Holy Spirit through Ananias, and Acts 8:14ff., esp., 17. For a recent discussion on this subject, see F.F. Bruce, "The Holy Spirit in the Acts of the Apostles," *Interpretation* 27 (April 1973), pp. 166-183.
40. Briefly, the questions include the relation of the apostle to the *shaliach* in Judaism, the place of the Twelve in the Book of Acts, and the election of Matthias. For all these, one is referred to T.W. Manson, *The Churches' Ministry,* 1948; A. Ehrhardt, *The Apostolic Succession,* 1953; Johannes Weiss, *Earliest Christianity,* 1973; Haenchen, *op. cit.,* pp. 163ff, and Simpson, *op. cit.,* pp. 67ff.
41. *Ibid.,* p. 116. "Until there is a common understanding of the nature of the church there can hardly be a common agreement on the nature and function of the ministry."
42. Elmer Homrighausen, "Lord-Servant," *Theology Today,* p. 7.
43. John Knox, *op. cit.,* pp. 1ff.
44. Quoted from "Unity and Multiplicity in the New Testament Doctrine of the Church," *New Testament Questions of Today,* 1961, pp. 256ff., by C.F. Evans in "Is the New Testament Church a Model?" *Is Holy Scripture Christian?* (London: SCM Press, 1971), pp. 86ff.
45. Schweizer, *op. cit.,* pp. 212ff.
46. Schweizer, *op. cit.,* p. 205: "There are three ways in which Church order can . . . remain open to God's active intervention. First, it can be broken through by God's giving an instruction to an otherwise uncommissioned church member. (1 Corinthians 14:30; cf. Acts 11:27-30) Secondly, God's initiative creates new ministries not hitherto foreseen. (Acts 13:1-3) This, of course, is true not merely in direct revelations by the Spirit, but equally so when the church listens to God as it confronts a new situation, (Acts 6:1ff) or when a new ministry is at first simply carried out on someone's own initiative and is recognized afterwards by the church. (1 Corinthians 16: 16) Thirdly, however, it is also possible that certain ministries have proved their worth and are being continued, but that the church tries seriously later on to find out who has received from God the gifts of grace that are necessary for them. (1 Timothy 3:1ff)"
47. Käsemann, *op. cit.,* p. 94.

The Holy Spirit and Sanctification: Refinding the Lost Image of Creation

Thomas A. Langford

We are dispirited. Walking the world in solitary aloofness, we have lost the image of our creation and we live in the midst of people who have lost the image of their creation. There is a malaise within and among us; our spirits have become estranged from the Spirit of God.

To be dispirited is to live with a lack in our humanity; it is to live as incomplete and as allowing for, resigning to, or affirming our incompleteness. To be dispirited is to live with attenuated relationships and with limited realization of corporate possibility. Living in isolation from the Holy Spirit, which creates and succors our spirits, we have lost the image of our creation.

To say these things is not to speak new truth; rather, it is to indicate the persistent tendency toward despoilation of human selfhood. People exist inauthentically, willfully rejecting their most distinctively human qualities, detracting from their freedom to be, to create, and to relate to others. Hence, as we find people on the street, in their homes, at their jobs, in their towns, in their cities, and in their churches, we find them living in truncated condition, lacking the power to express free and full lives.

This condition must be understood for what it is not, and for what it is. It is not relegation to a natural condition as opposed to a supernatural life; it is a deprivation of the fully maturing selfhood which was intended in human creation. To live as dispirited is to realize a less complete personhood than that which God intended: it is not to miss personhood completely; it is not to lack all creative vision and activity; it is not to live totally sundered from community; but it is to live with less than full realization of any of these possibilities and it is to live with unnecessary malformation. The failure to become fully human, not the failure to become more than human, is the resulting condition of dispirited life. *Gratia perficit naturam, non tollit.*

To understand this condition we need to return to first things, to primary reality. The Spirit of God and the spirit of persons are integrally, inescapably related. The human spirit has its origin in God who has created persons in his own image and with their own integrity. The human spirit has its definition in Jesus Christ who recreates persons and incorporates them into his life. The human spirit has its potential maturity given by the Holy Spirit who projects possibility by his continually nurturing presence.

The doctrine of the Holy Spirit, while immensely rich, is principally interpreted here under the ruling dynamic relationships. The integral community of God with persons and of persons with one another under God is the controlling theme. Throughout, there is reciprocal movement between the finding of selfhood in divine-human relationships and the finding of individual and corporate selfhood in human relationships.

Theological anthropology must take into account this movement from experience of community with God to the experience of community with other persons; and the counterposing move from experience of community with ʿother persons to an experience of community with God. The interaction and interfacing of these two realities always constitutes a difficulty for understanding and interpretation, but the composite reality is integral to our total experience. Our interpretations must include the reality of both aspects of this holistic experience. Community with God in the explicit relationship with Jesus Christ posits the norm by which all other relationships are to be understood, appreciated, and judged. From the perspective of this primary relationship with God through Jesus Christ one can recognize the wide-ranging and previous grace which has been present in general human experience. From the experienced meaning found in human relationships there is established the possibility of understanding the meaning of God's relating to us in Jesus Christ. Each relation contributes to the appreciation, evaluation, and projection of the other. Nevertheless, in terms of priority of values, the relationship with God in Jesus Christ functions as the more basic criterion and it is this relationship by which human relationships are ultimately judged, affirmed, annulled, and directed to new possibility.[1]

As viewed from the biblical perspective, the human being is brought into the world dependent upon the gracious community of God. In addition, persons progress in meaningful maturation where there is a mutual engagement of their spirits by and with the Spirit of God. Consequently, through God's initiation, continuing presence, and hopeful projection, we are created and challenged into growing selfhood.

In human society we can recognize an extension of this primal relationship in common grace through the created potential for personhood in community. The human child is born dependent upon community. The child remains dependent and can only live and mature if there is care—an attending to his or her needs and possibilities by others. Furthermore, the child can only come to meaningful personhood where there is an affirmation of his or her person and where that selfhood is defined in opposition to and in positive relation with other persons.[2] This need of relation continues throughout maturation, although its character goes through a variety of permutations. Dependence becomes interdependence, and mutual love, empathy, and support remain essential for meaningful life.

At the same time, to be a self also implies self-possession. There is an integration, an integrity by which the individual person is characterized, that is, by which he or she is given character. Selfhood is progressively realized as native potential grouped around a center of value; this is an ongoing, uncompleted, but essential motility of human self-development. Hence interior strength and personal definition are constituents of selfhood and are present where self-identification is found.

In maturing selfhood these two dimensions are always present: relation to others and possession of one's own person. There is a rhythm between, or a symbiosis of, these two elements: a going out from the self and reinforcing in the self; a reaching to the other and an affirmation of one's person. Each requires the other, each induces the other, each enhances the other.

But there is a priority. A child comes into the world dependent upon the approach of others; self-possession is responsive to affirmation by another or others. The quality of that affirmation determines the quality of the possession. The character and range of that affirmation determine the maturing potential of personal development. To be a self is to live in relation, but the person(s) to whom one is related is (are) fundamentally important in terms of the possible selfhood which may be realized. To be a self is to have a center around which life is organized; to be a self is, in that sense, to have a god. But now to take the next and critical step: to possess the possibility for actualizing the full potential for personhood requires that one be related to God; for it is only when we are related to that which calls forth our full humanity and offers the richest affirmation of our person that we have set for us the vision and the possibility of full personhood. It is God in Christ relating to persons through the Holy Spirit who establishes this full potential and evokes the response which issues in persistent maturation.

We are created *imago Dei,* for full relationship with God, for full possession of our persons. This is our heritage. But we have lost the image of our creation. We are fallen and so fail to realize the selfhood for which we were created. To fall is to be dispirited, to live apart from God's encountering presence, to live in truncated human community, and to be inadequately self-possessed. Because of the fall, there is dehumanization, that is, estrangement from God, and others, and ourselves; further, there is antagonism with ourselves, and others, and God. Hence, there is isolation and deprivation of spirit.

The tragedy of the human condition is located in this failure to realize the gracious possibility for fully maturing life. The hope for human development is located in the gracious possibility for the renewal of the lost image of our full humanity. The conditions of this recrudescence are justification and sanctification. Justification, as the gift of new possibility through forgiveness, reconstitutes the grounds for, even as it expresses the origination of, positive relationship. Sanctification, as the gift of new possibility through maturation, actualizes continuously enriching, challenging, fulfilling relationship. It is upon this possibility as given in sanctification that we shall now concentrate.

I. Sanctification: the Idea as Received

Sanctification is a theological notion long neglected—even by those who are in the Wesleyan tradition. The reasons for this neglect are complex and need exploration, and we shall touch upon this. But it is obvious that Methodists tend to look upon the doctrine with some uncertainty and with not a little embarrassment. It is like an heirloom which is presumed to have some value—how much no one knows and whom to ask no one is sure. We keep the doctrine, but with a degree of uncomfortableness, and are quite often relieved to have it hidden in an ecclesiastical lock-box.

I shall attempt to interpret sanctification as the re-finding of our lost human image. This interest is not located in an effort to reclaim an archaic word, "sanctification," although the word is significant; rather, the effort is to emphasize a dimension of experience which is a part of full-orbed Christian life and therefore requires theological interpretation. This dimension we need to keep before our attention and verify in our experience. But before we can undertake a fresh interpretation we need to look at the reasons why this doctrine has eroded.[3] First, however, let us begin with John Wesley and his definition of sanctification which was for him the chief concern. It was the primary mission of the church to spread "scriptural holiness over the land." There were three major emphases which Wesley made: (a) purity of intention, dedication of all life to God; (b) possessing the mind of Christ enabling us to walk as Christ walked; and (c) loving God with all our heart and our neighbors as ourselves. In all of these definitions the primal emphasis was upon the affections—upon the love of God—but in each case there was also a resulting moral style of life.[4]

Already in his time, Wesley was pressed to defend this position and attempted to say what he did not mean as well as what he meant.[5] But the doctrine was nurtured in uncertainty and continued in controversy.

A general examination reveals four major reasons why the teaching on sanctification declined into general disuse and often explicit rejection. First, the word "perfection" caused difficulty. Perfection seemed to imply a static, achieved state and in this it seemed to be an excessive claim. Perhaps modern psychology was the chief agent of this challenge. The psychological understanding of processes of growth and the continu-

ing character of maturation made questionable any
state which seemed static even though Wesley explicitly
said this was not so. Perhaps Wesley lacked clear con-
ceptualization or accessible illustrations to make his
point, "perfect and growing in perfection," clear. I
assume that he had in mind something like a person
who is entirely sensitive—if this were possible—to the
needs of another person but who constantly grows in
capacity to be sensitive and continues to be entirely
sensitive—now in expanded capacity— to the needs of
the other person. I assume something like this is what
Wesley had in mind, but again good illustrations are
difficult to find. In addition, the development of depth
psychology called into question undue reliance upon
the constancy and significance of our conscious awareness (which is what Wesley stressed). The vagrancy
of the unconscious, the deception of our conscious
thoughts, and the sense of dynamic growth all worked
to discredit the possibility of perfection. And perhaps
a proper Christian humility also worked to discount
the notion when it was falsely interpreted so as to
engender pride. In any case, the very use of the word
"perfection" limited the acceptance of the doctrine.

Second, there was a tendency to moralize the idea
of sanctification in such a way as to unbalance the fact
that sanctification was first of all a gospel and then a
life. Both grace and responsibility should be present
in creative tension. But the good person was often
judged to be so by his overt moral virtue. The emphasis
on moral qualities was transferred from a subordinate,
although necessary, role to the central role and, consequently, perfection was distorted. Rules and law—and
these often of a most parochial type—became the norm
by which sanctity was assessed. The primacy of religious affection was lost and such a tendency toward
moralism led to a demise of the doctrine.

Third, there was a tendency—at least in the United

States—to identify sanctification with a special form of Spirit-possession, namely, *glossalalia*. The manifest form of the second blessing or the second work of grace was speaking in tongues. But such ecstasy has always been confined to a minor proportion of Christians. Hence, when the experience of *glossalalia* was recognized as limited in the number of participants or as being eccentric to the mainstream of many persons' Christian development, interest in the entire doctrine waned.

Fourth, the doctrine of sanctification as taught by Wesley (although not lived by Wesley) and his followers was excessively individualistic in its form. Sanctification was thought of in private terms and therefore was separated from the experience of community as a community. Indeed, the notion of the "one, holy . . . church" seems to be shifted to the "one, holy" person. Such an emphasis was congenial, for instance, to the solitary character of the American frontier and modern American society, and possibly of western European life, but it did not speak to the need of community or to the possibility for church life. And this led to decline at least among those who had interest in the social character of life.

The idea of sanctification as received has, for the reasons indicated, become generally uncertain in meaning and unapplied in Christian living. Increasingly, the doctrine has become non-functional as a theological issue and as a moral force. Nevertheless, it continues to elicit some historical interest and, perhaps, solicits examination to determine its present value and applicability. It is the effort of this chapter to explore the possibility of new vitality for this theological concern.

II. Sanctification: the Idea as Reconceived

As already indicated, I want to speak of sanctification as the refinding of the lost image of creation. This means that sanctification is to be understood as the process of maturation through which persons progressively realize their potential for human growth as individuals and as participants in community with others and with God. Just as there is a wholeness in the action of God, there is a wholeness in Christian experience which, while it allows us to distinguish between such doctrines as creation, justification, and sanctification, always emphasizes the completeness of God's relation to persons and persons' relation to God. This is the fullness of redemption.

Let me illustrate the interrelated and complex wholeness.

God as Father is our creator; our life begins in him.

God in Christ is our justification; our justification is our dying and rising with Christ.

God as Holy Spirit is our sanctification. Our sanctification is the continuous interaction of the Holy Spirit with our spirits.

The one God acts to create and to promise full humanity. God as creator originates human life; Jesus Christ as justifier recreates human life; the Holy Spirit as sanctifier fulfills human life. Thus Christian experience extends from creation through justification to sanctification; and human maturation is the process of moving toward the full realization of personhood under the aegis of the encompassing grace of God as expressed in Christ Jesus through the Holy Spirit.[6]

We have spoken already of maturation. Now we should define the notion. The process of maturation is a continuous centering of life upon one prime object of affection. To will one thing, to love God only, is the chief end of persons. And Christian growth may be defined as the continual re-envisioning of that goal and the progressive integration of life around that center. To be a developing person is to be drawn by and to draw more and more of life under the aegis of a

supreme object of devotion. To be developing as a
community is to be drawn by and to draw more and
more of life under the aegis of the supreme object of
worship. Life for individuals and communities is established around a sacred center, around a constellation
of values.[7] Throughout experience there is necessary
reciprocation of individuals and community as a center
is shared and historically conveyed. In Christian faith
this center is God: God as he is disclosed in Jesus
Christ, God as he is present in the Holy Spirit. To love
God without measure and without demand, to love God
in and for himself—this is authentic relationship and
it is spirited life. To love our neighbor in unrestrained
caring, this is authentic relationship and it is spirited
life.

Human life becomes increasingly human—human
life is sanctified—by this focused love; and in this way
fullness of human life is dependent upon a transcendent
point of reference. There is a sequence of relationships.
The Holy Spirit confronts us soliciting our response in
the ordinary events of creation, but we are willfully
blind. The Holy Spirit meets us soliciting our response
in Jesus Christ and in faith graciously given our eyes
are opened. The Holy Spirit confronts us soliciting our
response to his presence and in love our sight is intensi-
fied and extended.[8] God in his fullness is present to us
throughout the ordinary and the special moments of
revelation. But we speak of Spirit-presence as having
that place in the ecology of spiritual life where attention
and devotion come to clear focus and life is drawn
around that nucleus and toward maturity. Sanctification
is the continuous consent of life to the lordship of
Jesus Christ as he is made present through the Holy
Spirit.

Now I want to add a comment. There is an incon-
gruity with our usual experience when we speak of
holiness. Sanctification is not to be understood or ex-

pected as a result of a review—even of the most careful sort—of the lower levels of experience. Rather, it represents a fresh and original integration of the given clues into a new configuration. An analysis of all of the ingredient factors which go into explaining this condition will not yield the new synthesis. It comes as a new vision of possibility which draws previous understandings into a new form, fulfilling their potential in unexpected ways. As a clock cannot be explained by an examination of all of the physical or chemical laws which are employed in its working, but in terms of its intended function, so sanctification is a new quality of life which results from a new vision for life. As a poetic achievement is not to be understood by an analysis of each word used, syntactical systems, and grammatical conventions, but in terms of its whole and unique character, so sanctification is a distinctive style of life established by a distinctive understanding of life. Holiness of life is not a natural, expected next step. It comes as unexpected discovery of a new integration of living with new dimensionality. Here the vision of Christian community establishes its own distinctive possibility.

Through this dynamic-of-focused-existence, life is released for expansiveness. There is a development of the rich possibility of personhood. Persons are emancipated to realize who they are and who they may become, and all of this in community. Sanctification means a new self understanding and realization; it means well-being. Sanctification means to be fully born and to be growing, to have a new capacity for others, for sympathy and love, for joy and sadness, for caring and sharing.

The order of priorities should be clear in this rhythm of being found and self-finding. The love of God initiates the response of persons. The holy life is built upon the gospel of prevenient, and continuing, judg-

ment and grace. Holy living is holy precisely because it
continually responds to the captivating power of that
grace. The holy life is drawn from the shores of shallow
security into the ocean where duty becomes freedom
and moral responsibility becomes the pulsation of a
life lived in trustful relation to God. The effect of the
relationship enacted in Jesus Christ is the opening up
of the whole, tangled, many-dimensioned creature to
the continuous presence and power of the Holy Spirit
and the resulting fructification as enriched maturation.

Sanctification is expressed as morality and, as such,
has implications for corporate life. We shall argue
shortly that sanctification as reinterpreted must become
more conscious of its embodiment as community. The
relation of spiritual righteousness to morality must be
carefully stated, however, for there is a direct bearing
upon theological assumptions as well as upon strategic
implementation.

Theologically and experientially we have to deal
with a persistent tendency to substitute moralistic ex-
ternalization of life for spiritual depth and range. When
persons become dispirited and live in solitary separation
they tend to relate to other people through the establishment of functional power bases by which they can affect their social context. When this political interest
issues from moral commitment it is, for the dispirited
person, often an expression of what Michael Polanyi
has called "moral inversion."[9] That is, it is a condition
which represents a loss of authoritative ground in
transcendent moral obligation and the affirmation of
an emotive morality of individual interests. Such private
convictions are often generalized, then absolutized and
imposed on others. These "homeless moral passions"
seek their dwelling place in centers of power which can
effect the will of the morally inspired person upon a
wider society. Several matters are crucial in this situation: the loss of a basic ground upon which communal

moral consent can be built, the substitution of pragmatic political power operations for more basic moral authority, and the subsequent destruction of authentic community as such.

The loss of transcendent grounding for morality is symptomatic of the loss of spiritual rootage in life. The isolated individual who has been sundered from primary partnership with God attempts to claim self-determined moral sovereignty—as an act of *hubris*—and to impose his or her moral convictions upon their context. Always involved in moral inversion is a hybrid of skepticism and perfectionism which leads to what may be called a "skeptico-fanaticism," that is, a skepticism about the source of moral life in any transcendent reality and a fanatical desire to impose privately conceived moral tenets or actions upon other people. What is at stake here is the basic loss of the relationship between God and persons at the ontological and axiological levels and a substitution of an individual's relation to his or her own self which is extended into imposed relations upon others.

The substitution of newly found centers of political power for the unself-claiming *diakonia* of Jesus represents a repudiation of the Protestant claim of justification by grace alone with a forthright effort to claim righteousness through moral exertion and with negative effect upon community life. This may be described as a pathological moral excess because it grows out of a sense of guilt over the loss of transcendent grounding and a sense of responsibility to serve and save the world. Such inauthentic rootage, however, always brings forth poisonous fruit; one cannot gather figs from thistles.

To claim that holiness is first of all a gospel, and then a resulting morality, is to lay hold upon the first principles of the Christian message. It is to claim that the foundation upon which Christian life is built is the redemptive work of God in Jesus Christ and it is to claim that the moral life which is built upon that foundation is the extension of God's redemptive activity as that grace is refracted through faithful discipleship.

III. Sanctification: the Presence of the Holy Spirit as Community

To speak of persons being focused upon God is to say that they are in living vital relation with the Holy Spirit. The focused life is the specifically related life; maturation means growth in and through specific relationships. Sanctification is the process of drawing together the disconnected strands of life by means of a central relationship. Throughout this discussion I have attempted to define personhood in terms of positively enacted relationships. To be a person is to be in relationship. To possess selfhood is to live in community with other selves. Hence, Wesley's notion of synergism is not to be eschewed. While it has always been difficult theologically to develop synergism without compromising God's sovereignty, it is necessary to insist that God in his creation of persons has limited his freedom by the gift of human freedom and has consequently made relationship more prominent than unilateral, omnipotent sovereignty. In his creation of persons for fellowship, God has, at the same time, limited himself and increased the free potential for responsible maturation of persons in community.[10] Forced relation is not love, for love requires fresh and free giving of each to the other.

Several times we have mentioned the word "freedom," and this notion is essential to sanctification. "For freedom Christ has set us free." (Galatians 5:1) Holy living is expressed through the liberation of persons who are becoming the persons God envisioned in their creation. The distinctive character of sanctity is best captured in the freedom of the human spirit as opposed to the atrophied life of bondage. Redeemed persons are those who are set free by God for their human fulfillment. But individual freedom is bound with communal freedom. Christianity, Charles Gore has said, "came into the world as a life to be lived by a community."[11] The single focus of worship draws the church as Christian community to God, and thence to freedom, and endorses the congregation as a liberated and liberating community. The sharing of freedom within and beyond the church is an essential element in the experience of liberation and is an authentic expression of sanctification. Again, we are not speaking of an achieved moral condition or a static state of community; rather, we are speaking of a community which matures toward its goal through responsive love (worship).

The cardinal issue is that in the present day it is a fundamental falsification to think of sanctification in radically individualistic terms. Holiness is to be found in and through Christian community. To be sanctified is to belong to the company of saints; it is to be in lively Christian comradeship; it is to make Christian community the agent of emancipated living in human society.[12]

The Holy Spirit is the *esprit de corps;* it is the Spirit which proffers community, which binds life together in community, and which extends the reach of community to those who are at present alien. The distinctive factor, however, is not that there is simply togetherness but rather the quality of the life which is experienced in community. Sanctification carries a connotation and a denotation of freedom, of openness, of fellow-affirmation, of concern for love and justice. Sanctification is the communal embodiment of crucifixion and resurrection; it is forgiveness, and new beginning, and renewed vision. Sanctification is life in the Spirit, among spirited persons; life grouped by the Spirit to extend and enhance the spirited possibilities of all persons.

In the New Testament, *hagios* designates all members of the congregation, not simply as a sum total of individuals but in virtue of their common life in Christ. Therefore, sanctification should apply to the common life of the congregation. Separated individualism is modified as the community realizes its own distinctive character and reinforces the distinctive character of each of its members. The church communicates to persons the assurance of their corporate—incorporated—reality in contrast to the isolated living which is typical of the present world. Ambiguity in the realization of this goal is ingredient to the life of the church, but within the community of the Holy Spirit the ambiguity is recognized and struggled with although it is never completely removed.[13]

Traditionally, creedal theology has started its description of the church as "one, holy . . . church." The oneness of the church is to be found in the singularity of its love. The church is the community of those who are in community with Jesus Christ. The congregation is convoked by the grace of God; it is continued by that grace; and it is commissioned for mission by that grace. The church is maturing where it responds to grace with understanding, trust, and obedience.

The holiness of the church has carried two meanings. Sanctity has often meant to be set apart, to be separated, to be drawn out of the world for special relationship. The prophetic critique in the Old Testament transformed the notion of sanctity so that it came also to mean righteousness, that is, the realization of meaning through faithful love of, and service for, God. It is this dimension which must, once again, be firmly grasped and faithfully pursued.

Here the theme of eschatology becomes important. Caught within the polarity of the kingdom present and the kingdom coming, the Christian community lives upon the realized fullness of life in Christ even as it moves toward the further and continuous realization of the intended image of creation. Hence, the church can represent in her own life and order a model of the ultimate destiny of persons in the kingdom of God. Sanctity, as found within a community whose historical existence makes our existence meaningful, also points toward a community whose full actualization always lies ahead. The presence of God as Holy Spirit creates our meaningful present; the promise of God as Holy Spirit creates our hope of meaningful future.

There is sanctification in church life. Once again, such holiness exists upon the base of the gospel and lives with eschatological fulfillment and expectation. Sanctification is the embodiment of the realized and coming kingdom of God. The configuration of the congregation which lives with the presence and power of the Holy Spirit takes distinctive shape as persons become free in community and as community seeks to free persons in the surrounding society. Both of these dimensions—living a free and maturing life and enlarging the context for freedom and growth—are important for the full and responsible life of Christian persons who constitute the Body of Christ.

It is the task of the church to witness to, even as it partially embodies, freedom and justice. Christian communities must become the place of free space among persons in which people share God's power as they live openly with one another and as they attempt to extend the character of the kingdom of God into the larger common life.

The meaning of human life, we have claimed, is relational and such meaning is progressively realized as there is mutual acceptance, affirmation, and acclamation. But a more fundamental point must be reemphasized: human community is established upon the ground of divine-human relationship, and this theme is found expressed at the nexus of the biblical tradition in the covenant. It is the covenanting of God which creates community—with himself and among persons—and by perpetuation through community provides the possibility for authentic personhood.

Conclusion

If this proposed reinterpretation possesses significance, then it does respond as an answer to the major causes for the decline of the doctrine of sanctification, and may point a direction for a revivification of the doctrine within the Wesleyan tradition. Holiness, as we have defined it, is not a realized state of being or a condition of affairs; it is, rather, a continuously realized and a continuous challenge to realization of the gracious presence of the Holy Spirit: sanctification becomes a process of maturation in which life undergoes constant reshaping through the primacy of the commanding relationship with God. The notion of perfection is released from a narrow moralization and is clearly built upon the gospel of redemption which undergirds the innovative possibilities for discipleship. The notion of perfection can no longer be interpreted in radically individualistic terms, rather it is now understood in terms of community for only in such a context may persons actualize their freedom to be and their struggle for the freedom of others. And in all of this the freedom of the Holy Spirit is also honored.

Now we return to our original theme. Through the experience of sanctification, dispirited persons find new spirit as the Holy Spirit meets our spirits in nurturing engagement. Spirit-with-spirit we mature in those special ways which are given to each Christian person and every Christian community. In engagement by and with the Holy Spirit we recover the lost image of our creation.

Notes

1. This approach is differentiated from that of some other
    theologians. For instance, Paul Tillich in *Systematic
    Theology* (Chicago: University of Chicago, 1963), III,
    22, writes: "Without knowing what spirit is, one cannot
    know what Spirit is." We are provided with a more suc-
    cinct statement of this position by Wolfhart Pannenberg
    in an article, "The Working of The Spirit in the Creation
    and in the People of God," *Spirit, Faith, and Church*
    (Philadelphia: Westminster, 1970), pages indicated. Pan-
    nenberg argues, ". . . we have to deal with the universal
    meaning in the origin of all life before turning to the
    particular presence of the Spirit in the Christian com-
    munity." (14) The ecstatic element in life is denominated
    "spirit." (18) This ecstatic element does not belong to
    "the natural equipment of men" even though it is
    ubiquitously present as a possibility for persons. (22)
    The divine spirit is the divine power that makes persons
    alive and which draws persons into ecstatic self-trans-
    cending experiences, some of which may be perverse and
    others fulfilling of the self in its relation to God and
    other persons. (22) On the basis of this general presence
    of spirit it is possible for Pannenberg to characterize the
    special form of spiritual presence in the Christian com-
    munity: "The Christian community lives on the basis of
    the message of a new life, which is no longer separated
    from the spiritual origin of all life." (23)

    My reasons for preferring to move in the other direc-
    tion are (1) that the experience of the spirit is retro-
    spectively recognized after the dominant clarification
    effected by the experience of the Holy Spirit as the Spirit
    of Jesus Christ; (2) the view of human nature and its
    condition as fallen I take to be more radically perverting
    than Tillich or Pannenberg; (3) I do not believe that
    the human spirit is given its full integrity when it is
    defined as participant in, but not possessor of, spirit, as
    Pannenberg seems to indicate. Because of these reasons,
    it seems truer to Christian experience and theologically
    more adequate to begin with the special characterization
    of the Holy Spirit as the Spirit of Jesus Christ and then
    move to the implications of this revelation for the general
    presence of spirit in human life.

    Tillich, it should be noted, differs from Pannenberg in that
    he emphasizes that human self-transcendence must be met
    by revelation to actualize its full potential (*Systematic
    Theology*, III, 112); this is a dynamic interaction with
    which I agree and which I think is basically significant.
    But I have reversed the weight of the dynamic inter-
    action. There is a universal spirit-presence and human
    beings are continuously engaged by this spirit; however,

even this experience is known for what it is only after
there is the dominant definition by the Holy Spirit as
the Spirit of Jesus Christ.

2. "We are not organisms, but persons. The nexus of relations which unites us in a human society is not organic
but personal . . . The baby . . . is made to be cared for.
He is born into a love relationship which is inherently
personal . . . he depends for his existence . . . upon intelligent understanding, upon rational foresight . . . . He
can live only through other people and in dynamic relation with them. In virtue of this fact he is a person, for
the personal is constituted by the relation of persons. His
rationality is already present, though only germinally, in
the fact that he lives and can only live by communication." John MacMurray, *Persons In Relation* (New York:
Harper Brothers, 1961), pp. 46, 48, 51. Also, ". . . children are born potentially human, that is all; they are
smiled and talked into being actually so." Austin Farrar,
Faith and Speculation (London: Adam and Charles Black,
1967), p. 6.

3. Two assessments of the development of the doctrine of
sanctification are of enough interest to mention. R.W.
Dale remarked, "There was one doctrine of John Wesley's
—the doctrine of perfect sanctification—which ought to
have led to a great and original ethical development; but
the doctrine has not grown, it seems to remain where
John Wesley left it. There has been a want of genius or
the courage to attempt the solution of the immense practical questions which the doctrine suggests." (Quoted by
Thomas Jackson, *Wesley Bicentennial 1703-1903* [Middle-
ton, Conn.: Wesleyan University, 1904], pp. 72-73.) John
Kent has more recently commented, "The point about
Methodism, as has become clearer with the passage of
time, was that so far from being raised up to spread
scriptural holiness throughout the land, it might be said
with more truth to have been raised up in order to show
that scriptural holiness could not be spread throughout
the land." (Martin E. Marty and Dean G. Pearman, editors, "Problems of a Protestant Spirituality," *New Theology, No. 4,* [New York: Macmillan, 1967], p. 215.)
Each of these assessments is partial and therefore of
limited truth, but they point to generalizations which
must be taken seriously.

4. Edward H. Sugden, editor, *Wesley's Standard Sermons*
(London: Epworth, 1921), II, 148. See also "Christian
Perfection" and "The Scripture Way of Salvation," *Ibid.,*
pp. 147-177, 442-460; also, "A Plain Account of Christian
Perfection," Thomas Jackson, editor, *Wesley's Works,*
Third Edition (London: John Mason, 1830), XI, 366-
445. It may be helpful to quote a statement to clarify
the character of sanctification in Wesley's thought. Justi-

fication "is not the being made actually just and righteous. This is *sanctification*; which is indeed, in some degree, the immediate fruit of justification, but, nevertheless, is a distinct gift of God, and of a totally different nature. The one (justification) implies, what God does for us through his Son; the other (sanctification) what he works in us by his Spirit . . . in general use, they are sufficiently distinguished from each other . . ." *Wesley's Works,* V, p. 56.

5. For instance, see Wesley's sermon, "Christian Perfection," *op. cit.,* pp. 150-174. See James M. Gustafson, *Christ and the Moral Life* (New York: Harper and Row, 1968), pp. 61-115, for the best recent study of sanctification.

6. "The thought is not that the Father alone is the Creator, the Son alone Redeemer and the Holy Spirit alone Sanctifier. The creation and preservation of the universe, the atonement for sin and its forgiveness, resurrection from the dead and the gift of eternal life—all these are the operations of the one Divine majesty as such. Yet the Father is especially emphasized in the work of creation which proceeds originally from him as the first person; the Son is emphasized in the redemption he has accomplished in his own person; and the Holy Spirit in the peculiar work of sanctification, which is both his mission and revelation. Such distinction is made for the purpose of affording Christians the unqualified assurance that there is but one God and yet three persons in the one divine essence—truths the sainted fathers have faithfully gathered from the writings of Moses, the prophets and the apostles, and which they have maintained against all heretics." Martin Luther, *Epistle Sermon, Trinity Sunday* (Lenker Edition), Vol. IX, nos. 16-23.

7. Edward Shils has written, "Society has a centre . . . . This central zone impinges in various ways on those who live within the ecological domain in which the society exists . . . .

"The centre, or the central zone, is the phenomenon of the realm of values and beliefs. It is the centre of the order of symbols, of values and beliefs, which govern the society. It is the centre because it is the ultimate and irreducible; and it is felt to be such by many who cannot give explicit articulation to its irreducibility . . . .

"The centre is also a phenomenon of the realm of action. It is a structure of activities, of roles, of persons, within the network of institutions. It is in these roles that the values and beliefs which are central are embodied and propounded." "Centre and Periphery," *The Logic of Personal Knowledge: Essays Presented to Michael Polanyi* (London: Routledge & Kegan Paul, 1961), p. 117.

8. Albert C. Outler has offered a definition of sanctification: "Holiness, therefore, is humanity raised to its highest

power *by the Holy Spirit,* . . . ." "The Doctrine of the Holy Spirit," *New Theology,* p. 207.

9. See *The Tacit Dimension* (New York: Doubleday, 1966), pp. 57ff.

10. John Oman, *Grace and Personality* (London: Collins, 1960), second edition. This is a theological treatise of unusual importance and especially in its sensitive and meaningful exploration of the themes of dependence and independence in persons' relation to God. See especially chapters VII-XI. Oman does not, however, develop the communal aspects in an adequate fashion.

11. *The Philosophy of The Good Life* (London: John Murray, 1930), p. 198.

12. Colin Williams attempts a "reconstruction" of sanctification following the lead of Walter G. Muelder by stressing its social implications for ethical responsibility (cf., Colin W. Williams, *John Wesley's Theology Today.* New York: Abingdon, 1960, pp. 182, 189-90). The difference I am attempting to express goes beyond the isolated individual who then relates to society, to a re-understanding of Christians as necessarily a part of a community which possesses unique potential for the fulfillment of life.

13. Cf., Paul Tillich, *Systematic Theology,* III, p. 173.

Charismatic and Pentecostal Movements:
A Challenge to the Churches

Walter J. Hollenweger

I. History and Phenomenology

A. Origins [1]

The Pentecostal movement originated in the year 1906 in a simple black church in Los Angeles.[2] W. J. Seymour, the minister of the congregation, was a descendant of the African slaves who had been shipped to America.[3] The first Pentecostal meeting place was a disused Methodist chapel with sawdust strewn on the floor; the pews were planks resting on wooden boxes. The leader of this revival was no great orator. It was his custom to pray from behind his pulpit which consisted of two packing cases nailed together, his head bowed and his face covered with his hands, his elbows resting on the pulpit top.[4] Yet that congregation in Azusa Street, Los Angeles, was the starting point for a Pentecostal movement which today embraces between fifteen and thirty-five million members.[5] Seekers from all over the world flocked to Los Angeles and there they found "the well-spring of spiritual life" and received a decisive impulse toward their ministry. It was justly said by the English Anglican minister, the Reverend Alexander A. Boddy, that "it was unheard of for white preachers from the southern states to be so eager to visit Negroes in Los Angeles, to share fellowship with them and by their prayers and intercessions to receive the same blessings as they had received."[6] And Frank Bartleman, an eye-witness at that first revival, proudly affirmed that in Los Angeles "the color line was washed away in the blood."[7]

In the period which followed, the Pentecostal movement succeeded in becoming a church of the poor in

Africa, Latin America, and Indonesia, primarily because it worked *with* the poor. Often, though not in-
variably, its missionaries themselves belonged to the
poor. For the most part the young mission congregations were allowed to create their own liturgy, their
own congregational life, their own forms of theology.
This policy explains not only the rapid growth of
the Pentecostal movement but also the diversity of its
forms throughout the world; it justifies the statement
that the Pentecostal movement was already an ecumenical movement in itself, with all the difficulties and
promises this implies.

B. The Pentecostal movement as an ecumenical revival movement

It is also a fact that from the very beginning the
Pentecostal movement thought of itself as an ecumenical revival movement within the churches.[9] In the first
years Pentecostalists had no intention of organizing
themselves into a new denomination. They believed
that "the human religious organization was by its very
nature in conflict with the community of the living
God."[9] "God had brought us out of old, dead ecclesias-
ticism and denominationalism. He has made us a free
people and we are not going back into 'Babylon' any
more."[10] They regarded the old organized power structure of the church as Babylon and there was no question
of imitating it.

The time before the birth of the Pentecostal movement is accordingly painted in dark and hopeless colors
and in fact as "a Babylonian captivity of the church."[11]
Then came the miraculous liberation movement, the
Pentecostal communities, to put an end to all strife
within Christendom. Doctrinal barriers were to be
overcome not by an agreed doctrinal minimum but by
the abandonment of fixed doctrinal statements of any
kind. The bond was to be the presence of the living
God, the reality of the Holy Spirit, which people longed

to experience in conversion, sanctification, baptism by the Spirit, and the gifts of the Spirit. Expecting as they did the speedy return of Jesus, they saw no need for theological explanations and paid no heed to political and social issues. Our calling, they said, is not to preach problems, but the gospel, the good news of salvation. Prior to the return of Jesus on the clouds of heaven there was only one legitimate goal: the sanctification and unification of the children of God and the evangelization of the world within a generation.

With the delay of the Lord's return, the diversity of ethical and doctrinal views within the Pentecostalist movement made a minimum of agreed doctrine essential. Only a dwindling minority—among them leading German Pentecostalists[12]—resisted the temptation to organize a large free church which would count for something in church affairs. This minority remained faithful basically to the Quaker position, renouncing obligatory dogma and rejecting majority decisions. The majority adopted their dogmatics from the doctrinal arsenal of the last century. Many Pentecostal denominations, especially in America, accepted permanent forms of organization and drew up doctrinal statements, which inevitably provoked new protest movements within Pentecostalism.[13] The exclusion of non-preachers from the main church offices of the Assemblies of God inevitably resulted in the formation of a Pentecostal laymen's organization, the "Full Gospel Business Men's Fellowship International." In the older congregations, zeal for sanctification and evangelism weakened. Specialists became needed to implement religious programs, and preachers began to be trained. Questions of congregational organization, baptism, and religious instruction arose. Although the fiction of the universal priesthood is still maintained, in the older denominations we find the majority of churchgoers listening to services conducted by a minister with a small staff of full-timers and voluntary helpers. The Pentecostal service does indeed still allow scope for active participation in prayer, testimony, and singing, but the actual participation of the ordinary member in worship is no longer the rule in all denominations. Occasionally, therefore, voices are heard calling for the old Pentecostal ideal.

C. Typology

Theologically one can divide Pentecostalism into the following types:

1. *Pentecostals who teach a two-stage way of salvation.*

This includes far and away the largest number of organizations. Representatives of this group are the American and British Assemblies of God, the French Assemblées de Dieu, the Italian Assemblee di Dio, the German Arbeitsgemeinschaft der Christengemeinden, the British Elim Pentecostal Church, the Brazilian Congregação Cristã do Brazil, and many more. *Theologically* the majority of the Protestant wing of neo-Pentecostalism also belongs to this category.

2. *Pentecostals who teach a three-stage way of salvation.*

This group is represented by the Church of God (Cleveland) and its missionary churches, the Pentecostal Holiness Church, and many more.

3. *The "Jesus only" groups.*

These accept only the baptismal formula "in the name of Jesus" and are—wrongly, I think—called unitarians by the other Pentecostals. In fact, they teach something of a modalistic trinitarian doctrine. The most important representatives of this group are the United Pentecostal Church, many of the black Pentecostal churches in the USA (Pentecostal Assemblies of the World, for example), and almost the entire Indonesian Pentecostal Movement.

4. *Pentecostals with a Quaker, Reformed Lutheran, or Roman Catholic doctrine.*

With the exception of the Roman Catholic Pentecostals and the charismatic movement within the historic Protestant churches in Germany and France, this type is not, as might be expected, to be found principally in the neo-Pentecostal movement within the historic churches. On the contrary, the bulk of the Protestant wing of the neo-Pentecostal movement within existing churches in the USA belongs to type "1." On the other hand, almost the entire Chilean Pentecostal movement has a Methodist doctrine, the German Mülheim Association of Christian Fellowship has a Lutheran Reformed doctrine, and the Quaker Pentecostals in the USA (i.e., Pentecostal free churches with a Quaker tradition; not Quakers within the Society of Friends who have made a Pentecostal experience) have a Quaker doctrine.

5. *Pentecostal denominations of the Apostolic type.*

These groups have institutionalized the offices of apostle and prophet. In the early stages of the denomination, prophecy played a major role and the church was guided by it. The theory has not altered, although the practice seems less spontaneous at the present day. This type is represented by the different apostolic churches in Great Britain, Germany, Denmark, France, and the Gemeinde fur Urchristentum in Switzerland.

6. *Independent African Pentecostal churches.*

Some of these churches (like the Zionists in South Africa) were founded by early converts of Pentecostal missionaries, others (like the Aladura and Seraphim and Cherubim churches in West Africa) have had at some time a link with some American and British Pentecostal churches. Others again (like the Kimbanguists in the Congo) historically do not belong to the Pentecostal churches. Yet it can be argued that, through the close similarity of their spiritual phenomena (speak-

ing in tongues, prayer for the sick, participation of all
in the making of the liturgy, etc.), they are close
enough to be identified with Pentecostalism.

There is still another distinction to be made; it is the
one between *classical* or *historical* Pentecostalism and
neo-Pentecostalism (Kilian McDonnell). By classical
or historical Pentecostalism, McDonnell means the
Pentecostal denominations. By neo-Pentecostalism he
means the charismatic revival in the historic churches.
This distinction is very useful in Europe and America
but less precise in Africa.

D. Protestant neo-Pentecostalism in USA

The known origin of neo-Pentecostalism in the USA
was a revival in Van Nuys, California. A young Anglican couple had received the baptism of the Spirit with
speaking in tongues at an Alliance meeting. From then
on they surprised the vicar of their Anglican church by
tithing regularly—i.e., giving ten per cent of their
income to the church—and by vigorous participation
in church life. The vicar's one fear was that they were
in danger of becoming fanatics. To sober them down,
he introduced them to another ordinary couple. There-
upon, these too experienced the baptism of the Spirit.[14]
Through the Full Gospel Business Men's Fellowship
International and the Ministry of "Mr. Pentecost,"
David J. Du Plessis, the movement invaded all churches
in the USA and its growth has so far not yet reached
its peak.

Theologically most of them teach an experience of
the baptism of the Spirit (mostly, but not always, with
speaking in tongues). Most of them, but not all,[15] are
rather evangelical. But all of them want to stay within
their churches and try very hard to remain faithful
to their liturgy and theology. Although most of them
are politically rather conservative there are some very
remarkable political moves to be observed (Pulkingham
in Houston, Texas) which could well represent a real

alternative to the false polarization between evangelicals and ecumenicals in the USA.

E. Protestant neo-Pentecostals in Europe

In England, France, and Germany there is a neo-Pentecostal movement within the historical churches which has existed since 1910, although this is generally unknown.[16] Their representatives are Alexander A. Boddy[17] (1854-1930, an Anglican priest in England); the brothers Dallière[18] in France (Reformed pastors of the French Reformed Church); the brothers de Rougemont[19] in Switzerland (Swiss Reformed Church); Karl Ecke[20] (Lutheran pastor, Germany); C.A. Voget[21] (Reformed pastor, Germany), and Jonathan Paul,[22] a Lutheran pastor in Germany and founder of the German Pentecostal movement. Jonathan Paul, although ignored in the present-day discussion, is one of the most important men for our topic. He was the founder of the Mülheim Association of Christian Fellowship, a Pentecostal organization in Germany which includes communities within the established churches and Pentecostal free churches. They also practice infant baptism *and* believers' baptism. Furthermore, they are not fundamentalist. It is therefore not by chance that the leader of this organization, Christian Krust, was the first Pentecostal to address an Assembly of the World Council of Churches.[23]

Through the mediation of Arnold Bittlinger,[24] a newer neo-Pentecostal movement has been growing in Germany since the sixties. It is probably theologically the most articulate neo-Pentecostal movement in the world. Its representatives are well-versed in modern exegetical literature and argue their case on the basis of Hans Küng, Nikos Nissiotis, Ernst Käsemann, and Eduard Schweizer. They do not teach a baptism of the Spirit; they are not evangelicals in the narrow sense, and have within their ranks Catholic[25] and Orthodox[26] theologians.

The British neo-Pentecostals follow more or less the lines of Protestant USA neo-Pentecostals.[27]

F. Catholic neo-Pentecostalism [28]

In addition to the French and German Protestant neo-Pentecostals the Catholic neo-Pentecostals are theologically the most interesting. Since they are the least known of all and seem to be of great importance for the future, and also because groups are known to exist in almost all the European countries, they are treated here in somewhat more detail. One of the most articulate of these charismatic Catholic theologians is the Dominican, Simon Tugwell from Oxford. He has presented several meditations at the British Broadcasting Corporation, one of them including singing in tongues by three Catholic sisters which provoked several hundred letters of thanks to the BBC. It was prayerfully and meditatively prepared in the studio—of course to the dismay of the technicians who did not appreciate the purpose of this "waste" of valuable studio time and technical facilities, "just for meditation." The actual meditation was then done extemporaneously.

In several publications Tugwell has defended the use of speaking in tongues which appears to him "to mean the production of genuinely linguistic phenomena, which may or may not be identified by one present as some definite language, but which do not convey any ordinary semantic significance to the speaker himself."[29] It is not simply identical with "praying in the Spirit," nor is it simply "God's kindergarten." "Prayer which we cannot ourselves fully understand is an essential part of Christian praying: tongues is a particularly straightforward embodiment of this principle."[30] But it is—from a phenomenological point of view—ambiguous. That applies, says Tugwell, to all *pneumatic* activities. He concludes that the New Testament does not put pressure on anyone to seek the gift of tongues, but it encourages those who receive it to use it to grow into fuller and richer experience of the Christian life as a whole. Thus Tugwell suggests that this gift does have a part in the wholeness of the Christian life. "This does not in any way commit us to accepting the Pentecostal understanding of it, nor to their kind of religion."[31]

Tugwell, in fact, goes on to state that "the Pentecostal doctrine is scripturally and theologically unwarrantable"[32] and is for the theologian "cause for alarm." Yet he maintains that "Pentecostalism does represent a genuine eagerness for the original, undiluted message of the gospel which is 'not in words of persuasive wisdom, but in demonstration of Spirit and power.' (1 Corinthians 2:4) This too makes a legitimate demand on the theologian's interest and sympathy."[33] He rejects the notion that the baptism of the Spirit adds anything *more* to Christian faith. "Anything *more* than fundamental Christianity is actually *less* than the Gospel."[34] Thus the "supernatural" can be seen within an old Catholic tradition as "being precisely the fulfillment of our nature."[35]

Tugwell uses categories of medieval mysticism in order to interpret his and his fellow Catholics' spiritual experiences. Mysticism, he says, "is not intrinsically Christian, but it can be *made* Christian."[36] He differentiates between oracles and prophecy, between idols and icons. "An idol is a god, or a manifestation of god, or an experience of god, or a doctrine of god, that one has 'made a thing of.' " But "Christ is larger than his media of communication."[37] Prophecy and icon "strip us down before God, peeling off our masks and pretences, our false selves,"[38] while those using oracles and idols always try to get power over God, showing thereby how right they are. Tugwell knows, of course, that definitions and names (also a kind of idol) are sometimes necessary for our sanity, but they never

capture God adequately. Only "when we have overcome" (Revelation 2:17) shall we find our full identity; only then will there be full correspondence between
the reality of the experience of God and its definition.
That is why Tugwell sees *no phenomenological* difference between Christian and non-Christian mysticism,
between oracle and prophecy, between idol and icon.
The difference does not lie on the level of phenomenol-
ogy, but in that of signification. From outside, both
these mysticisms look exactly alike. Only by its function, when it creates room for freedom, does mysticism
become Christian. From this Tugwell draws the conclusion that in a charismatic community there must be
freedom for speaking in tongues and extemporaneous
prayer, and also freedom for abstaining from such
kinds of spirituality without losing face.

So one comes to the somewhat astonishing conclusion
that the Dominican Tugwell has so far developed the
"most evangelical" understanding of *charisma,* i.e., an
understanding which rests on the plurality and freedom
of the Spirit, a thought which has been expressed by
Protestant and Catholic theologians simultaneously.
One of them, G. Hasenhüttl,[39] a student of Hans
Küng, describes *"charisma"* as "the ordering principle
of the church." Hasenhüttl, who dedicates his book
"to those who have left the church or are about to
leave it," works on the basis of a very careful exegesis.
He believes the World Council of Churches' study,
"The Church for Others," with its remarkable re-order-
ing of the structures of the church, should be defined
in terms of *charisma* (and not, as is usually the case,
the other way 'round!). Yet in his book he never
mentions the Catholic Pentecostals, although they
would perhaps be examples for his scholarly work.
The dialogue between those who "think" the Holy
Spirit and those who "hear" and "touch" the Holy

Spirit in their charismatic meetings is probably still missing!

G. The ecumenical significance of Catholic Pentecostals

1. The prayer meetings of the Catholic Pentecostals shattered the "economic-deprivation" theory that had customarily been set forth as an "explanation" of the older, classical Pentecostalism. It was not the uneducated, but the intellectuals, not the uncritical but the critical exegetes, not frustrated Puritans but quite normal Christians who took part in these meetings. There is not only speaking in tongues but critical discussion of theological and social problems; not only the singing of hymns, but the composition of hymns; not only praying, but eating, drinking, and smoking.[40] It is possible to laugh and weep, to clap hands—and also to leave the room (without being disqualified!) when one does not like this style.[41] The Jesuit Sudbrack, therefore, sees Pentecostal spirituality in relation to Harvey Cox's *Feast of Fools*.[42] Political and social topics are not excluded from their discussions. "The prayer meeting is not an end in itself, but its point is to build a mature community of Christians."[43] Since the autumn of 1971 they have experimented with commune-like communities.[44]

2. The Catholic Pentecostal movement has developed its own ecumenical momentum. It is true that it was only possible against the background of the Second Vatican Council, but the Catholic Pentecostals have translated this into the scope of experience of the *local congregation*. Here *oikoumene* is not discussed but lived (including its financial aspect). The Catholics accept the fact that this revival has its roots outside the Catholic Church. In spite of the fact that O'Connor does not allow any doubts about his Catholic orthodoxy, he answers the question whether it is thinkable that the Holy Spirit be more at work in the classical

Pentecostal churches than in that church which generally has been accepted to be the most authentic church, as follows: "This may be God's way of demonstrating to members of the Church that he alone is sovereign Lord, and that all institutions and hierarchs on earth, even in the Church, are nothing but instruments and ministers .... We need to have it demonstrated for us that God's action transcends the action of the church ...."[45]

3. In contrast to the Pentecostal revival sixty years ago within the Protestant churches, and the occasional social disqualifications within Protestant neo-Pentecostalism, the Bishops' Conference of the Catholic Church in the USA has rather friendly relations with Catholic Pentecostalism. It affirms that the movement has theologically legitimate reasons for its existence and rests on a solid biblical basis. There are abuses here and there, but the movement as a whole should not be hindered. "Prudent priests" should accompany the groups and help them to maintain the impetus which they have received from the historical Pentecostal churches without adopting their mistakes.[46] Understandably an observer mockingly criticizes the bishops[47] who prefer "tamed charismatics" to the revolutionary Berrigans.[48] Yet a much better informed specialist says that the charismatic groups and political movements, like "Black Power," are not opponents but should be seen as belonging to the same "movements of social transformation."[49]

II. Pentecostal Contribution to the Church Universal

Besides the obvious gifts which Pentecostal spirituality has to contribute (participation of everybody in the liturgy, a liturgy in the making,[50] involvement of the *whole* person in worship), and on top of the already mentioned ecumenical significance of Pentecostal spirituality, it has a far-reaching potential for alternatives in social theory and theology.

Let me begin with the latter, *the Pentecostals' contribution to theological study*.[51] In spite of the range of doctrinal differences there is in the Pentecostal movement something like a worldwide sense of belonging together. This means that the Pentecostal *oikoumene* is based not on printed and defined doctrine but on shared experience, namely, on the Pentecostal mode of communication transcending all barriers of education, color, social class, and nationality.[52] Taken seriously this offers a real possibility of discovering a methodology of theology in an *oral* culture where the medium of communication is—just as in biblical times—not the definition, but the description; not the statement, but the story; not the doctrine, but the testimony; not the book but the parable; not the *summa theologica* but the song; not the treatise but the television program. Whoever denies that one can do proper theology in these categories will have to prove that the Bible is not a theological book. Our way of doing theology is a culturally biased form (yet necessarily so, in our culture!). There are other equally relevant forms of doing theology. Pentecostalism offers raw material and elements for such an alternative methodology. How that works in detail I have described elsewhere.[53] One thing is absolutely sure: If theology wants to be universal (and it has to be by definition), then it has to be able to transcend the boundaries of literary culture. Only a theological method which gives equal theological weight to a parable, a dance, a song, a mime, a statement, or a definition meets the requirements of being ecumenical and universal. The ecumenical problem of the future will not be the discussion between the Catholics and the Protestants (this is a minor problem from an international point of view) but whether a dialogue will take place between the oral and the

literary theologians. This problem is increased because
oral theologians are mostly (but not always) poor and
black; literary theologians are mostly (but not always)
white and rich. I venture to say that this culture difference is as important as the economic one. Since a
great proportion of Pentecostals (not all—some, particularly the older denominations, have been "adapted"
and tamed by their Christian entourage) belong to
this oral culture, they are of vital importance for this
dialogue. That also explains why genuine, independent
Pentecostal churches (not the missionary-based Pentecostal churches; they have the same problems as other
churches) do not find it difficult to finance their own
programs and to train their own pastors. Since they
rejected the importation of a foreign and much too
expensive church organization from Europe and America with a university-based theological education, they
had to invent their own educational schemes. It was
a theological education in context, *"en la calle"* as the
Chileans say, based on the region in which they live
and without cutting them off from their secular work.

The *consequences for the development programs*
have been grasped only by very few people although
the results are obvious to everybody. The self-help
programs of the Kimbanguists in the Congo[54] or the
Indian Pentecostals in Mexico[55] may look primitive to
an expert of UNO or Christian Aid, but the advantage
is that they have invented the programs themselves.
They have financed them themselves. They do not depend on foreign skill, personnel or spare parts. They
have become aware of their own dignity. There is a
process of democratization in their worship services.
All of this has consequences for the structures of their
social and political life which go far beyond the influence of some so-called pressure groups which are often
just a new form of foreign ideology based on some
middle-class bourgeois groups. The latter's revolution

is by and large a paper revolution and will be reactionary in the long run, because it can never cope with the overwhelming technical means of any internal or external colonial power.

III. What Are Their Weaknesses?

The greatest weakness of the Pentecostal movement is that it is not aware of the potential power of its pluralistic approach. Pentecostals have so far not been able to present their experience other than in the very unsuitable categories of the rationalism of the last century. That is why their writings are, except where they are descriptive, so boring. Instead of developing a theological language which would meet their experience, they have borrowed *our* theological language which of course is a foreign language to them and which they will almost always handle less well than our experts. Nevertheless, there are exceptions to this, too.

Pentecostals try to win the fundamentalists and evangelicals to their cause. But these have proved so far the most stubborn antagonists to Pentecostalism. The modern charismatic movement has *not* broken into the evangelical churches but into the middle-of-the-road churches and into the Catholic church. That would call for a change of policy among Pentecostals. *Their friends are not where they expect them.*

The most difficult point of Pentecostal theology is, astonishingly, their pneumatology. Contrary to what one would expect, they have not developed a pneumatology which would match their experience. The pneumatology of Eduard Schweizer, Ernst Käsemann, Hans Küng, and others, is nearer to the Pentecostal experience than that of the Pentecostals themselves. The Pentecostal doctrine of the baptism of the Spirit can be seen as *one* possible way of describing the Spirit, but within the pluralistic framework of the New Testament there are others. Pentecostals upgrade Luke's approach to be *the* biblical theory although that is in contradiction to their own experience. The majority of Chilean Pentecostal pastors do not speak in tongues. In most Pentecostal congregations a great proportion, sometimes half, of the membership do not speak in tongues. That a Pentecostal doctrine of the baptism of the Spirit must create untold hardship and difficulties in such a situation is clear, not to speak of the difficulties it creates in relation to other churches. In my opinion the best criticism of Pentecostalism was formulated by a teacher of classical Pentecostalism, the British Bible teacher, Donald Gee (1891-1966),[56] who was for many years the leader of the British Assemblies of God. Already in 1962 he wrote to his "new Pentecostal friends," the neo-Pentecostals: "Many of you are trained theologians with a good academic background. Do not, now that you have tasted spiritual gifts, become fanatical in your repudiation of consecrated scholarship. Let the Spirit of truth set it all on fire and use it for the glory of God. Some of us in our early folly set a premium upon ignorance."[57] In my view, the balanced criticism of this Pentecostal has not been taken seriously enough, as can be seen from the fact that most of his critical writings have not been reprinted or translated. Those interested in a detailed criticism of Pentecostalism (classical and neo-Pentecostalism) will find the writings of this extraordinary Pentecostal teacher most rewarding.

In conclusion, this chapter suggests that the contribution of the Pentecostals must be taken seriously at the level where they are at their best, namely in their ability to create alternatives for theological education (education in the street, through apprenticeship, particularly in the Third World), alternatives for development programs, and liturgies which offer the possibility for congregational participation. On the other hand, it is my conviction that the systematic and rationalizing categories which they use in order to describe their activities fall short of conveying what they are actually doing. This might suggest that for the description of an un-systematic, or perhaps trans-systematic, reality, we might have to develop categories which are nearer to the narrative style of the Bible (or the modern writers), than to the Greek philosophers and the fundamentalist theoreticians.

Notes

Important Terms

Classical or historical Pentecostals: Those Pentecostals who are organized in denominations like the Assemblies of God and others.

Neo-Pentecostals: Those Pentecostals who belong to a Protestant or Catholic church.

Baptism in the Spirit: A religious crisis experience subsequent to and different from conversion; mostly, but not always, identified with speaking in tongues.

Speaking in tongues: A meditative, non-rational form of prayer, wrongly confused by non-specialists with ecstatic experiences; highly valued by Paul for private prayer, (1 Corinthians 14:4, 39) but regulated for liturgical use. (1 Corinthians 14:27) It sounds as if somebody has turned on the radio and picked up a broadcaster whose language he does not understand. Whether tongues are actual languages or not is controversial but irrelevant.

Abbreviations

PGG (German) Walter J. Hollenweger, *Enthusiastisches Christentum: Die Pfingstbewegung in Geschichte und Gegenwart* Zurich and Wuppertal, 1969.

PGG (English) —————, *The Pentecostals.* Minneapolis, Minnesota and London, 1972. French (*Le Pentecôtisme,* Geneva and Yaoundé, 1975) and Spanish versions (*El Pentecostalismo,* Buenos Aires, 1974) in preparation.

Handbuch —————, *Handbuch der Pfingstbewegung,* 10 Vols., 1965-67. Xerox and microfilm copies available from ATLAS, Board of Microtexts, Library of the Yale Divinity School, New Haven, Connecticut, USA. This is the most complete collection of Pentecostal documents, addresses, statistics, etc.

Notes

1. Some of the standard works: PGG (German, English, French, and Spanish; the different versions are not identical in content)—Handbuch—Nils Bloch-Hoell, *Pinsebevegelsen. En undersøkelse av pinsebevegelsens tilblivelse, utvikkling og saerpreg med saerlig henblikk på*

bevegelsens utforming i Norge, Oslo, 1956; abridged and revised English version: *The Pentecostal Movement: Its Origin, Development and Distinctive Character,* London, 1964; B.R. Wilson, *Sects and Society,* London, 1961; John T. Nichol, *Pentecostalism,* New York, 1966; Plainfield, New Jersey, 1972; Vinson Synan, *The Holiness-Pentecostal Movement in the United States,* Grand Rapids, Michigan, 1971; Arthur Sundstedt, *Pingstväckelsen—dess uppkomst och första utvecklingsskede,* 5 Vols. planned, Normans Forlag, 1969ff.; W.J. Hollenweger, (ed) *Die Pfingstkirchen. Selbstdarstellungen Dokumente, Kommentare.* Stuttgart, 1972; Paul Fleisch, *Die Pfingstbewegung in Deutschland. Ihr Wesen und ihre Geschichte in fünfzig Jahren,* Hanover, 1957.

2. There were some Pentecostal outbreaks in the USA before Los Angeles (Charles Parham in Topeka and the beginnings of the Church of God, Cleveland). Yet, with the exception of the different Churches of God, almost all Pentecostal groups in the USA can be traced back to Los Angeles.

3. A special area, which cannot be treated here, are the Black Pentecostals in the USA. On this, see V. Synan, *op. cit.,* passim; W.J. Hollenweger, *Black Pentecostal Concept,* June, 1970, WCC Geneva—PGG (English and German), passim; A.M. Brazier, *Black Self-Determination: The Story of the Woodlawn Organization,* Grand Rapids, Michigan, 1969; Luther P. Gerlach and Virginia Hine, *People, Power, Change: Movements of Social Transformation,* Indianapolis and New York, 1970; W. J. Hollenweger, "Pentecostalism and Black Power," *Theology Today,* Vol. 30, No. 3, October, 1973, pp. 28-45, *Handbuch,* 02a.

4. Best interpretation of the difficult sources in Bloch-Hoell, *op. cit.,* p. 38, note 99. Sources in Hollenweger, *Black Pentecostal Concept.*

5. Uncertainty on statistics is because many Pentecostal denominations do not care for exact numbers, and because a considerable number of large Pentecostal denominations are not known since they do not have any connection with a missionary society. Furthermore, researchers are not sure as to which denominations should be called "Pentecostal." I have proposed to call a church "Pentecostal" when it teaches at least *two* subsequent and different crisis experiences in the life of a believer, the second being usually—but not always—characterized by speaking in tongues. I am not very consistent in this as some of the most interesting Pentecostals (Simon Tugwell, Jonathan Paul, Louis Dalliére, and others), who are usually included in Pentecostalism, do not fit this definition.

6. Alexander A. Boddy, "Ueber Land und Meer," *Pfingst-*

grüsse Vol. 5, No. 8, November 24, 1912, p. 63. This is a translation from an early issue of the British Pentecostal periodical, *Confidence,* which I have so far not been able to find.

7. Frank Bartleman, *What Really Happened at "Azusa Street"?* (ed., John Walker), Los Angeles, 1962, p. 29.

8. Cf., the statement of the German Pentecostal minister, Christian Krust, at the Fourth General Assembly of the WCC in Uppsala: "The Pentecostal movement . . . originally hoped to become an ecumenical movement. This hope has not been fulfilled." (Christian Krust, "Pentecostal Churches and the Ecumenical Movement," in N. Goodall (ed.), *The Uppsala Report 1968,* Geneva, 1968, p. 343).

9. A. Reichenbach, "Sind wir deshalb eine Sekte?" *Verheissung des Vaters* (Zurich), Vol. 55, No. 10, October, 1962, p. 5.

10. E.S. Williams, "Forty-Five Years of Pentecostal Revival," *Pentecostal Evangel* (Springfield, Missouri, 1945), August 19, 1951, 3f.

11. G. G. Kulbeck, *What God Hath Wrought: A History of the Pentecostal Assemblies of Canada,* Toronto, 1958, p. 24.

12. PGG (English), pp. 231-243; PGG (German), pp. 216-230; W.J. Hollenweger, " 'Touch' and 'Think' the Spirit. Some aspects of the European charismatic movement," in a forthcoming collection edited by Russ Spittler (Plainfield, New Jersey, 1974); Christian Krust, *50 Jahre deutsche Pfingstbewegung Mülheimer Richtung.* Altdorf bei Nürnburg, 1958; Idem, *Was wir glauben, lehren und bekennen.* Altdorf bei Nürnburg, 1963; W.E. Failing, "Neue charismatische Bewegung in den Landeskirchen," in W.J. Hollenweger (ed.), *Die Pfingstkirchen,* pp. 131-145.

13. A recent example are the Jesus People. Most of their leaders in the USA are former ministers or members of Pentecosal churches. Best "history:" R.M. Enroth, E.E. Ericson, C.B. Peters, *The Story of the Jesus People. A Factual Survey.* Grand Rapids, Michigan, and Exeter, 1972.

14. PGG (English, pp. 3-20 and passim)—The literature is legion. A selection: Ivar Lundgren, *Ny Pingst: Rapport från en nutida väckelse i gamla kyrkor.* Den Kristna Bokringer, 1970; Don Basham, *A Handbook on Holy Spirit Baptism,* Monroeville, Pennsylvania, 1969; M.R. Carothers, *Prison to Praise,* Plainfield, New Jersey, 1970; D.J. Du Plessis, *The Spirit Bade Me Go,* Plainfield, New Jersey, n.d.; J.L. Sherrill, *They Speak With Other Tongues,* Spire Books, 1964; Larry Christenson, *Speaking in Tongues and its Significance for the Church,* London, 1968; D.J. Bennett, *Nine O'Clock in the Morning,* Plain-

field, New Jersey and London, 1970. Periodical: *Logos* (Plainfield, New Jersey). Extensive bibliography in, W.J. Hollenweger, *New Wine in Old Wineskins; Protestant and Catholic Neo-Pentecostalism,* Gloucester: Fellowship Press, 1973.

15. Morton Kelsey, *Tongue Speaking: An experiment in spiritual experience.* New York, 1964; J. Rodman Williams, *The Era of the Spirit,* Plainfield, New Jersey, 1971.

16. More on this in my essay mentioned, note 12.

17. Handbuch, 07.150.001 (Lit). "There is just as much danger sooner or later for a 'Pentecostal Church' (so called) as for any of the churches that have risen or fallen." (A.A. Boddy, "Unity, not Uniformity," *Confidence,* March, 1911, quoted by Boch-Hoell, *op. cit.,* p. 210)

18. Louis Dallière, *D'aplomb sur la parole de Dieu,* Valence, 1932—Handbuch, 07.334.001—French version of PGG in detail.

19. PGG (see index) and Handbuch, 08.211.001, 05.28.048, 08.212.001.

20. Karl Ecke, *Schwenckfeld, Luther und der Gedanke einer apostolischen Reformation,* Berlin, 1911; abridged 2nd edition: *Kaspar Schwenckfeld. Ungelöste Geistesfragen der Reformationszeit,* Gütersloh, 1952; revised 3rd edition: *Fortsetzung der Reformation. Kaspar von Schwenkfelds Schau einer apostolischen Reformation,* ed. by H.D. Gruschka in connection with the Schwenckfeld Library, Pennsylvania, Memmingen, 1965; Idem, *Der Durchbruch des Urchristentums seit Luthers Reformation: Lesestücke aus einem vergessenen Kapitel der Kirchengeschichte,* Altdorf/Nbg., 1952, 2nd ed. n.d.; Idem, *Die Pfingstbewegung: Ein Gutachten von kirchlicher Seite.* Mülheim/Ruhr, 1950; Idem, *Sektierer oder wertvolle Brüder? Randglossen zu einem Sektenbuch,* Mülheim/Ruhr, 1951; Idem, *Der reformierende Protestantismus: Streiflichter auf die Entwicklung lebendiger Gemeinde von Luther bis heute.* Gütersloh, 1952; Idem (together with O.S. von Bibra), *Die Reformation in neuer Sicht,* Altdorf/Nbg., 1952.

21. Handbuch, 08.543.001.

22. Ernst Giese, *Pastor Jonathan Paul, ein Knecht Jesu Christi: Leben und Werk,* Altdorf/Nbg., 1964. Further literature in Handbuch, 08.097 and in PGG (index).

23. Above, note 8.

24. Arnold Bittlinger, *Im Kraftfeld des Heiligen Geistes: Gnadengaben und Dienstordnungen im Neuen Testament,* Marburg a.d. Lahn, 1968; Idem, *Gifts and Graces: A Commentary on 1 Corinthians 12-14,* London, 1967.

25. Articles by Paul Verghese and Bishop Johannes in, R.F. Edel (ed.), *Kirche und Charisma: Die Gaben des Heiligen Geistes im Neuen Testament, in der Kirchengeschichte und in der Gegenwart.* Marburg a.d.Lahn, 1966. Period-

icals: *Aion* (Great Britain) and *Logos* (Ft. Wayne, Indiana, not to be confused with the periodical *Logos* which is published at Plainfield, New Jersey).

26. Wilhelm Schamoni and Eugen Mederlet in, R.F. Edel (ed.), *op. cit.*

27. Michael Harper, *As at the Beginning,* London, 1965 (and many more books published by the Fountain Trust, London). Periodical: *Renewal* (London).

28. Extensive bibliography in, W.J. Hollenweger, *New Wine in Old Wineskins.* A few important publications: K. Ranaghan, *Catholic Pentecostals,* New York, 1969; Ernst Benz, *Der Heilige Geist in Amerika,* Düsseldorf, 1970; Messlingberd Ford, "Toward a Theology of 'Speaking in Tongues,'" *Theol. Studies* Vol. 32, 1971, pp. 3-29; Virginia H. Hine, "Pentecostal Glossalalia. Toward a Functional Interpretation," *Journal for the Scientific Study of Religion* Vol 8, No. 2, 1969, pp. 211-226 (Lit.); Kilian McDonnell, *Catholic Pentecostalism: Problems in Evaluation,* Watchung, New Jersey, 1971; A. Bittlinger and K. McDonnell, *The Baptism in the Holy Spirit as an Ecumenical Problem,* Notre Dame, Indiana, 1972; Donald L. Gelpi, *Pentecostalism. A Theological Viewpoint,* New York, 1971; Edward O'Connor, *The Pentecostal Movement in the Catholic Church,* Notre Dame, Indiana, 1971; Francis A. Sullivan, "The Pentecostal Movement," *Gregorianum* Vol. 53, No. 2, 1972, pp. 238-265. Periodical: *New Covenant* (Ann Arbor, Michigan). There exists also vast French and Spanish literature (see W.J. Hollenweger, *New Wine in Old Wineskins).*

29. Simon Tugwell, "The Gift of Tongues in the New Testament," *Expository Times,* Vol. 84, No. 5, February, 1973, p. 137.

30. *Ibid.,* p. 139.

31. *Ibid.,* p. 137.

32. Simon Tugwell, "Reflections on the Pentecostal Doctrine of 'Baptism in the Holy Spirit,'" *Heythrop Journal,* Vol. 13, No. 3, July 1972, p. 268. Such and similar statements evoked the protest of Michael Harper. See his review on S. Tugwell in *Renewal,* Vol. 39, June-July, 1972, p. 8.

33. *Ibid.,* p. 269.

34. *Ibid.,* p. 280.

35. Simon Tugwell, *Did You Receive the Spirit?* London, 1972, p. 18.

36. *Ibid.,* p. 94.

37. *Ibid.,* p. 95.

38. *Ibid.,* p. 98.

39. G. Hasenhüttl, *Charisma: Ordnungsprinzip der Kirche,* Herder, 1969.

40. Descriptions of meetings in, Ranaghan, *Catholic Pentecostals;* O'Connor, *Pentecostal Movement;* and Ernst Benz, *Der Heilige Geist in Amerika.*

41. Tugwell, *Did You Receive the Spirit?*, p. 18.
42. Josef Sudbrack, "Streiflichter des nordamerikanischen Christentums," *Geist und Leben,* Vol. 43, No. 5, November, 1970, pp. 369-387.
43. *An Introduction to the Catholic Charismatic Renewal.* Communication Center, Notre Dame, Indiana, n.d., p. 10.
44. Stephen Clark, *Building Christian Communities: Strategy for Renewing the Church,* Notre Dame, Indiana, 1972; John Connor, "Covenant Communities: A New Sign of Hope," *New Covenant,* Vol. 1, No. 10, April, 1972, pp. 2-9; Max Delespesse, *Church Community: Leaven and Life Style,* Notre Dame, Indiana, 1972; "Families and Community Life," in, *New Covenant* Vol. 1, No. 6, December, 1972, pp. 6-8. On the influence on the convents: Sr. Cyprian, "I Will Pour Out My Spirit On All Flesh," *New Covenant,* Vol. 1, No. 9, March, 1972, pp. 2-5; Sr. Florette Amyot, "What is the Spirit Saying to Religious Today?" *ibid.,* pp. 6-8; Sr. Mary Reddy, "A Gate: Through Which Many May Pass to Jesus," *ibid.,* pp. 10-13, 21.
45. O'Connor, *Pentecost in the Catholic Church,* Watchung, New Jersey, 1971, p. 28; Ranaghan, *Catholic Pentecostals,* p. 153.
46. Quoted in O'Connor, *Pentecostal Movement,* pp. 291-93.
47. Catholic Pentecostalism finds support from Pope Paul (*Fatti Attenzione,* October 12, 1966, quoted J. Byrne, *Threshold of God's Promise,* Notre Dame, Indiana, 1971, p. 1), Cardinal Suenens "Cardinal Suenens on the Charismatic Renewal," *New Covenant,* Vol. 2, No. 1, July, 1972, pp. 6f.), and from well-known theologians (Karl Rahner, "Meditation on the Renewal of Priestly Ordination," *New Covenant,* Vol. 1, No. 12, June, 1972, pp. 8f.; Gregory Baum, "Ordination: On the Charismatic Renewal" *ibid.,* pp. 12f., p. 23) and from some of the American bishops: Joseph McKinney, "An Open Letter to Priests," *ibid.,* p. 11; Idem, "The Bishops, Atlanta, 1972," *ibid.,* pp. 10f.; Josef Hogan, "Charismatic Renewal in the Catholic Church: An Evaluation," *ibid.,* Vol. 1, No. 3, September, 1971, pp. 2-5; H.S. Cohen, "Contacts with Bishops in New Orleans," *ibid.,* p. 6; Hugh Beahan, "Interview with Bishop Joseph McKinney," *ibid.,* pp. 10-15; Stephen A. Leven, "What I Want for the Catholic Pentecostal Movements," *New Covenant,* Vol. 1, No. 5, November, 1971, pp. 24f.; E.E. Plowman ("Catholics Get the Spirit," *Christianity Today,* July 16, 1971) gives a more critical picture of the attitude of the Catholic bishops toward the charismatic renewal.
48. Karl Weber, "Katholische Pfingstbewegung in Amerika," *Orientierung,* Vol. 36, No. 7, April 15, 1972, pp. 84-86.
49. L.P. Gerlach and V.H. Hines, *People, Power, Change.*
50. On this see: W.J. Hollenweger, "The Social and Ecu-

menical Significance of Pentecostal Liturgy," *Studia Liturgica,* Vol. 8, No. 4, 1971-72, pp. 207-215.

51. On this see: Harding Meyer, "Die Pfingstbewegung in Brasilien" in, *Die Evangelische Diaspora: Jahrbuch des Gustav-Adolfvereins,* Vol. 39, 1968, pp. 9-50; Abdalazais de Moura, *Importancia das Igrejas Pentecostais para a Igreja Catholica,* Recife (duplicated typescript from the author, Rua Jiriquiti 48, Boa Vista, Recife); Idem, "O Pentecostalismo como fenômeno religioso popular no Brasil," *Revista Eclesiástica Brasileira,* Vol. 31, No. 121, March, 1971, pp. 78-94.

52. Most Pentecostals do not see the situation like this. They distinguish two crisis experiences in the life of a believer. The second is usually identified by speaking in tongues. This theory of the two experiences is found by Pentecostals in particular in the Lukan writings of the New Testament. The special characteristics of the Lukan pneumatology have been excellently set forth by Eduard Schweizer in his article in Kittel's *Dictionary to the New Testament.* Luke's particular interest in the Holy Spirit is clear from the very fact that the word *pneuma* as a designation of the divine Spirit occurs in his gospel three times as often as in Mark. The first twelve chapters of Acts provide the most frequent use of the term in this sense, with thirty-seven occurrences (E. Schweizer, art. *"Pneuma," Theol. Dict. of the New Testament,* Grand Rapids, Michigan, Vol. VI, 1968, pp. 332-451). Luke, who was not himself an apostle, appeals, as he expressly states, (Luke 1:1-4) to oral and written tradition. His editorial procedure is clear from one especially interesting passage where he cites verbatim from Matthew. (Matthew 7:11) His interest in the Holy Spirit is clear from his substitution of the words "Holy Spirit" for Matthew's "good things." The good thing which the heavenly Father wishes to give to those who ask him for it is, according to Luke, the Holy Spirit. Luke places this saying in a context different from that in Matthew, making it the conclusion of the parable of the Friend at Midnight. This is a way of saying we must ask for the Holy Spirit. Luke also distinguishes between the receiving of **salvation** and the receiving of the Spirit (contra J.D.G. **Dunn,** *Baptism in the Holy Spirit: A Re-examination of the New Testament Teaching on the Gift of the Spirit in Relation to Pentecostalism Today,* London, 1970; and F.D. Bruner, *A Theology of the Holy Spirit. The Pentecostal Experience and the New Testament Witness,* Grand Rapids, Michigan, 1970). According to Luke you can be a Christian without having received the Spirit. For Luke, as for the Pentecostalists, the Spirit is something additional to salvation. For example, the Samaritan Christians believed and had been baptized. Who but Luke and the Pentecostalists

would say of such Christians: "The Holy Spirit had not yet fallen on any of them but they had only been baptized in the name of the Lord Jesus"? (Acts 8:16) According to Luke, the reception of the Spirit is visibly marked by external signs, usually but not always including speaking in tongues. "Now when Simon *saw* that the Spirit was given through the laying on of the apostles' hands . . . ." (Acts 8:18) According to Luke, Paul had still to receive the laying on of hands *after* he had already encountered Christ. (Acts 9) How did Peter tell that Cornelius had received the Spirit? By his faith? By his love? By his fruits? Not at all! According to Luke Cornelius was already a devout man who feared God. Peter recognized Cornelius' reception of the Holy Spirit by his speaking in tongues. (Acts 10:46) The same is repeated in Acts 15. As a sign that the Gentiles had become believers Peter speaks of the fact that "God who knows the heart bore witness to them, giving them the Holy Spirit just as he did to us." (15:8) The Christians at Ephesus are not asked: Have you come to believe in Christ? Have you grown in faith, patience, and doctrine? The important question is: "Did you receive the Holy Spirit when you believed?" (Acts 19:2) This reception of the Holy Spirit can refer only to what then follows: "The Holy Spirit came on them; and they spoke with tongues and prophesied." (Acts 19:6) Schweizer sums up his account of Luke's pneumatology as follows: "The peculiarity of Luke's testimony lies in its demonstration that a Church which has no special power to fulfill its missionary task is a Church without the Spirit." According to Luke, the *believing person who prays* receives the Holy Spirit; according to Paul—as we shall see—*prayer and faith are a consequence* of the work of the Spirit.

Unlike Luke, Paul recognizes manifestations which are not distinguished by any extraordinary features. He differs from the Corinthians in including among the gifts of the Spirit: service, (Romans 12:7, 1 Corinthians 12:5) leadership, (Romans 12:8) mercy, (Romans 12:8) liberality, (Romans 12:8) and even being single or being married. (1 Corinthians 7:7) Yet Paul thanks God he speaks in tongues more than the Corinthians. (1 Corinthians 14:18) Nor is he any stranger to visionary experience. (2 Corinthians 12:2) He does not assign any priority to the exceptional as opposed to the normal or vice versa. "The greatest and most important gift is always the one which is most needed at any given time" (A. Bittlinger, in, R.F. Edel (ed.), *Die Bedeutung der Gnadengaben für die Gemeinde Jesu Christi,* Marburg, 1964, pp. 5-18), i.e., the gift most likely to serve the common good. (1 Corinthians 12:7) Paul makes a radical break with the notion that the exceptional (i.e., the supernatural) is the divine. For Paul there are no phenomena which because of their strangeness are nearer to God. But their strangeness, their unrational character, does not mean that they are nearer to the devil either. For Paul the criteria to be applied are: where faith is born and trust in oneself is conquered, where Christ is allowed to be Lord and where the body of Christ is edified, there is the Spirit. For Paul, the Spirit is not something additional to faith; this is where he differs from Luke.

Summa: The quarrel between Pentecostals and reformation-based theologians is an *inner-canonical quarrel.* A great deal has been written about the relationship between the Pauline and Lukan pneumatologies. In my view, they are not fundamentally contradictory, nor need we try to harmonize them in a system. Pentecostalists who presuppose that the Bible is a unified system solve the difficulty here by positing two modes of the Spirit's operation: a primary mode, essential for regeneration (the Pauline view), and a secondary mode, providing additional equipment for service (the Lukan view).

It seems to me, however, that the two pneumatologies raise afresh the question of the expression of unity in non-conceptual terms. The existence of a logical inconsistency is far from meaning necessarily a real inconsistency. Indeed, the above outline could be taken to suggest the unsuitability of a consistently systematic approach for expressing non-consistent and non-systematic realities.

53. W.J. Hollenweger, "Flowers and Songs. A Mexican Contribution on Hermeneutics," *Int. Review of Mission,* Vol. 60, No. 238, April, 1971, pp. 232-244 (detailed in PGG, Spanish).

54. See M.L. Martin, *Kirche ohne Weisse: Simon Kimbangu und seine Millionenkirche,* Basel, 1971; Martial Sinda, *Le Messianisme congolais et ses incidences politiques,* Paris, 1972; W.J. Hollenweger, *Marxist and Kimbanguist Mission: A Comparison,* Birmingham, 1973—PGG (Spanish and French).

55. Above, note 50.

56. Summarized in PGG (German, pp. 192-200; English, pp. 208-213). Handbuch, 07.496. See also a forthcoming thesis on Gee by Brian Ross (University of Toronto).

57. D. Gee, "To Our New Pentecostal Friends," *Pentecost,* Vol. 58, 1962, p. 17.

"The Spirit Groans"
The Sunday Sermon
José Miguez-Bonino

It is indeed an unexpected and bewildering privilege to be invited to preach in this city with its tradition of learning and distinction and, particularly as a Methodist, the place about which we learned as children in Sunday school—when we used to hear and even dramatize the story of Wesley and the birth of Methodism.

Together with my own gratitude for this opportunity I want to express the joy of our Institute for the privilege of sharing in the worship of this congregation of Wesley Memorial Methodist Church of Oxford and our deep appreciation for the hospitality which this church has offered us. We have indeed felt at home in this house. May I therefore convey to the congregation our gratitude as well as our love and blessing in Jesus Christ.

Romans 8:18-27

Whether out of courage or out of fear, I have chosen to comment on this section of the Epistle to the Romans which is supposed to be at the very heart of our Methodist understanding of the gospel.

It is rightly so, I think, because here the Apostle Paul makes it abundantly clear that faith is not merely an objective transaction, nor an intellectual conviction, nor, one should add, a set of resolutions, but a total involvement of God and the individual in a personal relationship. The name and reality of this total involvement is "the Holy Spirit." Or, to use Paul's and Wesley's expression, this one and twofold "witness" of God's Spirit is *in, with, to* our own spirit.

This, and this alone, is what allows us to address the Almighty by the name which Jesus used, and which otherwise would be blasphemy on our lips, *abba,* "my father." This, and this alone, is what entitles us to claim what otherwise would be sacrilege, a participation in the inheritance of Christ's Resurrection and glory. (Romans 8:15-17)

Here we are, therefore, at the very center of our personal, warm, intimate, living fellowship with God, in the sphere of the Spirit. And suddenly the Apostle turns on the lights, opens the curtains and we find ourselves, bewildered and gasping, surrounded, pressed, and questioned by all the forces and elements of creation. (verse 19) Our conversation with God does not take place in some shadowy corner of a temple where we can whisper outside the reach of other ears or in the recesses of the heart. It is a public affair, out in the open, where all creatures stand on tiptoe to see and hear what is happening. On this dialogue hangs their own future, their hope for liberation and fulfillment.

1. Exegetes are not agreed on the meaning of this "expectant groaning" of creation. It is not too difficult to discern the "groaning" of human creation expressed as slavery or meaninglessness. "For I have heard the *groaning* of my people, whom the Egyptians keep in bondage, and I have remembered my covenant." (Exodus 6:5) "For the oppression of the poor, for the *groaning* of the oppressed, now will I arise, saith the Lord." (Psalm 12:5) Although the word is not the same, can we not also hear: "The voice of thy brother's blood *crieth* unto me from the griund." (Genesis 4:10) "The wages of the laborers who mowed your fields . . , cry out, and the cries of the harvesters have reached the ears of the Lord of hosts." (James 5:4) Passages could be multiplied. The creation cries and groans on the lips of persons oppressed, tortured, exploited, cheated, and enslaved by others. Moreover, throughout Job and the Psalms is heard the groaning of human beings perplexed by the victory of evil and the silence of the Lord. Creation groans from the heart

of the individual who does not find meaning in a life which turns in a vacuum, without goal or direction. *Human creation* groans in the captivity created by human injustice, ambition, pride, and violence.

The *creation* of which Paul speaks may, nevertheless, have a greater scope; it includes things, energies, the whole realm of nature. Perhaps today we are beginning to hear at least something of this groaning of nature. We hear the groaning of the waters drained of life by pollution, the forests turned into deserts through irrational and profit-crazy exploitation, and the built-in obsolescence of the very stuff of our earth as it goes through the grind of our industrial and consumer society. The raped nature of Southeast Asia, the millions of tons of steel, the nuclear energy we have harnessed to our will to destroy and dominate—*they groan*. The nature which God subjected to us so that he might lead it to its goal is caught in our captivity to vanity and sin.

2. *Paul continues:* "... and *eagerly expects*"—its own deliverance—"the manifestation of the children of God." *We—those whom the Spirit has taught to say, "Abba"*—we are the meaning of creation, the answer to the groaning of earth and humanity, the hope of the world!

It sounds preposterous! But there is here no hint of triumphalism. We are shown here as we are. We are also trembling, groaning, perplexed, not knowing even what to ask or how to pray. But something has happened to us! Poor and perplexed as we are, we have received *the Spirit*. We have heard the word of promise and hope—and *know it to be true*. This is all we have, but it is enough!

What is Paul talking about? He is talking about those being *sanctified* in the Spirit—about those who have heard the gospel, believe and begin to move freely and unpossessively among things in the world because they know they are in their Father's house and do not need to steal or hoard. He speaks about those who have heard the gospel, believe and begin to give up all need to preserve their image, status, and self-respect because their dignity has been once for all ensured as children of God. He speaks of those who have heard the gospel, believe and begin to discern the meaning of life, not in their private satisfaction, fulfillment, or even holiness but in the fellowship and solidarity of love.

We are still in the beginning stages of our pilgrimage. We still live as captives of our fears, our isolation, our greed, our privacy, but the veil is torn. *We know* what truth is and what a lie is. The universe knows this is its meaning; its groans and strains itself to realize it! A dry and sterile earth groans expecting the love of a human community to make it fruitful. The dispossessed of the earth groan for the freedom to live fully as human beings and not as slaves. The youth and women of our time groan for the acceptance of love, but they find dehumanized institutions intent on making of them producing and consuming machines. Creation itself groans that its meaning may be finally realized! We Christians groan because we have tasted the reality, but are unable to live by it, to realize it. (verse 24)

3. This is indeed the ultimate truth of our life in the Spirit. Even though we groan in powerlessness, *we cannot abandon hope.* We have tasted the future, and we cannot renounce it. The person who has really received the Spirit is a *rara avis,* a strange creature, who has been convinced—against all evidence—that freedom, love, and community are the truth of creation. That individual will not cease groaning, struggling, seeking, hoping. That person will not cease straining toward the future, betting on God's tomorrow, ready to give up the security of today, even when unable to see clearly how the future will be—for hope that is seen is not hope. Why should one hope for what one sees?

Are we indeed *people of the Spirit?* Wesley's call for conversion is just as urgent as it was two hundred years ago. Are we really people of the Spirit, or deep down are we really of the flesh? Do we wake up each morning to the hope of the new, or do we simply expect the safety of the old, irritated when something disturbs us? Do we expect creation to move to its goal or simply to offer us a safe place for our own introverted and private satisfaction? Do we expect the Spirit to lead us to struggle for the newness of creation or simply to sanctify and preserve our "life in the flesh"?

4. *We cannot really answer these questions.* (verse 27) And here, finally, Paul opens a still larger scene—the curtains of heaven itself—to show us the ultimate dimension of faith. There, *God himself is groaning* because he is involved in the drama of hope. When we become restless and unable to accommodate our lives to demands of so-called "reality;" when we rebel against the meaninglessness of human suffering and deprivation, of waste and destruction; when we try, however hesitantly, to create a bit of freedom, love, fellowship, joy—it is the Spirit which groans in us.

And when we sleep, comfortably established within meaninglessness as if we know nothing, the Spirit groans with a betrayed creation and struggles to awaken us back to our true reality as God's children! It is only at this point that Paul can take us back to our dialogue with God. He can now tell us what *prayer* is. Prayer is the unity of the groaning of creation, the sigh of a restless faith, the expectation which strains toward the future, the praise for the victory which is certain. Prayer is our "yes" to our neighbor taking God as witness. Prayer is taking our place within the struggle of the creature for its liberation. Prayer is echoing the Spirit's own travail for the coming of God's kingdom. This is the dialogue of faith.

The Contributors

Arichea, Daniel C., Jr.   Translations Center, Indonesian
Bible Society, Jalan Jendral
A. Yani 62, Bogor, Indonesia

Hollenweger, Walter J.   Professor of Mission, Department
of Theology, University of
Birmingham, Birmingham, England

Idowu, E. Bolaji   Department of Religious Studies,
University of Ibadan,
Ibadan, Nigeria

Kirkpatrick, Dow   Co-Chairperson, Oxford Institute
Committee, World Methodist Council
Minister, First United Methodist
Church, Evanston, Illinois, USA

Langford, Thomas A.   Dean, The Divinity School,
Duke University,
Durham, North Carolina, USA

Meyendorff, John   St. Vladimir's Orthodox
Theological Seminary,
Crestwood, New York, USA

Miguez-Bonino, José   Instituto Superior Evangélico de
Estudios Theológicos, Camacuá 282,
Buenos Aires, Argentina

Pieters, André J.   Rue du Champ de Mars 5, B-1050,
Brussels, Belgium

Samartha, Stanley J.   Director, Dialogue with People of
Living Faiths and Ideologies,
World Council of Churches,
Geneva, Switzerland

Stephens, Peter   Randles Chair of Historical and
Systematic Theology, Wesley College,
Bristol, England

Tholin, Richard   Professor of Church and Society,
Garrett-Evangelical Theological
Seminary, Evanston, Illinois, USA

Wiles, Maurice F.   Regius Professor of Divinity,
Christ Church, Oxford, England

Reading List

The following titles have been suggested by the several partici-
pants. This list has been prepared by Dr. Lawrence D.
McIntosh, Rose Memorial Library, Drew University, Madison,
New Jersey, USA.

E. Bolaji Idowu—"The Spirit of God in the Natural World"

Evans-Pritchard, Edward Evan. *Nuer Religion.* Oxford: Clar-
endon Press, 1956.
Idowu, E. Bolaji. *African Traditional Religion: a definition.*
London: SCM Press, 1973.
————. *Olodumare: God in Yoruba Belief.* London: Long-
mans, 1962; New York: Praeger, 1963.
Lienhardt, Godfrey. *Divinity and Experience: the religion of
the Dinka.* Oxford: Clarendon Press, 1961; New York:
Oxford University Press, 1961.
Taylor, John Vernon. *The Primal Vision: Christian presence
amid African religion.* London: SCM Press, 1963; Naper-
ville, Illinois: Allenson, 1963.

Richard Tholin—"The Holy Spirit and Liberation Movements:
The Response of the Church"

Alves, Rubem A. *A Theology of Human Hope.* Washington:
Corpus, 1969.
Cone, James H. *A Black Theology of Liberation.* Philadelphia:
Lippincott, 1970.
Russell, Letty M. "Human Liberation in a Feminine Perspec-
tive: a working paper for the New York task force on
women in changing institutions." *Study Encounter,* VIII,
No. 1 (1972), pp. 1-12. Item SE/20, 1972.
Taylor, John Vernon. *The Go-Between God: the Holy Spirit
and the Christian Mission.* London: SCM Press, 1972;
Philadelphia: Fortress Press, 1973.
Tillich, Paul. *Systematic Theology.* Vol. III. Chicago: University of Chicago Press, 1963; Welwyn, Herts.: James Nisbet,
1964. Particularly Part IV, Section IIB., "The Manifestation of the Spiritual Presence in Historical Mankind."

Thomas A. Langford—"The Holy Spirit and Sanctification:
Refinding the Lost Image of Creation"

Bruner, Frederick Dale. *A Theology of the Holy Spirit: the
Pentecostal experience and the New Testament witness.*
Grand Rapids, Michigan: Eerdmans, 1970; London: Hod-
der and Stoughton, 1971.
Flew, Robert Newton. *The Idea of Perfection in Christian
Theology: an historical study of the Christian ideal for
the present life.* London: Oxford University Press, 1934.
Lindstrom, Harald. *Wesley and Sanctification: a study in the
doctrine of salvation.* London: Epworth Press, 1950.

Wesley, John. *A Plain Account of Christian Perfection*. London: Epworth Press, 1952.

Williams, Colin W. *John Wesley's Theology Today*. New York: Abingdon Press, 1960; London: Epworth Press, 1969.

Daniel C. Arichea—"The Holy Spirit and the Ordained Ministry"

Allen, Roland. *The Ministry of the Spirit; selected writings.* Edited by David M. Paton. London: World Dominion Press, 1960; Grand Rapids, Michigan: Eerdmans, 1962.

Glasse, James D. *Profession: Minister*. Nashville: Abingdon Press, 1968.

Goodykoontz, Harry G. *The Minister in the Reformed Tradition*. Richmond, Virginia: John Knox Press, 1963.

Hanson: Anthony Tyrrell. *The Pioneer Ministry*. London: SCM Press, 1961; Philadelphia: Westminster Press, 1961.

Minchin, Basil. *Every Man in his Ministry*. London: Darton, Longman and Todd, 1960.

Niebuhr, H. Richard, and Williams, Daniel D., eds. *The Ministry in Historical Perspectives*. New York: Harper, 1956.

Schmithals, Walter. *The Office of Apostle in the Early Church.* (A revised edition in translation of *Das kirchliche Apostelamt*, 1961.) Nashville: Abingdon Press, 1969; London, SPCK, 1971.

Simpson, Ervin P. Y. *Ordination and Christian Unity*. Valley Forge, Pennsylvania: Judson Press, 1966.

John Meyendorff—"The Holy Spirit, as God"

Lossky, Vladimir. *The Mystical Theology of the Eastern Church.* (Trans. *Essai sur la Theologie Mystique de l'Eglise d'Orient*. Paris, 1944.) London: J. Clarke, 1957; Naperville, Illinois: Allenson, 1957.

Pelikan, Jaroslav. *The Christian Tradition: a history of the development of doctrine.* Vol. 1: *The emergence of the Catholic tradition (100-600)*. Chicago and London: University of Chicago Press, 1971.

Prestige, George Leonard. *God in Patristic Thought*. 2nd ed. London: SPCK, 1952.

Titles Suggested by the British Committee:

Hollenweger, Walter J. *The Pentecostals: the charismatic movement in the churches.* (Trans. by R.A. Wilson with revisions by the author of *Enthusiastisches Christentum*, 1969) London: SCM Press, 1972; Minneapolis, Minnesota: Augsberg, 1972.

————. "Flowers and Songs: A Mexican contribution to theological hermeneutics." *International Review of Mission*, LX (April, 1971), pp. 232-244.

————. "The Social and Ecumenical Significance of Pentecostal Worship." *Studia Liturgica,* Vol. 8, No. 4 (1971-
72), pp. 207-215.

————. Articles—"Liturgies: Pentecostal" and particularly,
"Pentecostal Worship" in, Davies, J.G., ed. *A Dictionary
of Liturgy and Worship.* London: SCM Press, 1972; New
York: Macmillan, 1972.

Sykes, Stephen W., and Clayton, J.P., eds. *Christ, Faith and
History: Cambridge Studies in Christology.* London and
New York: Cambridge University Press, 1972. Particularly
chapters 1, 2, 7, 8, and 15.